The Consumer's Guide to
BANKS

by Gordon L. Weil

U.S.NEWS & WORLD REPORT BOOKS

TOO GOOD FOR THE RICH ALONE

The Complete Guide to Tax-Exempt Bonds for the Middle-Income Investor

by James F. Reilly

A division of U.S.News & World Report, Inc.   WASHINGTON, D.C.

U.S.NEWS & WORLD REPORT BOOKS

Directing Editor   Joseph Newman

Editors for this Dual Edition:
Roslyn Grant and Judith Gersten

Dual Edition Books, arranged with the original publishers and the authors,
are created and abridged especially for the U.S.News & World Report
Money Management Library.

The Consumer's Guide to Banks
Stein and Day Publishers
Copyright © 1975 by Gordon L. Weil

Too Good for the Rich Alone
Prentice-Hall, Inc.
Copyright © 1975 by James F. Reilly

ISBN 0-89193-421-9

Library of Congress Catalog Card Number 76-8702

Printed in the United States of America

Contents

Contents

Editor's Note

The books in this Dual Edition can be useful allies in the battle to increase one's financial worth. Banking is so fundamental to every other aspect of personal money management that it is hardly possible to contemplate achieving financial success without understanding how to use banks to the maximum advantage. Nor is financial success likely without sound investments, such as can be made in tax-exempt bonds. And tax-exempt bonds can indeed be a sound investment despite the problems encountered by holders of some "municipals."

As in all the volumes in this Dual Edition series, our editors have preserved the greater part of the original texts and the words of the authors of both books. In trimming less essential material, our editors have had the goal of bringing the essence of both books into sharper focus. This method enables the reader to save both time and money while acquiring the useful knowledge contained in these outstanding money management books.

Such knowledge can be difficult to obtain in other ways. Many banks are secretive about their operations, and even the most inquisitive customers may not be able to learn all they want to know about the banks they use. *The Consumer's Guide to Banks,* by Gordon L. Weil, may prove helpful. Armed with the information provided by Mr. Weil's book, the consumer should be able to shop knowledgeably for every type of banking service: loans, checking and savings accounts, mortgages, retirement accounts, credit cards, safe-deposit boxes, travelers' checks, and the many other services banks offer individuals. By shopping around for whatever service is required, the consumer may be able to save or make money on various types of bank transactions.

Making money is the theme of James F. Reilly's *Too Good for the Rich Alone,* the second book in this Dual Edition. This complete guide to tax-exempt bonds points the way to an unusual avenue of investment for the middle-income individual.

Many persons who could invest profitably in tax-exempt bonds have not done so in the mistaken belief that this source of income is the preserve of very rich individuals and of such institutions as banks and insurance companies. Mr. Reilly refutes this widespread belief in his easy-to-read book. He explains why investment in tax-exempt bonds should be considered by every middle-income person seeking a reliable source of additional funds without the worry of possible loss of capital. Anyone who is wary of tax-exempt bonds at the present time should take note of the fact that professional investors are continuing to invest heavily in high-quality tax-exempts—those that have a triple-A or double-A rating.

Tax-exempt bonds have for too long been a subject of mystery and misunderstanding. Mr. Reilly turns a bright light on this mysterious corner of the market in this first book about tax-exempts for middle-income investors.

Roslyn Grant, Associate Editor
U.S.News & World Report Books

The Consumer's Guide to
BANKS

CHAPTER 1

The
Buck
Stops
Here

There are more of them than post offices.

You'll visit them more often than you'll go to a doctor's office.

They are inspected by the government more than anything but prime beef or buck privates.

But unlike post offices, they are not official institutions.

Unlike doctors' offices, they dispense cash, not care.

And unlike bad beef or raw recuits, they are almost never rejected by the inspectors.

They arc banks.

They are perhaps the most pervasive single institution in your life. Their checks create more money than does the United States Treasury. Their loans make it possible for millions to purchase their own homes, send their offspring to college, and provide for their retirement. Even after a person dies, a bank may well manage the wealth left behind.

The bank itself is a go-between—a "financial intermediary"—between savers and borrowers. It collects a fee both
for safeguarding your money and for making loans, and pays
you for the use of your savings.

What banks do

Banks provide services that are some variation on the basic
function of acting as an intermediary between savers and
borrowers.

The most common service is the checking account. In almost
all cases, the consumer gets a convenient and safe way to handle his or her funds and the bank gets a service fee and the
right to lend the money in the checking account and to charge
interest on such loans. In only a few instances does the bank
pay the depositor interest on the money left in the checking
account. The customer is likely to purchase other services from
the bank, once he or she has a checking account. For example,
the bank must have a safe place to keep its cash, so it installs a
vault. Then it rents safe-deposit boxes in that vault to its
customers.

If you put your money in some kind of savings account, the
bank will pay interest for the use of your funds. Within limits
set by law, the savings business is highly competitive because a
variety of institutions vie for your dollar.

When you want a loan, chances are good you will go to a
bank. Indeed, you may find yourself becoming a borrower almost painlessly by using "loans" created by bank credit cards
or by an account that permits you to write checks for more
than your balance. From these kinds of loans, you may progress to a consumer loan to finance the purchase of a car and to
a mortgage loan, probably the largest debt you will ever incur.

Some people leave to the trust departments of banks the
supervision of their funds, both while they are still alive and on
behalf of their estates. And you may find yourself the beneficiary of a trust account, often without knowing it, because trust
departments handle a great many pension funds.

In providing these services, another thing banks do is make
profits. In the decade between 1962 and 1972, their profits
rose at an annual rate of 7.2 percent. That growth rate was
four and a half times greater than the annual profit increase of
manufacturers. The information in this book was current in
late 1974 and early 1975, and may now be different in some

specifics; it nonetheless gives an indication of the relative charges at many banks and the variety of their services.

Dog eat dog?

In a free-enterprise economy, the push for profits is supposed to heighten competition. Banks like to point out that banking is perhaps the most competitive industry in the United States.

For example, on November 1, 1973, the day when savings banks were first allowed by the government to begin paying as much as 7.5 percent interest, ten large display ads placed by ten large banks on ten successive pages of *The New York Times* attempted to convince depositors of the special merits of each institution. That's what the banks mean by competition, since the law required that the accounts offered by each of them be absolutely identical.

At most midtown Manhattan intersections, three, if not all four, corners are occupied by bank branches begging for business. Many people who run banks believe that convenience—even the convenience of not having to cross the street to get to the bank—is the most important aspect of competition. And that kind of thinking is not limited to big cities. For example, the small and obviously thrifty hamlet of Quakertown, Pennsylvania (population: 2,500), has no fewer than three banks, each within a stone's throw of the others.

A wealth of banks

You may find that the competing claims of banks are further confused by the different kinds of institutions. By a tradition that has long since been frozen into law, various kinds of banks have been forced to specialize in certain services.

Take, for example, these three hypothetical institutions: the First National Bank and Trust Company, the First Savings and Loan Association, and the First Mutual Savings Bank.

First National Bank and Trust Company is a "commercial" bank that may provide all kinds of banking services, including checking and savings accounts. There are over 14,000 commercial banks in the country, not counting their branches. Most claim to be "full-service banks," implying that all of your banking needs can be handled by one-stop shopping.

Because commercial banks have tried to offer the greatest convenience by opening legions of branches, and because of their wide range of services, they are the dominant group of banks. They have a virtual monopoly on checking accounts and specialize in relatively short-term consumer loans. In addition, the words "trust company" in the name of many commercial banks indicates that they have a trust department.

The First Savings and Loan Association and the First Mutual Savings Bank are both "thrift institutions." With the exception of three states, these institutions cannot offer checking accounts. But they are authorized by law to pay a slightly higher rate of interest on savings deposits than do commercial banks. With the savings placed on deposit, they frequently make mortgage loans. In fact, in some places they are banned from making consumer loans. Thus, the typical loan by a commercial bank is likely to be one for the purchase of a new car. The purpose of the slight advantage given to the thrifts in attracting savings is to ensure adequate financing for needed new housing. There are only six thousand thrifts, far fewer than commercial banks.

Credit unions are still another kind of thrift institution, although they are not banks. The chief distinction between them and other thrifts is that depositors must be members of a specific group, for example, the employees of a single firm or the parishioners of a single church. The members of a credit union get better loan rates than are available from banks, and they may receive dividends after administrative costs have been paid, because credit unions are not operated for profit. In fact, credit unions come the closest to the classical notion of a financial intermediary. They usually make only consumer loans. Increasingly, they are trying to offer expanded banking services without losing their special character.

Beyond these distinctions, commercial banks and thrifts may be chartered either nationally or by a state. Thus, our hypothetical commercial bank might have been called the First State Bank and Trust Company. That distinction affects the consumer merely in terms of the regulators who supervise the institution and to whom complaints may be directed. In practical, everyday terms, there's no difference between national and state banks.

The variety of banks and their number, to say nothing of the variety of services they offer, means that the consumer has a variety of choice. By now, it should be obvious that all banks are not alike. It will become evident just how worthwhile it is to shop for banks and banking services just as you would shop for a new car or a television set.

Of course, a new-car dealer is a new-car dealer, and that's pretty simple. By contrast, the names for the different kinds of financial institutions may be confusing. In general, the word "bank" means all of the main financial institutions except credit unions. Among "banks," you can distinguish between "commercial banks" and "thrift institutions." The "thrifts" include "mutual savings banks" and "savings and loan associations."

Who's who

While banks may be institutions, you have to deal with people. Bank personnel are organized much like the United States Army.

The bank "officers" include the various treasurers, cashiers, and vice-presidents, plus the president and, in some cases, the chairman of the board. Even the directors of the bank themselves take part in high-echelon decision making, because, under law, they are personally responsible for bank actions.

The "enlisted personnel" of the bank are the tellers and bank-office paper processors. They handle all routine banking operations involving deposits and withdrawals. In larger banks, they may eventually get to handle specialized functions such as issuing letters of credit and transferring funds. Generally, one person is designated chief teller, similar to a top sergeant. In many banks there's also a guard.

An officer will want to see you if you have overdrawn on your account or have missed a loan payment. You will want to see an officer if you want to open an account or to make a loan. While tellers, and particularly the chief teller, can be most helpful, most often you will want to see an officer (or a "warrant officer") for anything other than the most routine question. The next problem is how to find one.

Most of the time, the customer's stop at the bank will mean going to a teller's window to complete a simple transaction. The teller's area is known as the "cage." One window is reserved for the chief teller, and another window—or in larger banks a separate "general cage"—is designated for handling more complex transactions such as foreign-exchange transactions.

In every bank, there is a "platform." What distinguishes the platform from the rest of the bank is that the personnel are sitting down. This area is not usually raised above floor level, although it once was. Now it is separated from the rest of the floor by a rail. There, behind desks, sit what most people think are the officers

Actually, there may be only one officer on duty, and he's the one farthest away from the entrance to the platform. The absence of office walls gives the aura of openness, but the officer is stationed so that a customer will have to run the gauntlet of underlings—either junior officers or platform assistants—before reaching him.

Everybody gets to the platform at least once—to open an account. The bank would like to see you there again, asking for a loan. But if you have a question or complaint about bank service, you should go to the platform and request to see an officer.

Big brother is watching

Banking is a serious business—deadly serious. Banks hold a large part of each person's assets. If a bank were to fail, those assets would simply vanish.

Government regulators set limits on what banks may do, mostly as a way of making sure they are not grossly mismanaged. In the wake of the Great Depression, several agencies were given authority to ensure that banks are operated responsibly. Deposits were covered by federal insurance. And the number of bank failures dropped until now and then only a small bank would be forced to liquidate.

While it might appear that the regulators have done a pretty good job, three major federal agencies stood by in 1974 as the Franklin National Bank sank out of sight. It was the biggest bank failure in American history. Two other large banks—the United States National Bank of San Diego and the Security National Bank on Long Island—also went under in a relatively short period.

While these events have worried depositors, perhaps more than is warranted, they ought to be equally concerned about the amount of policing that the regulators leave to them. Few bank examiners check the bank's arithmetic to ensure that you have been paid the proper amount of interest. And they may not verify the amount of interest you have to pay on credit-card purchases.

In order to look out for your own interests, you need information. Many banks are notably reluctant to make full disclosure, and the regulators are just as likely to side with the bank as with the consumer on matters involving disclosure. In short, while the regulators try to make sure that the bank is managed well enough to prevent it from going bust, they leave it to you to protect yourself.

If Benjamin Franklin was correct in summing up human aspiration as a desire to be "healthy, wealthy, and wise," then banks must take their place in society alongside the doctors and the schools. But if you hope to be wealthy, you'll have to be wise, and by all means, the sooner the better.

2

Your Friendly Neighborhood Bank

Most people simply don't know what they are getting themselves into when they open a checking account. What they are told is merely the tip of the iceberg, and what remains hidden may do them a lot more harm than good.

In part, that's the customer's own fault. Too many people assume that all checking accounts are alike and simply take whatever their friendly neighborhood bank has to offer. Perhaps they will never come to grips with costs of checking because they will never get into an unusual situation such as overdrawing the account. Other charges, deducted automatically, will be considered a normal price for doing business with a bank.

The convenience of being able to create your own money is obvious—so obvious that the vast majority of adult Americans maintain checking accounts. When you write a check, you "create" money just as surely as the U.S. Treasury does.

The check makes payment easy. Check writing can settle the month's bills. And the canceled checks constitute proof of payment and help in record keeping for the tax man. In addition, checks are a lot safer to carry around than cash.

There are more commercial banks than any other kind of bank, and more than anything else, commercial banks are specialized in the handling of checking accounts. By the end of 1974, 14,456 commercial banks plus 28,434 of their branches dotted the landscape. And checking accounts make up a large share of the total funds left with the banks—some $226.3 billion at the end of 1974. Most of those funds are used for making the loans on which most bank profits are based.

Personal checking accounts are good business. Large banks report that they derive net earnings of 66 cents monthly on each personal checking account—regular or special. Small banks earn as much as $1.84 each month on a personal account. In short, it's just as Willie Sutton is supposed to have said when asked why he robbed banks. "That's where the money is," he replied.

As part of their effort to attract new customers, banks offer a surprising variety of checking accounts. Each of them is governed by rules covering service charges and penalty charges, and each customer has to decide on the basis of his or her own use of a checking account which specific plan is appropriate.

Regular checking

Traditionally, regular checking accounts were reserved for those people who could afford to leave a sizable balance in their account, in return for which the account was exempted from any service charge. Of great importance to the depositor was the belief that a check written on a regular account would be more readily accepted than a check written on an account where no minimum balance is required. Prestige was attached to having a regular account.

With the wider acceptance and use of checks and greater consumer concern about getting full value for the money spent, this attractiveness of regular-checking prestige has sharply diminished.

In a few places, banks offer completely free checking accounts, thus abolishing at a single stroke any distinction among kinds of accounts. All customers simply have the same kind of account. The American Bankers Association has estimated that

13 percent of the banks provide such accounts, mostly in the Northeast. Banks throughout the country may offer free checking accounts to special groups—students, servicemen, and retirees. Obviously, a completely free checking account is the most desirable for the consumer, except for a very few people who would benefit more from a "package" account. But even in that case, the checking-account portion of the deal has to be the equivalent of cost-free for it to compare favorably with a completely free checking account.

More frequently, regular-checking-account charges are based on either the maintenance of a minimum balance or a combination of minimum balance and the activity in the account—the number of checks written and deposits made. The minimum-balance account requires the customer to maintain a certain amount in the bank, in return for which the account is exempted from service charges. But as the balance falls below the minimum, the charges are gradually increased. At each level down the scale there is a flat service charge, completely unrelated to the number of checks written or deposits made during the month.

There are wide variations among banks in determining the minimum balance for cost-free checking, the steps, and the associated care. Indeed, differences even exist in the calculation of what determines the minimum balance.

The Basic Checking Plan at the Bank of America provides free checking if the monthly balance either averages $600 or does not sink below a minimum of $300. This incorporates both of the most commonly used methods for determining the minimum balance. The average method involves determining balances daily, totaling them, and then dividing by the number of business days in the month. That means a fair amount of math for the bank, but it is a most beneficial account for the customer whose balance is likely to fluctuate considerably. The minimum-balance approach simply requires the bank to determine the lowest balance in the account at any one time during the month. For the consumer who has maintained a consistently high balance but whose account dipped below the minimum on a single day, the service charge may seem unwarranted.

When banks describe regular checking accounts, they usually don't reveal their method for determining the minimum balance. Almost none is as explicit as the Bank of America. For example, when the Chase Manhattan Bank speaks of a $500 minimum-balance account, it means the lowest balance. When the Beatrice State Bank of Beatrice, Nebraska, speaks of a $500 minimum-balance account, it means the average balance for the month.

Of course, a minimum-balance checking account is not actually free. The consumer loses the interest that could be earned on the balance he must leave in the bank. That money is invested by the bank and earns interest, none of which goes to the depositor. If, for example, the $500 minimum were placed in a savings account in the commercial bank for a month, it would pay $2.08. On all regular checking accounts—lumping business and personal accounts together—banks have net earnings of over $5 per account each month. In part, of course, these high earnings are the result of customers usually keeping balances above the required minimum. This is particularly true when the lowest-day-of-the-month minimum balance is used. In such cases, the account is almost always above the required minimum, but the bank, not the customer, gets all the benefit in the form of interest when that "excess" money is loaned out.

The most frequent minimum balance required for cost-free checking is $500, but the figure may go as low as $200. Most often, charges are increased by $1 as each $100 step is passed, down to a floor varying between $300 and $100. The highest flat charge is usually either $3 or $4. These figures are determined by the bank on the basis of the overall behavior of all consumer checking account holders. As a result, any single customer may find that they are either especially economical or unusually expensive for the services rendered.

Charges on "analysis accounts" are based on a specific examination of just how much the depositor uses the account and how much money the bank has made from lending funds left in the account. These relatively unusual regular checking accounts have been reserved for business customers and individuals with large balances. Because the volume of funds in the account is sufficiently high to provide a portfolio income to the bank far in excess of the cost of maintaining the account, it will pass along some of its profit to the customer by reducing or eliminating service charges.

While it is impractical to offer analysis accounts to all customers, some banks have been able to develop fee schedules based on their actual experience that more closely reflect reality than does the flat rate. The Beatrice State Bank, for example, makes no charges for accounts with a minimum balance of $500. For accounts with a balance of less than $100, it charges 5 cents per check and 75 cents per month. For each additional $100 balance, the 75-cent fee is cut by 10 cents. While the Beatrice Bank is a small institution, the giant Bank of America also provides a rudimentary analysis account. Below the $300 minimum, charges range down from a 50-cent monthly charge and 7 cents per check to an 80-cent charge and 9 cents per check.

Special checking

People who have never had a bank account and who may have limited funds are often reluctant to open a regular checking account because of the requirement of a large noninterest-bearing deposit. As a result, banks developed special checking accounts intended especially for people who both write few checks and do not want to maintain a minimum balance.

Frequently, banks are reluctant to promote special checking accounts because the fees they generate may not cover their maintenance costs. These accounts often have little or no balance that the bank can use to make loans. In addition, these accounts may not lead to use of other services. In fact, many special checking account holders are students and newlyweds and can be expected to use other services later.

Costs and services vary widely. Some banks provide statements only once every two or three months instead of monthly as in regular accounts. While the special account is considered "pay-as-you-go," many banks levy a monthly service charge in addition to a per-check charge. In a small bank, a special account may cost as little as 10 cents a check. By contrast, at the Chase Manhattan Bank, charges reach 15 cents per check, with a 75-cent monthly service charge.

It's worth shopping around for a special checking account because of the wide variation in charges. Within a three-minute walk of each other near Broadway and Fifty-seventh Street in New York, the customer can find the Chemical Bank (75 cents, plus 15 cents a check), the First National City Bank (25 cents, plus 15 cents a check, and a maintenance fee that is dropped if twelve or more checks are written), and the Amalgamated Bank (no charge but possible disadvantages for frequent check writers).

The "package" deal

Increasingly, banks are offering a variety of services, including checking accounts, in return for a fixed monthly fee. All of the other services are less frequently used, so the checking account remains the principal service rendered for the fee.

These arrangements come under many names, with a wide range of charges covering a variety of services. That means that the customer must take paper and pencil to determine if any package deal is advantageous and to compare one with another. Here's how a few of them work:

At the Bank of America, two plans are offered. The All-in-One Checking Plan is available to those with sufficient credit to qualify for a BankAmericard and Instant Cash, a check-overdraft-loan feature. For a $2 monthly fee, the customer receives personalized checks, a check-guarantee card, the Instant Cash feature, a monthly Timesaver statement with checks arranged in numerical order, a BankAmericard, the right to purchase commission-free travelers' checks, and automatic transfer service into, say, a savings account.

Personalized checks would otherwise cost about 30 cents per month. Once a customer purchases these checks, he or she automatically gets the Timesaver statement at no extra charge. All other elements in the package are free to customers who qualify, except for travelers' checks. Using twenty checks per month, which the Bank of America says is average, the package would be cheaper than the bank's Basic Checking Plan if the customer did not maintain the $300 minimum balance. If he or she could keep a balance of $300, the interest the consumer would forfeit is $1.25 a month, plus the personalized-check cost of 30 cents, for a total of $1.55, some 45 cents less than the flat package rate.

For $2.50 a month, the Bank of America offers the same package without BankAmericard, the check-guarantee card, and overdraft protection. At first glance, it may appear that the bank is actually offering fewer services for more money, and closer examination indicates that credit services, on which the bank expects to make additional income, have been deleted. Without loan income to offset the costs of the package plan, the bank presumably raised the cost to the point where the plan will pay for itself. Once again, unless the customer is likely to use a lot of travelers' checks, he or she may find another account more desirable. Fortunately for the customer, the Bank of America provides prospective account holders with sufficient information about each account to allow this kind of careful choice to be made.

Elsewhere, Houston's Allied Bank of Texas offers its President's Account for a flat fee of $3, which covers twelve services, including free money orders. First National City Bank has had a similar Everything Account. European-American has the Bank Pack. The included services are usually free checks, gift checks (fancy drafts to be used when the depositor makes gifts of money), overdraw-loan privileges (but not free overdrawing rights), travelers' checks, certified and cashiers' checks, money orders, comprehensive bank statements, credit cards, check-guarantee cards, safe-deposit boxes, and sometimes reduced loan rates. While all of these features sound impressive, especially for a monthly fee ranging from $2 to $4, many are free in any case. Many customers probably won't use more than half of the features provided. Finally, by careful shopping in one or two banks, the customer can probably put together a tailor-made package at lower cost. For a person who makes heavy use of those services for which charges are usually made, the package deal may be a real advantage.

Strings attached

Frequently, accounts are promoted as "free," but most of them have some strings attached. Only a few are actually free of fees and do not require a minimum balance. Often, "free" checking accounts are package arrangements, with the bank implying that the service charge covers all other services. Closer examination will almost always reveal that the service charge is essentially related to checks and not to less frequently used services. In other instances, "free" checking accounts involve a minimum balance, perhaps lower than those associated with regular checking accounts. If, for example, an account were "free" except for a minimum-balance requirement of $200, the actual cost would still be far less than the service charge for a regular or special checking account. The interest that you would lose on the $200 would be no more than $10.94 a year. Service charges would surely be more.

NOW is the time

With the exception of the relatively unusual free checking account, you have to pay for the privilege of having a checking account, even though the bank may be earning interest on the funds you leave on deposit. Businesses and large depositors who have a lot more clout than the average customer were able to induce banks to create analysis accounts, which might at least eliminate service charges. Then, some businesses insisted on unused funds in checking accounts being automatically shifted into interest-bearing accounts. That meant that interest payments on short-term deposits could actually exceed service charges.

The individual was pretty much left out of such arrangments unless the account involved was quite large. Then came the NOW account.

The Consumer Savings Bank of Worcester, Massachusetts, recognizing that a statement savings account was quite similar to a checking account, sought approval to allow account holders to withdraw funds from their accounts, not by presenting a withdrawal slip to the bank, but by giving the slip to a third party who could present it at the bank. Previously, when the account holder had been required to make all withdrawals directly from the bank, the withdrawal order was considered "nonnegotiable," or nontransferable. But by passing what in effect is a communication between the account holder and the bank through a third party, a "negotiable" order of withdrawal was created. It took a favorable decision by the Massachusetts Supreme Judicial Court before the NOW account became legal.

NOW accounts—in effect, checking accounts on which interest is paid on the unused balance—were soon offered by other thrift institutions and then commercial banks in both the Bay State and neighboring New Hampshire. But soon after the thrifts began popularizing the NOW accounts, commercial banks brought pressure in Congress, which blocked their extension into other states. The legislative rationale was that NOW accounts were experimental and their impact on commercial banks had to be tested.

In fact, NOW accounts are immensely successful because they come closer to fairly repaying the depositor than any other kind of account. But they obviously reduce bank profits on each individual account. If they failed to attract new funds into the bank, the amount of funds available for longer-term loans would be reduced.

At first, Massachusetts and New Hampshire banks levied service charges of 10 and 15 cents per check, much like a special checking account. Since the accounts obviously involve expense for the banks, such charges seemed fair as long as interest was paid to the depositor. Even if a very small balance is maintained, the NOW account is preferable to a special checking account because the interest will reduce the fee. The Provident Institute for Savings, a large Boston mutual savings bank that quickly followed the lead of Consumers, levies no charges if the minimum amount in the account exceeds $500. But the depositor receives interest on that minimum account. In short, with or without service charges, the NOW account is better for the consumer than any checking account.

The commercial bank response was to create NOW accounts for their savings account customers. At the same time, they waged an ad campaign to discourage use of these NOW accounts on the grounds that people would be tempted to tap their savings. They argued that savings should be kept inviolate and inviolable.

The greatest obstacle to attracting new customers has been the service charge, and as a result, more than half of all banks offering NOW accounts have dropped them.

Due to the congressional action resulting from commercial bank pressures, the NOW-account banks are not to solicit accounts from out-of-staters, and most have discouraged such accounts for fear of stimulating even more restrictive legislation. Even without advertising, they received requests to open such accounts and have done so, although in some cases they have imposed high minimum balances.

Some savings institutions are authorized to open checking accounts, but they cannot pay interest on unused balances. According to Consumers Union, all savings banks can also provide checking accounts, as can large, state-chartered credit unions in Rhode Island. The Kansas Credit Union League has actually purchased a bank and has offered free checking to members. The Credit Union National Association has started a pilot program in five credit unions for the issuance of "share drafts," which are actually checks. But savings accounts and checking accounts have been kept strictly separate. In the credit union experiment, no interest is paid on that portion of the deposit used at any time during the quarter to cover a share draft.

In 1974, an effort was made by New York banks to get around the law. They offered an arrangement allowing for either automatic transfer of funds from a savings to a checking account or transfer made in response to a telephone request. The New York Banking Superintendent cracked down, forcefully reminding savings institutions that they could not make transfers, except in writing.

Of course, a do-it-yourself NOW account is possible if funds are left in a day-of-deposit-day-of-withdrawal account and withdrawn, say, only once a month. As many checks as possible should be written at the same time as the transfer has been made or perhaps a day or two in advance. That means interest will be paid up to the last minute, when the funds are needed to cover the checks. Such a system requires either a trip to the bank or making a mail withdrawal regularly.

For those who need few checks and do not mind an occasional trip to a thrift institution (or making a mail withdrawal), the use of savings bank or savings and loan association checks may take the place of a checking account. On day-of-deposit-day-of-withdrawal accounts, interest is paid until the check is written. The thrift's check is made payable to any third party at your request. This amounts to an interest-bearing checking account.

A Chicago bank has worked out another account, marketed with a lot of razzle-dazzle, that is actually two accounts. You open a savings account and automatically receive what amounts to a line of credit of the same amount as your balance. You may write checks up to the full amount of your savings account balance. However, no interest is paid on that part of the savings account balance equal to the value of outstanding checks. If you do not deposit money to cover the outstanding checks by the fifteenth of the month following the one in which they were written, you begin to pay 6 percent annual interest on the amount of the checks for which a new deposit has not been made. There are no service charges.

The Chicago bank says it has 190,000 holders in all fifty states and abroad. Even though the bank provides an identification card, it is likely that some people would encounter difficulties if they tried to pay for the week's groceries with the bank's check, which does not even look like an ordinary check. The account is perhaps best for a person who can have a deposit made regularly to the account and who writes relatively few checks. Indeed, the bank uses the testimonial of a foreign correspondent in Cairo to sell the virtues of the account.

But this account may be useful for those people who can manage with two accounts—one for local needs and the other for mail payments and for those local merchants who will accept it. The problem with local acceptance is not only that merchants question the validity of the check; it may take several days longer for funds in a Chicago bank to be credited to their account.

The Chicago bank pays the highest day-of-deposit-day-of-withdrawal rate allowed to commercial banks. In 1975 that was 5 percent. But remember, if you don't make a deposit equal to the dollar amount of the checks you've written, you must either tell the bank to withdraw the necessary amount from your savings, or "borrow" the money to cover the checks. This "loan" carries a monthly interest rate of $1/2$ of 1 percent, a 6 percent annual rate. You pay interest only on the outstanding loan balance, not on any interest that may still be due. And because your account balance continues to earn interest at almost the same interest rate as you pay on your outstanding loan, the net cost of the account is likely to be less than the cost of an ordinary checking account.

This account has not been copied by other banks, although it now has been offered for several years. In part, managing the account is more costly than an ordinary account. Of course, the bank knows that its account holders will not write a great many checks on their accounts. Thus it profits from a higher rate of return on the investment of deposits than is ordinarily possible for a commercial bank that cannot expect deposits to remain in the account for so long a period. In addition, most commercial banks want to avoid for as long as possible paying interest on checking accounts or even seeming to do so.

In April 1975, the Federal Reserve Board in Washington announced that it would permit banks to allow their depositors to withdraw funds from their savings accounts by phone. For the preceding thirty-nine years such withdrawals had been banned.

The impact is obvious. If a customer can transfer funds from a day-of-deposit-day-of-withdrawal account into a checking account when they are needed to cover a freshly written check, he has what amounts to a NOW account. Banks would not be required to offer such an arrangement, but those that did so would presumably permit transfers into any of their checking accounts.

Many banks can be expected to provide such a service. In fact, it should break down the barrier between the states with NOW accounts and the others. As a first move, Maine authorized thrifts to offer checking accounts. Federal regulators are prepared to allow commercial banks and thrifts to pay their customers' bills directly out of their savings accounts. If the federal regulators adopt these rules, the overwhelming majority of banks in the United States will be able to offer what amounts to interest-bearing checking accounts.

Self-expression on the cheap

It's a good picture. It lifts the spirit. The crystal-blue surf pounds the rocks at the base of a towering cliff. Bright sun and fluffy clouds promise a splendid day. Matisse? Gauguin? Grandma Moses? No. Behold the lowly bank check in all its glory.

In 1965, Wells Fargo Bank sold checks to only 5 percent of its customers. The rest simply used the standard stock checks issued by the bank. But the bank figured that people really wanted checks that would help them attain individual identity in an age when the Social Security identification number and the computer threatened to take away what little personality remained to anyone. So, Wells Fargo designed a check to meet this psychological need. These checks, with a stagecoach design, were sold, not given free. Now more than 60 percent of Wells Fargo's customers purchase checks. And of course, the picture check brought the bank a lot of new customers.

The Wells Fargo story is not unique. Banks all over the country now sell so-called scenic checks. In addition to providing a little something for the soul, they also provide the convenience of printing the name and address of the account holder on the checks, a convenience when cashing them, plus prenumbered checks. Prenumbering allows the bank to list the checks in numerical order on the statement, which helps some people get through the onerous task of reconciliation.

The American Bankers Association reports that scenic checks have been so successful that banks have been able to avoid the effects of competition that would otherwise have required that they install free checking. Customers so badly want to express themselves when they write checks, that they prefer to pay a charge to get a scenic check rather than no charge at all for a plain, old-fashioned bank check.

When a customer opens a checking account in most banks, he or she will automatically be offered the opportunity to purchase scenic or at least personalized checks. Mention is often made only in passing about regular bank checks. Alternatively, the customer may actually be given these special checks as the first supply from the bank. The reorder form urges purchase of the same kind of check or another scenic type. It does not mention cost. Instructions for ordering regular bank checks are usually in smaller print and more difficult to find.

Even if the customer wants scenic checks, he or she will have a hard time figuring out the cost. The sample books do not contain prices, and frequently the platform personnel are completely uninformed. As a result, you may have to wait until you have actually begun to use the scenic checks and have received your first statement before the cost of the scenic checks is stated. In a survey of banks in the New York area, the cost of an order of scenic checks (usually 200) ranged from nothing to $5.10.

Only a few banks do not issue cost-free stock checks. If the way a customer wants to manifest his or her personality is not pictorial but pecuniary, then the free check is the best way to a better life. Unless, of course, you'd like the ultimate—the check with your own picture on it.

Check clearing

Obviously, the check is at the heart of a great number of the financial transactions in an average person's life. By the time the customer gets his or her canceled check back with the monthly statement, this bit of paper may have made a long and sometimes tortuous journey, much of it recorded on the back of the check. The whole process is called "clearing."

Ordinarily, check clearing should be a matter of small importance to the customer, but in fact, it may be a matter of money. Most banks tell you in the fine print on the signature card when you open your account that you cannot draw checks against other checks you have deposited until they have cleared. That means that your bank wants to make sure that the person who wrote you a check has sufficient money in his account to make good on it before the bank lets you use that money. Fair enough.

The trouble is that the individual depositor has no idea just how long it takes a check to clear, and he or she may draw on uncleared funds. If so, the depositor's own check will bounce. In fact, the most frequent cause for a check's being returned for insufficient funds is drawing on deposits not yet credited to the account. In most cases, depositors do not run into this problem, of course, because their own checks are in the process of being collected a few days after their deposits enter the same process. As a result, the individual is in effect gambling that his or her own check will not reach the bank until after the check deposited clears.

The best bet is for the depositor to ask just how long the banks allow for checks to clear. The survey of New York area banks by the New York Consumer Assembly showed that banks allowed from one to eight days for in-state checks to clear and from three to twenty days for out-of-state checks to clear. There is virtually no justification for such a variation because all banks use the same facilities for clearing checks. In New York, in-state checks—and certainly those within New York City itself—can be cleared within twenty-four hours by a continuous computerized process. In any case, banks that say they require as much as eight days are obviously giving themselves a wide margin of security.

In fact, they are doing more than that. They are making money. When a prospective customer asked at one bank how they could offer completely free checking, he was first told that statements were issued less frequently than normal. When he pressed for a better explanation, he was told that his initial deposit would not be credited to his account for eight days.

What happens is that the bank is informed that the check has cleared within twenty-four to forty-eight hours on local checks. But it delays depositing the money to your account for another few days. During that period, the bank can use your money for a variety of purposes that will earn it interest. This procedure is actually not one of the traditionally legitimate earnings functions of a checking account.

At another bank, a customer was told that although the bank had been credited with funds from a local check within forty-eight hours, that money would not be deposited to his account for an additional forty-eight hours. The bank argued that it would wait to see if the check bounced. It preferred to withhold the customer's money while waiting rather than run the risk of having to withdraw money from his account later to cover the bad check.

While few banks will state just what proportion of their customers write bad checks, Chase Manhattan says that 2 percent of its personal accounts are overdrawn at any given time. It's questionable whether or not it's fair for banks to refrain from depositing 100 percent of all funds that have cleared on the grounds that 2 percent might have to be withdrawn again.

Checking account customers should understand that the delay in crediting deposits to their accounts can cause a real inconvenience. Of course, for some customers the problem of delay will never be of any real importance. If it is a potential problem because, for example, you need to withdraw money from an out-of-state paycheck, you should ask a bank officer for special authorization to draw on uncollected funds—uncleared checks. Particularly if you maintain a reasonable balance and are a good customer, the bank should be willing to grant you this convenience at absolutely no cost.

A simple declarative statement

Next only to the fun of writing checks is the joy of receiving a bank statement and trying to reconcile what the bank says you have with what your checkbook says you have. Many people don't even try, although the process is not as complicated as it seems. The bank is not infallible and the only real check on the accuracy of its bookkeeping is the customer's reconciliation of his or her checkbook with the statement.

Either way, it's useful to receive the statement as often as possible—in most cases, monthly. Some banks that offer low-cost special checking accounts or free accounts provide statements only once every three months. These will be satisfactory only to the person who makes light use of the account. Unless you're a very good keeper of the book, you're bound to make some error in a three-month period. So it's worth deciding whether the extra cost of the service charges for monthly statements isn't warranted.

Banks have been introducing consolidated or comprehensive statements that provide information not only on the checking account, but also on outstanding loans, savings accounts, and credit-card accounts. The benefit for the customer is that he or she can see at once the status of all accounts and loans. Yet many customers do not want others, even at the bank, to see the status of all accounts and loans. As a result, banks have had to offer customers the right to delete any information they wish. That's important to know if your bank uses a comprehensive statement as a matter of standard practice.

The bank probably benefits more from the comprehensive statement than does the customer, because the statement itself is a powerful selling tool for a variety of services. Unless you have a savings account where you normally receive a statement instead of having entries put in a passbook, much of the information will be of only limited use. You will still need to use your savings passbook, and you will still receive a separate credit-card bill. Of course, when the customer sees just where he stands, he may notice that he's paying the bank more for a checking account than the bank is paying him interest on the savings account.

While the consolidated statement doesn't make money for the bank or cost the customer anything, it is primarily a marketing tool. Before a customer is attracted to a banking service by the existence of this statement, he or she should probably weigh the utility of what's being offered.

A little something on account

Banks like deposits and provide special services in order to make sure they attract all they can. Only in certain activity accounts do the banks charge for deposits. Some banks will even pay your postage on deposits by mail.

Preauthorized deposits can often be arranged with disbursing agents of companies and with employers for the automatic deposit of dividends or salary checks. The bank likes this procedure because it has funds on hand it is certain will clear, perhaps a day or two earlier than otherwise would have been the case. The customer is discouraged from spending more of the funds prior to deposit. At the same time, the customer can probably draw on the funds earlier and is saved the inconvenience of making a deposit. In case of either a dividend or a payroll deposit, the customer should receive notification at the time the deposit is made from either the depositor or the bank, or both.

Frequently, banks will offer to make automatic transfers out of the checking account into savings or loan accounts. This saves the customer the need to write checks and removes the problem of remembering the required loan payment. Usually, this automatic transfer feature is free. But the customer should ask an officer, because some banks charge the same amount as if a check had been written to cover the cost of the transfer.

Cash and carry

Sometimes the customer will want to make sure that his check will be as acceptable as cash. In short, he wants the check to be accepted immediately, not subject to collection. If, for example, you have to do business with the United States Postal Service, that's the only kind of check they'll accept.

A customer can obtain a certified check simply by using one of his or her own checks. It must be taken to a teller's window. The teller checks the amount of money in the account and immediately withdraws an amount equal to the check. That means that funds are immediately deducted from the account, not when the check clears. The bank will identify a certified check by strange strips and punched holes, so that when it is processed, funds are not inadvertently deducted a second time. This service should be absolutely free because it amounts to nothing more than writing a check and preclearing it. Yet the New York area bank survey showed that most banks make a service charge. Often, on request, they will forgo the charge.

A cashier's check serves the same purpose. It is a check signed by the bank itself and thus widely acceptable if the bank is well known. In order to obtain a cashier's check, the customer must present cash. Of course, funds can be drawn out of a checking account, so the customer will not have the cost of a check. And there is almost always a service charge for a cashier's check. In addition, not all banks make them available to the public. Occasionally, banks issue so-called gift checks, which are nothing more than cashier's checks in a fancy wrapping. It's actually more economical for a customer who is confident that his or her check won't bounce simply to write a regular check and send it with an appropriate greeting card.

In most cases, a savings bank or savings and loan will issue a cashier's check at no charge to cover a withdrawal from the account.

Most banks also issue money orders, which are virtually the same thing as cashiers' checks. The cost of each money order, as high as 60 cents each, is usually set at a level aimed at discouraging their use in lieu of checks. In fact, unless the purchaser wants a relatively large amount of money converted into a money order, he or she might do better purchasing a postal money order, costing 30 cents for up to $300. Money orders are designed primarily for use by people who do not have bank accounts. Their cost might be high enough to encourage you to open an account.

For all of those monetary instruments that are as good as cash, the bank service charge should only cover costs and not provide a profit. Regular bank customers should make a point of determining if some or all of them are provided free.

And away you go

Banks make a big point of offering travelers' checks as part of their package plans. Generally, they advertise that the customer can obtain travelers' checks without paying the usual service charge. That can mean a savings of $1 for each $100 worth of checks purchased. The willingness of banks to throw in the purchase fee for travelers' checks indicates both that many people seldom, if ever, buy them and that banks can do without the service charge.

With the advent of the credit card, the need for carrying travelers' checks has been reduced. Thus, the potential account holder should determine just how much of an actual savings can be realized from a package plan. Unlike a credit card, where the bank in effect grants you an advance, travelers' checks are based on the customer's giving the bank a cash advance. The bank makes its big profit on the "float"—the funds that people have paid to purchase travelers' checks that they have not yet cashed. Until the traveler's check is used and returns to the issuing bank, the bank can use the purchaser's money for other purposes. In the New York area survey, only one bank provided travelers' checks free. Actually there is no reason why a bank should charge a fee for checks it issues.

Even if they don't issue their own checks, banks can make money by using the funds used to purchase them. They can reinvest those funds before they pass them on to the issuer of the checks. In short, travelers' checks are moneymakers for the bank, and the fee is just the icing on the cake. If you're a frequent user of travelers' checks, it's worth shopping around. Many of the holding companies that own banks, like Citicorp in New York, or American Security in Washington, have travel agencies, and if you use a bank's own agency, it's worth asking for free travelers' checks in return for doing business there. After all, the travel agency is also getting a commission on each ticket it sells.

Play it safe

Every bank must have a vault in which to store its own cash. As an extra service, designed to attract customers, almost all banks make space available within the vault for safe deposit. Usually, safe-deposit boxes are not available to people who do not have accounts.

This is one service that is of far greater benefit to the customer than to the bank. In fact, virtually all banks lose money on the operation of their safe-deposit vault for customers. The average annual loss by big banks amounts to more than $6 per box per year.

The customer, on the other hand, has a safe place to leave important papers and other valuables, although they are not accessible except during banking hours. They may also be difficult to get at in case of the death of the box holder, because the Internal Revenue Service will want to know the contents of the box before it can be emptied. The IRS also offers an advantage to the box holder: the annual cost is usually tax deductible for those people who itemize deductions.

The only hitch is that a safe-deposit box is not quite so safe as most customers think. Of course, a lot less can happen to your valuables in a safe-deposit box than under the mattress, but if something happens to them in either place, you're a loser.

Thieves "dropped in" to the vault of a California bank at Laguna Niguel once, and walked off with the contents of 451 safe-deposit boxes. The property owners claimed they were out some $5 million and asked the bank to make good. The bank pointed to the fine print, which limited its liability to "the exercise of ordinary care" and included the understanding that "under no circumstances shall the lessor be liable for the loss or destruction of any other property, including money, placed in said safe."

Personal insurance policies may cover some or all of the contents. Aetna Life and Casualty offers a special policy for safe-deposit box holders.

When banks promote safe-deposit boxes, they stress safety and convenience. Both are relative.

At your service

Many banks offer a variety of other services worth inquiring about. For example, the Bank of America has a special student account called the College Plan. Students pay only a $1-a-month service charge during the academic year and nothing during June, July, and August or when they maintain a minimum balance of $300. Scenic and personalized checks are available at low cost. Obviously, the College Plan is an excellent way to attract new customers.

Senior citizens also get special treatment by many banks. The advantage to the customer is the lower fees charged. The bank hopes for arrangement of automatic deposit of Social Security or pension checks and recognizes that many senior citizens use checking accounts less often than younger people. The New York area survey indicates that small banks offer senior citizen accounts far more frequently than large banks.

Where either student accounts or senior citizen accounts do not exist, organized groups in a community may be able to convince a local bank to institute them.

The First National Bank of Lake Forest, Illinois, has provided for over sixty years a multiple-payee check. This enables customers to pay a number of bills by writing a single check, which is actually a payment order sent to the bank. The bank then deposits the proper amount in the accounts of the business firms or sends them a cashier's check.

The multiple-payee check has real advantages for both the customer and the businesses, finding funds deposited to their accounts faster than usual. And it reduces paperwork caused by processing many separate checks, thus cutting bank costs. The bank may attract additional accounts in this way. This system could reduce or eliminate checks altogether.

Another service operated by the Chemical Bank but available to other banks is the Braille Checking Account, which makes it possible for the blind to handle their own financial affairs.

Some major banks act as paying agents for municipal or corporate bonds. All the customer has to do is arrange to collect the funds payable in person or by mail. If he lives near one of these banks, he would do well to stop in on the payment date. Otherwise, the bank can hold the funds for a few days, and the interest goes to the bank, not the customer.

If you have an account at a thrift institution or credit union, it may have a special arrangement with a commercial bank that could reduce service charges. For example, the Kansas Credit Union League has recently purchased the State Bank of Lancaster, Kansas. This alliance will allow credit unions, normally just a place for savings and consumer loans, to provide free checking, credit lines secured by credit-union balances, credit cards, and overdraft accounts. In New York, the mutual savings banks can extend the scope of their services through the Savings Bank Trust Company, which they own. It's always worth asking at a thrift if it has any special arrangements with another kind of banking institution.

Finally, banks provide an additional form of identification—a bank-identification or check-guarantee card for use in a world that seems to thrive on numbers and signatures as a sign of trust. At First National City Bank, these cards allow the customer to find out his account balance by inserting the card in a special machine. In large cities, where big banks have many branches, they serve as identification in any branch when a customer wants to cash a check, usually of $100 or less. That saves time. In addition, a check-guarantee card tells any merchant that the bank vouches for the check up to $1,000. Of course, the banks will issue such a card only to customers who do not overdraw. The card may be useful as identification for other purposes, particularly if it bears a photograph.

The fine print

When the average customer opens a checking account, he or she generally knows little about the terms governing such an account. Most banks claim they make full information available in brochures they leave in their main banking lobbies. Of course, many customers don't even examine these brochures, because they choose a bank on the basis of convenience and on the presumption that all banks are pretty much alike. Indeed, banks do not expect potential customers actually to shop around for an account by picking up the brochures from several banks and comparison-shopping.

The brochures accentuate the positive and eliminate the negative. There is no mention of how the bank treats overdrawn checks. What fees are charged when checks deposited bounce? How is an inactive account defined, and what are the maintenance costs of such an account? What is the cost of a stop-payment order? Does the bank have the right to withdraw money from the account without the consent and possibly without the knowledge of the customer?

Brochures are designed to attract customers, not to inform them of the drawbacks connected with opening a checking account. Obviously, banks believe that people need not become aware of some of the hidden costs until some time after their funds are on deposit. Among the major exceptions to this general rule of nondisclosure is the Bank of America, which grew to its great size as a consumer-oriented bank. It publishes a brochure called "The Facts," which explains the advantages and then some of the costs of its accounts. The brochure refers to "special situations [which] may be rare with your account, but it is important for you to understand them and be prepared." Yet even with the Bank of America, the customer is unprepared for the offset (or setoff).

Offset, sometimes called the "banker's lien," is perfectly legal. The bank may withdraw from your checking account those funds needed to cover a debt to the bank, usually an outstanding installment or credit-card loan. The bank requires no court order, and it need not inform you that it has this right or that it is making use of it. Of course, an unknown withdrawal from your checking account can cause you to overdraw your balance unwittingly.

While a customer may not like the idea of offset, it is perfectly legal and avoidable. All the customer need do is keep his checking account in a different bank from the one where he borrows money, or avoid borrowing beyond what can easily be paid back. The bank will continually urge the customer to borrow more, so abstinence will, as usual, require willpower.

The main problem is in the failure of banks to disclose what they can or will do. In early 1975, the Bank of America was in the process of revising disclosure statements to inform customers of offset.

Citibank says it does not put this information on checking account forms, but does include it on the loan agreement. Offset is used only on loans more than ninety days overdue, and the bank attempts to warn the customer first.

Most banks appear not to include information about offset when a checking account is opened and do not plan to change their policy on this matter.

Of course, any bank may have to comply with a court order relating to funds they hold in your name (and also the contents of a safe-deposit box). Almost none will tell you in advance if they will levy a charge. The Bank of America will charge your checking account $7 if any such order is processed.

Everybody runs the risk of depositing a check to his or her

account that is returned for one of a variety of reasons, most often because of insufficient funds. Indeed, the possibility of this happening is one reason given by banks for delaying in crediting funds to your account. Some banks will charge for the extra work involved in processing a return item; almost none will tell you they do. The Bank of America says it may charge 50 cents an item.

Of course, you may write a check that "bounces." Unless you know you're doing that at the time, overdrawing may be due to the failure of the bank to credit a deposit in the time you thought adequate. If you shave the margin thinly on a regular basis, just how long the bank requires for clearing and crediting is of vital importance.

Once a customer has overdrawn, the bank has two options. It may choose to process the check anyway. If the check is relatively small and if you generally maintain a good balance and ordinarily don't write bad checks, chances are that the bank will accept the overdraft. In the New York area survey, half of the big Manhattan banks said they would notify a customer before bouncing a check. That would give him time to increase his balance. Chances are pretty good that many banks will act without contacting the customer.

The bank may choose to reject the check, in which case it's sent back to the person the customer paid with it. That relieves the bank of any collection problems.

In either case, the bank will levy a fee for handling an overdrawn check. All banking surveys indicate that charges range from $2 to $5. They may be waived in certain cases. For example, Chase Manhattan says it does not charge the first time a customer errs and will waive charges for certain customers. The Beatrice State Bank in Beatrice, Nebraska, will charge $2 for the first overdraft on a given day and $1 each for all others on that day.

Many customers are unhappy about overdraft charges, particularly when they appear to be unjustified because they are based on delayed check clearance or unknown withdrawals from the account. Accounts that allow for overdrafts have been created, but they are, in fact, high-interest loans.

Another checking account feature is the stop-payment order. You may write a check and then decide that you should not have written it. In that case, you will ask your bank to stop payment. If the check has not yet returned to the bank and been debited from your account, the bank can issue an order for which it may charge. The cost ranges from nothing, where competition among banks is sharp, to $5. The order may be ineffective, even if issued in time. If you write a check to a merchant and he endorses it over to another party instead of depositing it, the innocent third party may well be able to collect from your account. In the case of a bank with many branches, even another branch of your own bank can be that innocent third party. Only the Bank of America among those surveyed explains this feature to potential account holders.

Finally, you may simply not use your account very much, even though you have left a small balance in it. The bank is incurring very few costs, if any. But many banks levy a charge that is supposed to cover their costs. The Bank of America charges $1 per month. In some states, if the account remains inactive, the funds are turned over to the state. This applies to both savings and checking accounts. With proper identification, they may be retrieved later.

All of these hidden charges cannot always be uncovered merely by reading the brochures banks make available or even by asking personnel. The bank regards the signature card that is used when an account is opened as a contract but it is unusually vague for a legal document. More often than not, the card will simply refer to the bank's rules and regulations and not include details of what the account might cost the customer. Whatever the card says, it's usually difficult for the account holder to get a copy of it. And if the potential customer doesn't like what he reads while sitting on the platform, how likely is it that he will walk away? That makes shopping for a checking account complicated if not occasionally embarrassing.

Check it out

The first thing a potential checking account customer should do is make up a list of questions, not for the bank, but for himself or herself. Only by determining what you want from a checking account can you determine which checking account is best. Here are some of the questions:

- Do I write enough checks each month to require a checking account?
- How many checks will I average each month?
- How much money am I likely to have in the account at any one time?

• Do I have a savings account in an institution that has links with a commercial bank?

• Will deposits be fairly regular?

• Do I use travelers' checks? How much and how often?

• Do I need a safe-deposit box?

• Do I qualify (as a student or senior citizen) for a special account?

• How often do I need or want to receive a statement?

• Do I deposit many out-of-town checks to my account?

• Am I likely to overdraw the account or stop payment?

Having answered these questions for yourself, it's time to ask banks a few questions. You can ask your questions by phone or in person. You're likely to get fuller answers in person, but you have to be willing to spend a few minutes. Chances are you will have to speak with a senior person on the platform, if not the branch manager. Some banks will be more cooperative than others. Since your mental well-being is at least as important as your financial well-being, how you are treated should influence your choice of a bank. Ask these questions and write down the answers:

Choosing an account. What are the service charges of all accounts offered as well as the per-check charges, the required minimum or average balance (if any, and what interest income is lost), and the cost of checks?

What is the comparative cost of accounts, given my circumstances? (If the bank won't help you figure this answer out, promise to return only after you have made such calculations for yourself.)

Deciding on a package plan. What are the charges for travelers' checks, safe-deposit boxes, certified and cashiers' checks, and loans? (The value of these answers depends on how often you would use these services.)

Deciding on a bank. What are the costs of overdrafts (and are you notified), returned checks, inactivity, stop-payment orders, and does the bank use offset?

What additional features are offered, like automated teller and multipayment checks, and what do they cost?

How frequently are statements provided?

What special accounts are offered?

Can I obtain immediate crediting for deposits of checks to be collected later?

Only when you have all the answers should you choose the

bank for your account. There's no indication that you are likely to do better in obtaining the kind of checking account you want according to the size of the bank or part of the country in which it's located. Of course, the exceptions are those two states in which NOW accounts are available. Competition appears to be a factor in all markets, but in many respects banking markets are isolated from each other. Convenience is important, but if you can save several dollars a month by using a more distant bank, it may be wise to consider banking by mail. If a NOW account appeals to you, consider the advantages of having two accounts.

It's more than possible that you will not get satisfactory answers to many of your questions from any bank. But banks are sensitive to public pressure and you may be able to organize with others to improve your chances of finding a bank that suits your needs. For example, a university student council could organize a drive for student checking accounts or a civic organization could muster support for senior citizen accounts. The organizing group should represent enough potential customers that local banks will listen to their demands.

3

No
Saving
Grace

Like a lot of other working men, Mike Pellegrino, a New York television news film editor, had always wanted to set some money aside for his kids. Finally, he saw a bank ad for "Golden Growth bonds." Attracted by the interest rate and the promise that interest would be paid from the day of deposit to the day of withdrawal, he opened an account. In the next week, he opened two more accounts, each with identical initial deposits.

Four years later, Mike went back and cashed in each account on its anniversary. He was amazed to receive three different amounts in return for the accounts, because they had all held the same basic deposit for exactly the same period. When he questioned a bank officer, Mike ran into a stone wall. Months later, he was still waiting for a promised explanation.

Mike's case illustrates two of the most important characteristics of bank savings. First, he was attracted to the bank by its advertising and its convenience to the place he worked. Second, neither he, the depositor, nor the bank officials fully understood the rules governing his savings accounts. About the only untypical aspect of this case was Mike's persistence in trying to find out why he had not received the same return on identical accounts.

People save money in a lot of ways. They put their extra money into the stock market, United States Savings Bonds, Treasury securities, municipal bonds, pension funds, life insurance, money market funds, and gold. Obviously some of these investments represent more than simple savings.

Investments, such as those in common stock, may offer the best hedge against inflation, because they tend to grow as the economy grows, but they offer little security, since they may slump substantially when the economy slows down. Saving in a bank means less growth than is possible in the good times on the stock market—but absolute security. That's why most saving takes place in commercial banks and in thrift institutions— savings banks or savings and loan associations.

Banks, thrifts, and accounts

More people save at commercial banks than at other institutions, because they are convenient and offer one-stop shopping for banking needs. But commercial banks usually pay lower interest than thrift institutions. Commercial banks come in all shapes and sizes. Much depends on what government agency regulates them—state or federal—and whether they are insured by the Federal Deposit Insurance Corporation (FDIC), by a state agency, or not at all. Almost all commercial banks are insured by the FDIC. Don't put your money in a noninsured bank; it offers far less security than an insured bank.

Government regulators allow commercial banks to provide a wide variety of savings accounts. Technically, money placed in an interest-bearing account that may be withdrawn without advance notice is called a savings deposit. Money that can be withdrawn with interest after a fixed period of time is known as a time deposit. Under government rules, set by the Federal Reserve, maturities on time deposits are 30 to 89 days, 90 days to 1 year, 1 to 2½ years, 2½ or more years, 4 to 6 years, and 6 years and above. These periods are tied to interest rates in such a way as to ensure that savers who are willing to leave their funds with the bank for longer periods will receive higher rates of interest. By setting such rules, federal authorities regulate competition to protect smaller banks from being driven out of business, thus reducing consumer choice. Often, banks will impose a maximum length on open-ended periods in order to avoid being locked into paying a high rate of interest at a time when interest rates may again have fallen.

These account periods relate to amounts of less than $100,000. For the big customers, the Federal Reserve Board, a regulatory agency for all national and some state banks, may well choose not to set any restrictions and let the bank and the customer negotiate terms. Generally, on large accounts, banks offer very high rates for short-term deposits but do not want to promise high payments long into the future.

After commercial banks, most people favor savings and loan associations. They, too, are subject to a dual state-federal system of regulation. Just as the Federal Reserve is responsible for commercial banks, the Federal Home Loan Bank Board (FHLB) watches the savings and loans. At the end of 1974, there were 2,221 state-chartered savings and loans and 2,060 federally chartered savings and loans.

Federal associations are required to have their deposits insured by the Federal Savings and Loan Insurance Corporation (FSLIC), an institution similar to the FDIC. In addition, state associations may obtain such insurance, and many do. In three states—Massachusetts, Ohio, and Maryland—state insurance plans are used instead of FSLIC.

At most savings and loans, if you're a depositor, you're a part owner. Some savings and loans are owned by shareholders, as are almost all commercial banks (except those few individually owned). That means they must use some of their income to pay dividends to shareholders.

Like most commercial banks, savings and loan associations are now authorized to provide a wide variety of savings accounts. Until 1966, setting rates and kinds of accounts was strictly up to association managers. As a result, they often set rates so that the associations were at a competitive advantage in relation to commercial and mutual savings banks. In those days, California savings and loans, paying high interest, actively advertised for customers, even in the New York newspapers. Because savings and loans must dedicate their deposits to home mortgage loans, government policy favoring as much housing construction as possible meant that they were given preference in the money market.

After 1966, federal regulators placed limits on the interest rates that the associations could offer. In part, these limits reflected concern that the associations would push rates higher than would be wise for their own long-term stability. They might offer high rates but have too many low-rate mortgages to be able to meet their own interest bill. The ceilings did not reduce the savings and loans' ability to attract savings, because of their established positions in their communities and the slightly higher interest that they may offer as compared with commercial banks.

Savings and loans offer regular passbook accounts and a number of time-deposit arrangements. These include 90-day accounts, 90- to 179-day, 180- to 364-day, 1- to 2-year, and 2- to 10-year accounts, each with a progressively higher interest rate.

Because the chief purpose of savings and loan associations is to provide funds for the home mortgage market, those who save at savings and loans are better off if they turn to the same association for a mortgage loan. While they will not get preferential rates, their own credit will already have been, in part, established. Merely having left funds with a savings and loan over a period of a year or more will indicate a degree of stability in managing your affairs that will please a potential lender.

Savings and loans lack the convenience of the many-branched commercial banks, which are spread across the face of the land in great profusion. Almost half of the associations are located in Pennsylvania, Illinois, Ohio, New Jersey, Texas, Maryland, and California.

Mutual savings banks, the third-ranking type of banking institution for savings deposits, are even less widely spread. There are 486 of them, located in seventeen states and Puerto Rico. Well more than half of these are located in Massachusetts and New York, with all but a handful located in New England, New York, and New Jersey. They're likely to be larger institutions than savings and loans. The assets of the average savings bank are likely to be greater than those of the average savings and loan association.

Deposits in these banks are insured by the FDIC, in most cases, or by state insurance funds, notably one in Massachusetts. Only one mutual savings bank is not insured.

Although the Federal Reserve Board keeps tabs on them, the mutual savings banks are state regulated. As their name implies, these banks are owned by their depositors. But as with corporate stock ownership, people with savings accounts are hardly in a position to set corporate policy.

Because most savings banks are members of the FDIC, they are subject to federally imposed interest-rate ceilings. Until savings and loan associations were placed under similar regulation, the mutual savings banks generally offered lower rates of interest. Recently, however, savers have found the same array of savings choices at the same interest rates available in both kinds of institutions.

As with the savings and loans, savings bank customers have a built-in advantage should they wish to borrow money from a bank where they have an account. If the customer seeks a mortgage, he is already known by the bank. A fully secured loan on the pledge of a passbook is easy to obtain and available at about as reasonable a rate as possible. The advantage of a passbook loan is that you do not dissipate your savings but instead pay for a purchase out of current income. Your funds continue to earn interest, so the net interest cost is only the difference between the interest paid and the interest charged. The interest paid is deductible on income taxes. Such loans are easy to obtain. Finally, by using money in a savings account to guarantee a loan, you do not run the risk of losing any interest because of a withdrawal made before the end of the period during which you had promised to leave the money in the bank.

The smallest of the savings institutions in terms of deposits are the credit unions, but they are the fastest growing. Over 23,000 cover the country, with major concentrations in the largest states—California, Pennsylvania, Illinois, Ohio, and New York.

For the consumer, the chief distinction between credit unions and other savings institutions is that he or she cannot just walk in off the street and open an account. Credit unions consider themselves part of a movement to offer people an opportunity to help those they know and work with rather than the unknown borrowers at banks. In addition, credit unions distribute any "profits" they make in the form of dividends to their members. Management is often voluntary rather than paid, with officers elected by the members. Of course, the larger credit unions have paid staffs.

Many of the credit unions are quite small, with more than

half of them having assets of less than $500,000. They can be either federally or state chartered, but both can obtain $40,000 per account deposit insurance from the National Credit Union Administration (NCUA). The NCUA acts as the federal regulatory agency, while state banking departments supervise credit unions that they charter.

Credit unions are the odd birds among financial institutions. They are exempt from federal income taxes, are not held to the same monetary reserve requirements as banks, and may have their operating costs subsidized by the host company or organization.

At this time, the credit unions are relatively limited in the services they can provide to their saver members. They generally offer one kind of account, with the interest ceiling set by the NCUA or state banking departments. This rate, for what amounts to accounts containing a minimum deposit for at least one quarter, usually exceeds rates payable on similar passbook accounts. For example, some credit unions offer 6 or 7 percent, while the highest bank rate on a 90-day savings account is 5.5 percent. A few issue credit union certificates as a way of raising additional funds for lending. Such certificates may be available even to nonmembers.

Members enjoy an absolute preference when it comes time to borrow relatively small amounts from credit unions. Perhaps the most frequent loan is for the purchase of an automobile. In addition, credit unions provide life insurance on outstanding loans at no extra cost.

A matter of great interest

Once a saver is able to sort out the various kinds of institutions and accounts, he or she will probably find the same account labeled in two different ways in two different banks. With interest rates so closely regulated, just about the only way one bank can attract savers as opposed to any other bank is through marketing. It's a case of putting basically the same product in a fancier package.

Savings accounts have all kinds of names, most of which do little to explain the nature of the account. It's up to the consumer to strip away the frills to determine which of the basic accounts is being offered.

In 1974, allowable rates were just about as high as they had ever been, reflecting tight-money policies and the willingness

Interest Rate Ceilings on Consumer-Type Savings and Time Deposits
(as of January 1, 1975)

	FDIC Mutual Savings	FHLB Savings and Loan	FDIC Commercial
Passbook accounts	5.25%	5.25%	5.00%
Time deposits maturing in:			
90 days to 1 year	5.75%	5.75%	5.50%
1 to 2½ years	6.50%	6.50%	6.00%
2½ years or more	6.75%	6.75%	6.50%
4 to 6 years (minimum of $1,000)	7.50%	7.50%	7.25%
6 years or more (minimum of $1,000)	7.75%	7.75%	7.50%

of banks and thrifts to bid high for the funds they needed to make loans. Of course, interest rates change often. But they tend to remain in the same general relation to each other, whatever their actual level.

Rules and regulations

After July 1973, federal regulatory agencies began to bring the variety of savings accounts into line, whatever the banking institution offering them. Top interest rates payable on a comparative basis are shown in the above table. The NCUA permits federal credit unions to offer as much as 7 percent on their savings accounts, which are called share accounts because savers buy "shares" of the credit union and become part owners. More than half pay between 6 and 7 percent. Others pay little or no interest.

No such ceilings exist on "nonconsumer-type" savings deposits, those about $100,000. This distinction may look like a rather obvious attempt by the regulators to favor the rich, but actually the ceilings are dictated by conditions in the money market. This is the "market" where all those who want to borrow—business banks, governments, and individuals—"meet" all those who want to lend. It exists in no single place, but New York is its focal point. Generally, higher interest rates are offered in the market for larger amounts of money. It's easier to raise $100,000 from one person than from one hundred people, and it's reasonable that the one person should get some sort of financial reward resulting from the economy to the borrowing institution. Hence, a higher interest rate.

By 1973, big depositors were increasingly attracted by the higher interest rates they could obtain by purchasing United States Treasury bills like savings bonds but costing at least $10,000 and maturing in a period of months, and similar items in the money market, and the banks feared that they would lose their deposits. The regulators lifted the ceiling in order to let banks compete, and rates immediately rose from 6 percent to above 9 percent.

All this was of little interest to the average saver who would not have enough money to become a lender in the money market. When the regulators want to allow banks to attract funds from smaller savers, they authorize increases in the ceilings on deposits of less than $100,000. That's just what happened after the ceiling on larger deposits was removed.

When states have lower ceilings than those dictated by the federal regulatory agencies, even those banks that are federally chartered and regulated must adhere to the state ceiling.

Obviously, federal rule makers want to keep commercial bank interest rates slightly lower than those offered by thrifts. Without this distinction, there would be no way for the savings and loans and savings banks to compete against the commercial banks.

The difference between the rates offered by the thrifts and by commercial banks is generally no more than ¼ of 1 percent. For accounts of one and one-half to two years, the gap widens to ½ of 1 percent. These differences may seem virtually meaningless at first glance, but they may not always be. Thrifts and commercial banks may not have the same objectives and so they stress different aspects of the rate structure. The thrifts lend out money for longer periods than the commercial banks so they seek longer-term deposits. As a result, they advertise the interest they pay on higher-rate, long-term accounts. Commercial banks, with shorter-term loans, push lower-interest, short-term savings accounts. Most savers put their money in the short-term savings accounts, where they are not committed to leave their funds. Many people who have checking accounts at commercial banks make the extra effort of going to a thrift to get the slightly higher interest for pass-book accounts.

In short, the interest-rate differential, coupled with the banks' own needs for specific kinds of deposits, ensures customers for each kind of institution.

Why do the federal authorities get involved in setting interest ceilings at all? Actually, putting different interest lids on savings accounts is designed to ensure that funds will be available for a variety of purposes, but most importantly for mortgages. Without controls, regulators fear, thrifts would offer too high rates of interest in order to attract more funds. But the income to pay these high rates would have to come from a mix of old and new mortages. Given the low rates on older mortgages, income would not be sufficient to meet interest payments at levels to which they might freely float. Rates on new mortgages would have to move to even higher levels to compensate. Hence, ceilings on interest. And as we have seen, differentials are meant to provide funds for both consumer loans by commercial banks and mortgage loans, mostly by thrifts.

The case of the "wild card"

Of course, either unforeseen circumstances or mistakes by regulators in setting ceilings can lead to savings flowing into the wrong kinds of accounts, in terms of national objectives. For example, this occurred for a few months during 1973.

In July 1973, commercial banks were allowed to pay any interest they wanted on four-year accounts with a minimum deposit of $1,000. In order to limit transfers of funds from traditional savings accounts to the new accounts, federal regulators said that only 5 percent of a bank's time deposits could be in no-ceiling accounts. In some commercial banks, interest rates immediately took off. Chemical Bank New York Trust pegged its interest rate on these "wild card" accounts to the going rate for United States Treasury bills. Citibank set its rate one-half point below the prevailing prime rate—the short-term interest rate charged big borrowers with the highest credit ratings. But as an added inducement, the rate payable during the first quarter was set at an astronomical 10 percent, whatever the base rate did.

The "wild card" accounts suddenly allowed the small saver the same kind of potential gain that had been reserved for those saving more than $100,000. Obviously, there was more risk in a "wild card" account than in a traditional savings account because of the possible fluctuations in interest rates. To reassure savers, banks made interest floors a part of the arrangement. For example, Citibank set a 5-percent minimum and Chemical Bank set a 6-percent minimum, well above the passbook rate. On a four-year account, then being offered by the thrifts, the saver was guaranteed 7.5 percent.

Despite the element of risk on return, savers began withdrawing funds from savings banks and savings and loans to put into the fluctuating-interest accounts. This sudden transfer of funds out of thrifts is called disintermediation. In simple language, those banks losing accounts stopped playing their expected role as intermediaries between savers and borrowers. Some borrowers, notably those who needed mortgages, began to run into problems finding funds at the thrifts, because money was flowing to the commercial banks. At those banks, the new receipts were used to finance short-term loans on which it was possible to charge higher interest than on long-term mortgages. Higher interest income enabled the commercial banks to pay at a higher rate.

The federal regulators had mistakenly calculated that higher interest rates at the commercial banks would draw more spending money into banks. They did not expect that most of the money going into "wild card" accounts would simply be coming out of other savings accounts. Perhaps, too, they did not expect the commercial banks to offer rates as high as 10 percent.

The thrifts were quick to move. They warned Congress that massive disintermediation, with a related reduction in mortgage money, was sure to result if the "wild card" accounts remained in effect. Within two days of the first alarm, a bill was introduced and passed that simply overruled the regulators and set a ceiling on four-year deposits at commercial banks. Thus ended the short history of interest-rate competition for small deposits among banks.

Even congressional action did not stop some banks from trying to offer higher rates. Instead of the banks themselves, their holding companies took the next step. In July 1974, Citicorp, which owns First National City Bank, marketed floating-rate notes. These issues promised to pay 9.7 percent interest until May 1975 and then interest at one point above the Treasury bill rate. After June 1976, purchasers could cash the notes in and receive the full purchase price.

Citicorp was promptly followed by seven other banks and two industrial corporations. Corporations? Yes, because the notes were not insured at all, as are bank deposits, since even the bank issues were technically made by corporations. The higher interest rate was in part compensation for the lack of insurance. Some $1.3 billion worth of floating-rate notes was sold in two months.

Three things happened that slowed and eventually stopped sales. First, Congress threatened legal action against the notes, unless they were made somewhat less attractive. As a result, the Federal Reserve was able to prevail upon Citicorp to make it somewhat more difficult to cash in the notes and not to guarantee the high return for a long period. Second, interest rates began to fall. Floating-rate notes are just that, and the interest paid can go down just as easily as it can go up. These notes looked a lot more attractive as rates rose than they did when they fell. At that point, an insured 7.5 percent account looked pretty good. Third, when Franklin National went broke, depositors with insurance were paid immediately. Anybody who held notes had to wait, like any other creditor, for the division of what was left. That did a lot to weaken enthusiasm for uninsured notes.

Congress and the federal regulators have come to understand that their efforts to prevent disintermediation require full-time surveillance. Even the Treasury itself, in 1969 and again in 1974, issued high-interest paper that sopped up savings account money like a sponge. The first time it was a mistake and the Treasury acted to cut off the savings outflow. The second time was no mistake, for the Treasury was willing to pay high interest and attract savings account money at about the very same time it was trying to discourage the sale of floating-rate notes.

An interest-rate menu

Of course, interest-rate maximums are just that—the most that the law will allow. No bank or savings institution is required to pay interest at those rates. Competitive conditions in a particular market will determine the interest rates that will be offered. Most institutions operate on the theory that the saver will not wander outside his immediate home market, thus relieving them of any obligation to offer rates competitive with those available elsewhere. Some undoubtedly believe that because of convenience and perhaps market domination, they can afford to offer lower rates without losing deposits.

Look, for example, at First National City Bank (Citibank) which is located in the heart of the highly competitive New York City market. In 1974, on a passbook account, Citibank offered 4.5 percent and only provided the maximum 5 percent if the saver was willing to accept a statement, similar to a checking account statement, instead of having each transaction entered in his or her passbook. Citibank says that it saves on expenses this way.

Citibank's Golden Passbook Account allowed withdrawals at the end of each calendar quarter or on ninety days' written notice. In line with interest-rate regulations, it would not pay 5.5 percent interest unless the money was left on deposit for at least ninety days. The minimum deposit was $500, an amount not required by regulation.

Next step up the ladder was the Premium Golden Passbook Account, which was offered for two and one-half to ten years at the maximum allowable rate of 6.5 percent. Again, the minimum deposit, not required by regulation, was $500. The saver had to pick his own maturity date. In that way, he could guarantee himself the interest rate offered for as long as ten years, whatever may happen later to allowable maximums. He might prefer to be assured of 6.5 percent for ten years than to get 7.5 percent for seven years, the maximum then available from savings banks in the New York market. He was, in fact, betting that interest rates would decline later, and especially after the seventh year. Over the long run, rates don't usually come down, but the precipitous climb in recent years allows for some expectation that they'll fall again.

Finally, Citibank offered Investment Certificates of Deposit. For all practical purposes, certificates did not differ from savings accounts. These were issued for periods from ninety days to five years at a guaranteed interest rate of 5.5 percent. A minimum deposit of $500 was required. Actually, these certificates "overlapped" the Golden and Premium Golden accounts without offering any appreciable advantage to individual savers. (They are also sold to corporations, which can't open savings accounts.) They could be issued with any maturity date within the deposit period selected by the saver in advance. If the saver chose a maturity of more than two and one-half years, he would have done better to choose a Golden Passbook Account. After two and one-half years, the certificates offered an interest rate a full percentage point below the allowable maximum.

Many commercial banks offer completely different varieties of savings accounts. Almost none is likely to provide the full range of savings choices at the maximum rates allowable by law. Indeed, a random sample of small-town commercial banks indicates that they tend to offer fewer of the high-interest accounts. With relatively small assets, they simply cannot afford to commit themselves to pay a high rate of interest over a long period of time. As a result, they will offer passbook accounts at the lowest interest rate the market will allow.

At the end of 1972, savings and loan associations were paying an average interest rate about three-quarters of a point higher than commercial banks. This lead reflected the higher passbook rate they were allowed to pay (5 percent as opposed to 4.5 percent) and the willingness of savers at the associations to leave money in accounts paying a higher rate of interest.

But like commercial banks, savings and loans do not necessarily pay at the maximum allowable. A case in point is the Home Savings and Loan Association of Los Angeles, the largest in the nation and located in an area where most of the association giants operate. While it offered passbook and time-deposit accounts at the legal maximums in 1974, it offered no 7.5 percent four-year accounts on amounts of $1,000 or more as authorized by federal regulation. Even this $5-billion association did not find it sufficiently profitable to make such a big bid for the average saver's money, although in the ceiling-free area of deposits of $100,000 or more, it was prepared to pay 7.5 percent for a deposit left for one year.

Smaller savings and loans follow the same conservative pattern as the smaller commercial banks.

The largest mutual savings banks, many of which are located in New York City, break the pattern. They usually offer interest rates at the maximums allowable by law. On accounts other than passbook or the highest-interest accounts where a $1,000 minimum is required by regulation, the mutual savings banks require a minimum deposit of $500 in the account at all times.

Once again, smaller savings banks tend to offer fewer high-interest accounts. Of two banks in Vermont, for example, which operate in different markets, one provided the full range of accounts at the maximums, while another would pay no more than 5.5 percent on a ninety-day account.

Perhaps as a reflection of the savings orientations of consumers in various parts of the country, the average interest rate paid by savings banks, concentrated in the East, was almost a fifth of a point lower than in savings and loans, concentrated in the West.

As for credit unions, they operate under a flat ceiling. Until recently, the top interest rate they could pay was 6 percent. A national survey indicated that a great many of them paid substantially less than the maximum. In some cases, state law set the maximum a full point below the federally permitted level. In three of the states with the largest number of credit unions—Pennsylvania, Ohio, and Michigan—the maximum rate was 5 percent.

The applicable maximum interest rate permitted in 1975 was 7 percent. In the face of climbing interest rates, more credit unions moved toward higher payouts. For those few large credit unions that offer certificates, the interest rates may go as much as a point higher than the allowable maximum payment for share accounts. Maturities on these certificates range from those that were redeemable at any time after issue to those that must be held one year. Thus, they may, where available, amount to the most attractive savings choice, because they combine high interest and relatively short maturity.

When the potential saver is faced with the impressive publicity each of these institutions puts out in an attempt to attract his or her money, there are a few items in the fine print that are worth watching closely.

The rock bottom

As already indicated, many of the higher-interest-paying accounts require that a minimum deposit be kept in the account at all times in order for the account to be kept open at all. These minimums are generally on the order of $500 or $1,000. Even a regular passbook account at a savings bank may require $25 to $100 in the account in order for interest to be paid, although the account may be kept open with a lesser amount. When the interest already due on a day-of-deposit-day-of-withdrawal account is not paid until the end of a quarter, the saver must be careful to keep the required minimum in the account for that time in order to get the interest already due. So it's important for a saver to know exactly how much will have to be committed to any savings plan, keeping in mind that at some time in the future he or she may want to make an unplanned withdrawal. If such a withdrawal would bring the balance in the account down below the minimum required for payment of a high interest rate, you are unwise to choose it in the first place.

Minimum deposits get tricky when it comes to adding money to an account of a fixed maturity that is already open. The saver cannot add to an existing account and expect to have the additional deposit treated the same way as the initial deposit unless he or she extends the life of the entire account. For example, an executive who thought he would put his extra cash into a 90-day account at the savings bank in order to receive 5.75 percent interest, came back a month after opening the account with an additional deposit. He was barred from simply adding his second deposit, even on the commitment that he would leave that deposit with the bank for 30 days beyond the first one. He was told that he either had to extend the first deposit to a 120-day account or meet the minimum to open an entirely new account for the second deposit. That's why banks may call anything beyond a passbook account a savings certificate or bond or certificate of deposit, because, in most cases, time requirements make it virtually impossible to add to an existing account.

Paying the penalty

Federal regulators have attached high penalties to the premature withdrawal of principal from a high-interest savings account. Banks can afford to promise high interest only on the understanding that they will have the saver's money over a definite period—usually a relatively long one. That way the banks can be certain to commit their funds to loans that will cover the cost of the depositor's interest. The reason higher interest is paid is that the depositor is willing to leave the money for a predetermined period. From the depositor's viewpoint, if interest rates decline later, it was a wise move to get the money tied up in a high-interest account for a long period.

Of course, some people have to lay their hands on their savings at short notice. Anybody can withdraw the interest already earned and paid without any hindrance whatsoever. But such a withdrawal will reduce the effective yield of the account, which is calculated on the basis of both principal and accrued interest's being left on deposit until the account runs its course.

All banks are required to inform the depositor in advance about the penalties attached to early withdrawal. On some older accounts, most of which have been closed, the depositor had to prove to the bank's satisfaction that the withdrawal was made necessary by dire personal circumstances, like a death in the family. Later the regulators retreated from imposing such strenuous terms. Now, almost no bank will refuse to permit the withdrawal, although it must exact the penalty.

Publicity for savings accounts must include the disclaimer describing the penalty. If it is couched in the official regulator's language, the depositor is going to find it tough to understand just what toll is exacted for early withdrawal.

Here's how the penalty works. The interest rate paid on the amount withdrawn is not the high rate originally offered, but the passbook rate provided by the institution during the time the money was on deposit. Thus, in a savings bank, if a person takes money out of a 6.75-percent account, the interest payable on that money is 5.25 percent. Of course, the saver must leave in the account an amount greater than the required minimum deposit. Otherwise the entire account is closed by the withdrawal. Then, the interest that is to be paid on the amount withdrawn, at the reduced rate, is further cut by a total forfeit of three months' worth of interest. For an example of an actual loss, Home Savings and Loan of Los Angeles provides this case:

Example of Penalty on a 6.75% Account

If $1,000 is withdrawn one year after the account was opened, the penalty would be $28.45. The penalty is based on the following calculations:

1. Loss of one year's interest at 6.75% $68.08
2. Payment of nine months' interest at 5.25%   39.63
3. Total penalty loss $28.45

Some banks may insist that they have the right to refuse a withdrawal even with these penalty provisions. If the saver contemplates the possibility of a premature withdrawal, he or she should discuss the matter in advance, and if in any remaining doubt, get a statement in writing that he or she will be able to make the withdrawal. Despite their strict statements, designed to discourage early withdrawals, most banks will, in fact, permit them.

Making a person who has left funds in the account for a considerable period pay the same penalty as a person who has withdrawn funds earlier in the planned life of the account strikes some as unfair. After all, the bank has enjoyed the use of the funds for a considerable period and ought to pay for that use.

One way would be to pay interest according to the duration funds were actually left in the account. This method would not require a decision in advance by the saver on just how long he or she would leave funds in the account.

"Roll-over" provisions

What if the saver leaves his funds in the account beyond the maturity date?

Banks and thrifts should tell the depositor, before the account is opened, what will happen to the deposit in this case, but many don't so it's wise to ask. The least desirable possibility is that the institution will simply hang on to the money without paying any interest at all. Without contrary advice from the depositor, that's what the Federal Reserve requires its commercial bank members to do. Some institutions will automatically place the funds on deposit in a passbook account, thus assuring at least a minimal rate of interest. Generally, this will allow the customer to withdraw the money whenever he or she wishes (although the saver may be required to wait until the end of a quarter), and to avoid losing any interest. Other savings institutions have automatic "roll-over" provisions, which means that the funds on deposit will be placed again in exactly the same kind of account they were in, provided that kind of account is still available. The danger here is that the depositor may not want to have his or her funds tied up again for a considerable period of time. A good bank will notify the depositor well in advance of the termination date of the account and offer all alternatives, including payment of all the proceeds to the depositor. A good saver will keep records, permitting prompt action to reinvest funds most profitably.

Guaranteed return

The higher-interest-rate accounts "guarantee" the rate until the specified maturity. But since interest-rate maximums are subject to government regulation, can't one of the regulatory agencies require that the rate be lowered at any time? In fact, there is nothing that would prevent an agency from doing just that, except for the inevitable public outcry. Thus, in order to maintain public confidence in savings institutions and in their inducements to attract savings, it is virtually inconceivable that such an action would be taken.

But savers should be careful to see if, in fact, they are being guaranteed an interest rate. If "interest" is called "dividends" on the passbook account, no return is certain. Dividends are payable on earnings. Mutual savings banks pay dividends, not interest, on their passbook accounts. Both are careful to tell customers that the interest rates they are paying at the moment a deposit is made is only the anticipated rate for the future. In recent years, these rates have gone above anticipated levels, but they can go down just as easily. High-interest accounts are not usually subject to fluctuation, but rates on passbook accounts can be adjusted. If they do change, the rate is adjusted automatically, and there is no need for the depositor to open a new account.

A member of the club

Christmas Clubs and similar devices have always been the stepchildren of savings. For a long period, banks paid no interest at all on deposits made by individuals seeking to save up enough to pay for Christmas presents. That practice is virtually ended, but there are still "costs" to savers who continue to participate. Presumably, the additional paperwork of preparing coupon booklets and posting the number of the payment due each week justifies these "costs."

Most important, the depositor is almost always required to complete all payments to the club before any annual interest is paid. Obviously, banks want to make sure their administrative expense is justified before they pay for the use of savers' money. In that case, savings banks will often pay interest at the same rate as the passbook account. Commercial banks may offer less. In some cases, banks pay higher interest to people who have funds transferred automatically from their checking accounts to the clubs than they pay to coupon rippers.

Banks report that the clubs actually cost them money. Each club member makes about thirty-five deposits a year, more than the average saver. And a great number of accounts are opened and closed each year, unlike savings accounts, which may remain open for extended periods. But banks find that the clubs are one way of attracting customers and a competitive device that they must maintain simply because others do.

The interest paid on club accounts averages well under 3 percent, a sure indication that some banks pay little or no interest and many depositors do not keep up their payments regularly. One missed week, and all the interest for the year is lost.

Clearly, unless the saver is so weak-willed as to require constant reminders provided by the club, he or she is far better off placing funds regularly in a passbook account. The bank will probably be happier, too. Of course, the saver has to be able to withstand the temptation of taking money out of the account before there is enough on hand to pay for gifts. Interest may well be paid both on the money withdrawn and on the money left in a passbook account, while all interest may stop when any withdrawal is made from a club.

For retiring people

Anybody saving for retirement can use his savings to set up his own plan. The pension law, passed in 1974, spreads the benefits of so-called Keogh Plans to virtually everybody.

You can withdraw money from your current income and lock it into a retirement plan and not have to pay taxes on that income now. You must leave that money in the plan until you reach the age of fifty-nine and a half. If not, you pay a 6-percent penalty on the amount you withdraw, plus income taxes. The bank will simply deduct that penalty from the balance you then have. If you leave the funds alone until your retirement, principal and dividends are only taxed when they are withdrawn, almost certainly at a time when your reduced income has put you in a lower tax bracket.

Self-employed people can place 15 percent of their income each year into such a plan, but no more than $7,500. Those who are not self-employed but who work for an employer who does not have a pension plan for them can funnel up to 15 percent of their salary or $1,500 (whichever is less) each year into an Individual Retirement Account (IRA).

While you may establish a Keogh Plan or IRA in stocks and bonds, the most secure plan is probably at a savings bank. The funds must be in the account before December 31, but they need not be deposited on a regular schedule. There is almost no more red tape in opening a Keogh Plan or an IRA than in opening an ordinary savings account. In effect, it's simply a long-term account.

The saver should make sure that he or she gets the best rate possible. In case of premature withdrawal of funds, the 6-percent penalty is far less tough than the standard penalty on time deposits, which means a reduction in the interest paid for the full amount withdrawn for the entire time it was in the account, plus a partial forfeiture of all interest on the amount withdrawn. The retirement fund penalty comes off the top of the amount withdrawn and does not reduce the interest rate paid on the funds for as long as they have been on deposit.

For anyone saving for retirement anyway, a Keogh Plan at a savings bank may be a very good deal.

The three Cs

Interest rates should be expected to tell the whole story about where to put your money. But things are seldom what they seem. Even the banks themselves tell the saver that the effective annual yield is higher than the posted rate. That's only possible, of course, if the saver leaves the interest already earned on deposit in the account so that interest will be paid on interest.

There's even more to it than that. The banks have considerable discretion in determining the way they will pay interest. How often will they calculate the interest on the money deposited? That's *compounding*. How often will they add that interest to the principal so that it can earn additional interest? That's *crediting*. What sum will be used as the basis for figuring interest, especially when withdrawals and deposits are made at odd moments during the life of the account? That's *computing*.

If a bank wants to boost the posted interest rate as far as possible, it will use its discretion on the three Cs in the most liberal way. But if it wants to seem to be offering a lot more than it does, it can reduce the effective yield considerably by a narrow interpretation of these bases for calculation. On longer-term deposits, these factors are far more explicit than in pass-book savings accounts, the type most frequently held.

Compounding: interest on interest

When the bank calculates interest, adds it to principal, and then calculates interest on the new amount, that's called compounding. Banks compound interest more frequently these days than a few years ago, because they want savers to believe that their funds are earning as much interest as possible.

Yet the mere speeding up of compounding is misleading. For one thing, the differences in actual interest received are small when compounding is accelerated beyond the quarterly period—once every three months. Look at the interest on $1,000 at 5 percent annual interest, when the interest is compounded:

Continuously	$51.27
Daily	$51.27
Monthly	$51.16
Quarterly	$50.95
Semiannually	$50.63
Annually	$50.00

With interest rates, banks pay attention to the frequency of compounding. Daily compounding or even continuous compounding sound most impressive. How do they work?

The daily rate is determined by dividing the annual interest rate by the number of days in the year. Banks may use either a 360-day year or the actual year of 365 or 366 days. In 360-day years, each month is considered to have 30 days and each quarter 90 days. Using a 365-day year, the number of days in each quarter varies—90, 91, 92, 93. As a result, even with quarterly compounding on a 365-day account, the amount of interest paid for the fourth quarter is likely to be more than the amount paid for the first quarter of the following year. That may seem odd, if you think that interest should be increasing each quarter when all funds are left on deposit.

In an effort to increase effective yields, some savings institutions use a combination of the 360-day and 365-day years. Obviously the daily interest rate for a 360-day year is slightly higher than for a 365-day year (at 5 percent, it's .0001389, as compared with .0001370). Some banks pay the 360-day rate for 365 days. That's why banks can claim an effective yield of 7.9 percent on an annual rate of 7.5 percent. Without this unusual rate mixture, the yield would be only 7.79 percent.

While continuous compounding sounds extremely impressive, for any practical purpose it is essentially a mathematical exercise that yields the same result as daily compounding. At 5 percent on $1 million left in the bank for a year, the difference between continuous and daily compounding would be $4.

According to a 1973 survey by the American Bankers Association, most commercial banks compounded interest quarterly or daily. Generally, it's the smaller banks that compound less frequently. The rate of compounding has been stepped up over the years as competition for savings increased. As money gets easier, savers should be careful to watch whether banks slip back on compounding. Read the fine print in their ads.

All the advertising about compounding and, indeed, all calculations about differing interest payments depending on frequency of compounding mean little if you don't know the rules covering crediting interest to the account.

Crediting: the money's yours, or is it?

You will learn a lot more about the interest you can receive from the frequency of crediting than from how often interest is compounded. For example, a few commercial banks compound and credit daily. But one major bank says it compounds interest daily and pays (another word for credits) it quarterly. Another compounds daily, but credits annually. If you left your money in any of these banks for the full year, you would get the same interest. But if you withdrew funds before the end of a crediting period—in the last case, a full year—you would lose all interest. (Besides crediting rules, you probably need to make sure that a minimum balance remains until the end of the quarter even at banks that compound and credit daily.)

The most recent ABA survey indicated that 93 percent of commercial banks credit interest twice or four times a year. Small banks tend to credit less often. Because only 5 percent of commercial banks credit interest as frequently as monthly or daily, the implication that most frequent compounding means more interest may be misleading. That depends on how long you leave money in the bank and on crediting rules.

Obviously, the more frequent the crediting, the better the yield for savers. But the chances are great that you won't find banks crediting interest more frequently than four times a year. Even on day-of-deposit-day-of-withdrawal accounts, interest probably isn't credited more than quarterly, although it may be compounded for every day you have it on deposit. If, say, you withdraw funds on October 31, interest on those funds for the calendar quarter beginning October 1 won't actually be paid to you until December 31, and then only if you have maintained a minimum balance until the end of the year.

Mike Pellegrino, who left no balance when he cashed in his accounts, lost interest because the accounts were closed before the end of the calendar quarter. The fact that he had left the money for exactly four years was of no importance. Because the accounts began and ended on different dates relative to the end of the quarter, the lost interest varied, thus accounting for the different amounts he received on each account.

Computing: LIFO, FIFO and grace

Almost every saver has heard of compounding. A few are familiar with crediting. But almost none has ever paid any attention to computation. Yet computing methods can have a far greater impact on the interest received than either of the other two elements.

Commercial banks, in particular, use a wide variety of methods for determining the balance on which interest will be calculated. The American Bankers Association has surveyed its members over the years and has found literally scores of variations. Most related to savings accounts in which withdrawals and deposits can be and are made at any time. Many people may not realize that when they withdraw money, the bank will determine which of the dollars in the account—those deposited a long time ago or those deposited recently—are actually paid. That determination can affect how much interest you receive.

Professor L. D. Morse of Kansas State University and Ms. Jackie Pinson, one of his former graduate students, have done most of the detailed research that reveals just how wide the variations can be among banks. They have found six basic computing methods used by most banks:

1. *Low balance.* Interest is calculated only on the lowest balance in the account at any time during the crediting period.

2. *Day of deposit to day of withdrawal.* Interest is calculated on all funds in the account for as long as they are on deposit.

3. *Day of deposit to end of crediting period.* Interest is calculated only on funds left in the account until the end of the period.

4. *FIFO, beginning balance.* Interest is calculated on funds in the account after withdrawals are deducted from money in the account for the longest period of time, beginning with money in the account at the beginning of the crediting period. FIFO means "first in, first out."

5. *FIFO, first deposit.* Same as FIFO above, except that withdrawals are deducted from the earliest deposits during the crediting period.

6. *LIFO.* Same as FIFO above, except that withdrawals are deducted from the most recent deposits and then other deposits in reverse chronological order. LIFO means "last in, first out."

The 1973 ABA survey reflected the growing popularity of the day-of-deposit-day-of-withdrawal method. It was the most frequently used method, favored by 46 percent of the commercial banks, and is most advantageous to consumers.

The low-balance method was still favored by 30 percent of the commercial banks. It is most advantageous for them because they do not have to pay any interest on funds left in the account in excess of the minimum during the compounding period.

The FIFO approach was used by 16 percent of the banks. This method, too, is more advantageous to the bank than to the customer. A distant fourth was LIFO, which is fairer to the customer, whose "old" money is left untouched until recent deposits are withdrawn. The other methods trailed in popularity.

Grace days

Although the method of determining the balance for the purpose of calculating interest is in itself quite significant, other factors come into play in the calculation process. One of these is "grace days."

On certain types of accounts, banks will allow grace days to depositors. If, for example, a deposit is made to a passbook account on the tenth of the month, interest will be calculated from the first of that month. Because interest is actually paid on deposits that were not in the bank, the interest rate is, in effect, increased. The ABA survey found that four-fifths of commercial banks allow grace days, normally up to ten days, although some allow fewer days. Generally, the grace period covers the first days of the month at the beginning of the quarter. This feature will be of importance mainly to people who want to make deposits at quarterly intervals, but who do not receive the funds they want to save until the first day of the quarter. Some day-of-deposit-day-of-withdrawal accounts now include grace-day features for deposits at the beginning of a quarter (and for withdrawals at the end). That's a good deal.

Savings accounts may also include a grace period for withdrawals. A saver may be allowed to withdraw funds before the end of the period and yet be paid interest as though the funds had remained in the bank until the last day of the period. Only about a quarter of the banks offer this feature, and the normal grace period is three days.

Many consumers would find that grace days for withdrawal are far more useful than grace days for deposits. Frequently a tax or other bill is due at the first of the month and a savings account will have to be tapped in order to meet the expense. It's far better to be able to withdraw the money in time to pay the bill without losing any interest than either to lose interest or be late in making the payment.

Grace days can be used by what might be called "money jugglers" to increase the effective yield on savings. Most of the juggling these people do, often based on shifting money between banks and using uncollected funds—balances against which they have written checks that have not yet cleared—is too risky for most people. The way they use grace days will illustrate the method.

On January 2, Mr. Jones deposits $1,000 at a thrift paying 5 percent in a day-of-deposit-day-of-withdrawal account with interest compounded daily and paid quarterly. This account, number one, also gives ten grace days at the beginning of each quarter and three at the end. On January 10, he withdraws the $1,000 from account one and deposits it in an identical account, number two. By the end of March, the $1,000 will have earned $12.50 from account two and $1.09 from account one. On March 29, taking advantage of the withdrawal grace days, Jones the Juggler takes $1,012.50 from account two and puts it back into account one, where it will remain until April 10.

Then the process is repeated at the beginning of each quarter.

By redepositing interest and juggling his funds, Jones obtains an annual interest rate of 5.85 percent. If he had merely left his funds in account one for the entire year, he would have had an effective rate of 5.13 percent. In short, the juggling put Jones $7.20 ahead for the year. He worked for that money.

About one-fourth of the commercial banks may penalize their depositors for making too many withdrawals. Two withdrawals every three months may be all you get. If you take money out of your savings account too often—the amount doesn't matter—the bank may slap on a fee. Most charge from 50 cents to $1 for each withdrawal beyond a certain number during a specified period. This fee is charged no matter what the remaining balance. A smaller number of banks link the fee to the balance. This kind of activity fee is designed to discourage withdrawals, which will make it difficult for the bank to plan on how much money it has available to lend, and to prevent savers from using their accounts like checking accounts.

Using five of the computation methods listed above plus the four other variables (compounding, crediting, grace days, withdrawal penalties), Ms. Pinson constructed forty different model savings accounts using exactly the same data. In the six months for which she kept her hypothetical accounts open, they never had a balance exceeding $4,000. The interest yield for the forty accounts ranged from $29.95 to $79.13. That amounts to a difference of 264 percent between the highest and the lowest. She also checked on seven banks and found the range between $36.67 and $58.72—a 60-percent difference. Later checking indicates that Ms. Pinson's survey findings continue to be borne out. Those banks using FIFO practices and semiannual compounding and crediting bring up the rear in interest payments. Banks with quarterly compounding and crediting on a day-of-deposit-day-of-withdrawal basis provide substantially better yields. The best deal, although virtually impossible to find, would be daily compounding and crediting on a day-of-deposit-day-of-withdrawal basis.

Other factors affecting the return on savings are penalties for closing an account early, minimum-balance requirements, and charges for "inactive accounts."

You may have to pay from 50 cents to $5 if you close out an account before a fixed period has elapsed—usually a month or a quarter, but in one case in California, a year. Some banks won't pay you a cent of interest if you don't leave a minimum balance in the account throughout a quarter. The lowest required balance in any bank is $1. But in some banks you can have $99 in your account and receive no interest because the minimum is $100. Of course, the bank is receiving interest on every cent in the account.

A California study by San Francisco Consumer Action found that if there are no deposits or withdrawals for five years, the account is considered inactive. Then, the banks begin charging "maintenance" fees, which can go as high as $2 a month. Nationally, these charges go as high as $4 a month. Consumers Union says that commercial banks levy these fees more often than savings and loans. Almost 200 years ago, Benjamin Franklin left $5 to the city of Boston on the condition that the funds be left on deposit for two centuries. Had the "inactivity" rule been in effect, that account would have been wiped out. Instead, Boston will receive some $14 million as a result of the bequest.

Annual yield stressed

Savings institutions, like other commercial enterprises, seek to make their product appear as attractive as possible through their advertising. In general, that means stressing the annual yield more than the actual annual interest rate, even though that yield rate is based on the depositor's leaving all interest on deposit and interest being paid on that interest. Following are the maximum yield rates, using the 365/360-day year and with interest left in the account.

	Rate Ceiling	Annual Yield
Passbook accounts	5.25%	5.47%

	Rate Ceiling	Annual Yield
Time deposits maturing in:		
90 days to 1 year	5.75%	6.00%
1 to 2½ years	6.50%	6.81%
2½ years or more*	6.75%	7.08%
4 to 6 years	7.50%	7.90%
6 years or more*	7.75%	8.17%

*Generally, no more than 7 years.

Actually, most of the added interest results from leaving interest in the thrift rather than from the 365/360-day compounding method.

As we have seen, the actual yield depends not only on the funds left on deposit, but also on the three Cs. As a result, Professor Morse developed a "truth-in-savings" bill, which Senator Vance Hartke has introduced in Congress. This bill would require a considerable amount of information to be given to each potential depositor, including the annual percentage rate, the minimum length of time funds must remain on deposit, the annual percentage yield, the percentage rate for each crediting period and the method used to determine the balance for computation of interest, the number of times each year that interest is compounded, the dates on which earnings are credited, any "costs" and their method of computation and limits on them, and any other conditions that alter the rate of earnings payable.

The Federal Reserve and the FDIC have already issued rules requiring that yields not be given greater prominence in ads than actual interest rates and that withdrawal penalties be stated.

Banks have been asked by the Federal Reserve to comment on the desirability of establishing a single method of computation. The commercial banks oppose any single method. The American Bankers Association says that commercial banks can partially close the rate differentials, established by regulation, between commercial banks and other savings institutions by using liberal computing methods. Savings and loans argue against a single method of computation on the grounds that it would reduce competition among banks by narrowing the variety of choices available to consumers. While the mutual savings banks make similar arguments, they indicate willingness to accept day-of-deposit-day-of-withdrawal or daily compounding with monthly crediting (although they do not indicate the computing method for deposits of less than a month). Finally, the credit unions would accept a uniform computation method that required funds to be left until the end of a crediting period, using day-of-deposit-day-of-withdrawal for computation. But they would prefer a variety of computation rules in order to permit the widest competition among institutions.

Bankers say they are willing to see greater disclosure of information about savings accounts. "Full disclosure will result in

A Savings Plan Checklist

Savings are a lot more complex than they appear, but the consumer who takes the time to figure out the best deal is almost certain to come out ahead. Here are some things to watch for:

1. The bigger the savings account balance, the more important it is to maximize interest. Don't just look at the dollar amount involved; calculate how much better you do on interest on one account as compared with another.

2. Remember that commercial banks, while more convenient, cannot pay as high interest as savings institutions. Of course, if you have no checking account, use a thrift for savings. It is often worthwhile to have an account at the institution where you will later apply for a mortgage. Go to the bank that offers the best interest.

3. An almost iron law of banking says that the larger the institution, the more likely it will be to pay the maximum interest the law will allow. But they do not offer the same kind of customer service as smaller banks, because they have so many customers that they don't know their own account holders.

Just because the big banks generally pay at a higher rate than the small ones does not mean that you should accept this as automatically true. About a quarter of commercial banks pay below the ceilings. A higher percentage of both savings and loans and savings banks pay at the ceiling rate than commercial banks, but the size rule remains valid for them as well.

4. The part of the country where you have your savings account can make a difference. Not only do variations exist for the prevailing interest rate, but also for such matters as frequency of compounding and crediting and the basis for computation.

For commercial banks—the great majority of all banks—the American Bankers Association has found that the customer gets the best deal in the Pacific states and New England and the worst in the North Central part of the country. Although the Mid-Atlantic region does not rate particularly high, it's likely that the New York City area is as favorable as the Pacific region—at least among big banks.

It's wise for the saver to consider opening an account where the terms are best. There may be no need to keep a seldom-used account right in town. Virtually all the banks that are likely to offer attractive terms also offer cost-free bank-by-mail arrangements.

5. Analyze your future needs before you select an account. If you can set a portion of your fund aside for a relatively long period, you can consider a higher-interest account.

For example, if you put $2,000 in a 7.5-percent four-year account and decided to withdraw $500 at the end of two years, the net interest paid for the two-year period, even taking into account the penalty of the amount withdrawn, would be $295.34. If you simply put that same $2,000 in a standard 5.25-percent account on which there would be no penalty for the $500 withdrawal, the interest paid at the end of two years would be $224.78. As a result, you would gain $70.56 by placing your money in a higher-rate account, even if you expected to withdraw a part of it.

For those who may have to withdraw their savings at any time, the best account may well be a day-of-deposit-day-of-withdrawal account. If you can leave your money at least until the end of a calendar quarter, and if you can qualify, the best deal is probably a credit union. The interest rate it pays exceeds the rate paid in so-called grace-day accounts, which are equivalent at the bank. In addition, credit unions offer extremely favorable lending rates to their own depositors.

6. Check to see if the savings institution is insured (it almost certainly is), but don't place too much stock in what account insurance can do. Of course, it will protect up to $40,000 per account in case of bank failure. That means that federal and state examiners are interested in determining if the bank is managed properly. But they do not check the math on your account or determine if your interest has been calculated properly. That's up to you, and you can get some help at the bank on request.

7. Don't be overly impressed by how often interest is compounded unless you know how often it is credited or paid into the account. The best deal is day-of-deposit-day-of-withdrawal with daily compounding and crediting.

8. Check into how interest is computed. The computation method may lead you to try another bank. If not, it will help you to determine the effect of withdrawals on the interest you are paid. Occasionally delaying a withdrawal a couple of days can make a difference. For example, if interest is calculated on the basis of the lowest balance in the account during a quarter, it would be unwise to make a withdrawal just a week before the quarter ends. All of the interst on those funds withdrawn would be lost. That's also why it's a good idea to know about grace days. Aim for as low a minimum balance as possible.

9. Unless you are terribly weak-willed, you should stay away from Christmas Clubs and the like. You can accomplish the same purpose with a savings account. In a club you can lose all the interest on all of the money in the club simply by missing a single deposit. And some banks offer little or no interest at all.

10. If you are eligible, consider establishing a Keogh Plan or an IRA. The money you deposit and the interest that money earns will not be taxable. It will be taxed only when withdrawn for retirement purposes. Because your income is likely to be lower then, you'll pay less in taxes.

11. Ask questions. Bank disclosure, even the best, is not likely to give all of the information you need to get the best deal. The bank is in business to make a profit, and the customer is responsible, as in all transactions, for looking out for himself.

a more informed savings public able to understand and compare interest rates, yields to maturity, computation of interest, and other terms which will result in better service and increased competition between financial institutions for savings deposits," says James D. Farley, executive vice-president of Citibank. What "increased competition" generally means is that all banks in a market area have to offer the same return, generally at the highest level permitted. But as long as the consumer remains in the dark about interest calculation, they may only seem to be offering the same interest.

The Bank of America says that it favors full disclosure, but maintains that it would be impractical to include all details of interest calculation in advertising. Instead, it suggests that the information should be made available when the account is opened. At the moment, almost no bank provides written information on interest calculation to new-account savers. Very often the depositor doesn't have the opportunity to read all the literature he's been given until after the account has been opened. If the Bank of America is correct, then the regulators will have to prescribe an explanatory text and require that a person opening a new account sign, indicating that he or she has read it. Incidentally, the Bank of America went further than other commercial banks in favoring a single calculating method—day-of-deposit-day-of-withdrawal for a 365-day year. That's the most beneficial for consumers.

Without full disclosure, bank advertising leaves a lot of questions unanswered and can easily mislead the customer. It's all intended to bring in customers, and obviously, some banks believe that full disclosure will undermine the attractiveness of the accounts they offer.

Some banks don't just sell their accounts, they use merchandise as a "come-on." Gifts are offered to people opening a new account or adding a deposit to their present account. Gifts don't indicate much about the terms of the bank's accounts themselves and may very well represent interest in another form. For example, a bank might use semiannual crediting rather than quarterly crediting, with the difference in interest going toward the purchase of the gift. And even if the gift does not detract from interest, the saver should be careful not to lose any interest in the process of transferring funds from an old account to a new one. Finally, the bank revenues that go to gifts may be taken away from another service you desire.

One woman saw that a local bank was offering a "free" tree for each new $1,000 account. She promptly put no less than $17,000 in the bank, hoping for enough trees to landscape her yard. She was crestfallen when she learned that she would get only one tree because she had opened only one account. Presumably, her backyard is still barren. Still another incentive to putting at least $5,000 in a thrift and leaving it there is a free private club for big savers. First organized by State Mutual Savings and Loan in Los Angeles, the clubs have spread East. It took eight years for them to make it to New York, where First Federal opened a club in 1975. With all their comforts and facilities, the 100 or so clubs discourage depositors from making withdrawals below the minimum.

4

The
Legal
Loan
Shark

Fortunately for most people, the only contact they have with a loan shark is in the movies. Few of us have to do with people who lend us money without any fixed date for repayment and keep piling on exorbitant interest charges all the time the loan is outstanding.

Or do we? Loan sharks actually do flourish. But as the saying goes, "for those who qualify," there is a better way. For a mere 18 percent you can borrow money from the bank. You can borrow a couple of thousand dollars from a bank without even setting foot on the premises. You can take just about as long as you want to repay the loan. All you have to pay is 18 percent annual interest, and the bank will probably find a way to calculate the interest that can drive the effective rate up another three points. In addition, the bank probably won't let you borrow the money at any lower rate, so if you want consumer credit and can't put up collateral, you have to borrow at these prices. At least you probably meet a better class of people at the bank than at the loan shark's.

What made free-and-easy mass credit possible, more than anything else, was the development of the plastic chip, the stuff credit cards are made of. In 1951, the ill-fated Franklin National Bank issued the first bank credit card, the forerunner of today's mammoth BankAmericard and Master Charge cards. Even in the early days, Franklin National and others quickly learned that operating a credit-card system could be costly and cumbersome. So the new form of credit sputtered along and was joined in 1955 by a check-credit plan, designed to make it possible to extend credit to bank customers without all of the complications of the credit card. Check-credit allows the account holder to write checks for amounts exceeding his or her balance, thus automatically borrowing money from the bank. Begun by Boston's First National Bank, check-credit began to attract other banks that wanted to keep out of the credit-card business. But banks generally stayed away from both of the new forms of credit until ten years later, when they realized that they could bring about a credit explosion and sharply increase their loan portfolio by pushing the plans.

By the end of 1972, the bank credit card and check-credit had swept the country. Credit cards were available in every state, while check-credit, far less popular, was concentrated in the Northeast and Far West. Neither appeared to be limited to those states that permit the highest interest rates to be charged. Between 1967 and 1974, the amount of credit outstanding in credit-card schemes had increased some 895 percent. Check-credit outstanding balances had jumped by 364 percent. By way of comparison, the growth in credit in non-installment retail charge accounts was only 33 percent during the same period.

At the end of 1972, the last year for which complete figures have been published, some 8,574 banks participated in credit-card plans, with 1,621 operating check-credit plans. Of course, there was some duplication. The amounts of money involved were even more striking. By the end of 1972, some $10 billion in credit had been extended through bank credit cards and $2.5 billion through check-credit. Together, they represented more than 21 percent of all consumer installment credit extended by banks. As recently as 1967, they had amounted to only 3.8 percent of all consumer installment credit.

Pick a card

The bank credit card is, above all, a way of charging retail purchases. The customer gets a monthly bill including purchases made in the last thirty to sixty days. If the bill is paid promptly, there is no interest charge. In effect, the customer has borrowed money from the bank for about a thirty-day period without paying any interest. The bank receives from 1 to 10 percent of the amount of the sale from the merchant.

Credit comes into play when the customer does not immediately pay all of the amount owed. At that point, the bank begins to levy a finance charge and may also exact a number of other fees. Some two-thirds of all people who use bank credit cards take advantage of the credit made available and, in effect, borrow money from the bank. In addition to the interest, the bank still receives the merchant discount fee.

Subject to the limits in state law, the bank can set the interest rate far higher than it charges for regular consumer loans. In most cases, the interest rate is 1.5 percent each month on the unpaid balance, which amounts to an annual interest rate of 18 percent.

The customer is usually required to pay only a minimum. For example, if the balance is $10 to $200, a customer might be required to pay at least $10, but no more than 5 percent of the balance if it exceeds $200.

The bank credit card is what is called revolving or open-end credit. That means there is no fixed deadline to have repaid all that you have borrowed. You may have a virtually permanent debt, which means that the bank is continuing to collect interest. Indeed, most monthly credit-card statements have emphasized the minimum payment due rather than the total balance as a way of encouraging customers to borrow money. That is plainly against the law. Obviously, the bank hopes you will be hooked on credit and keep charging and then paying only the minimum required. You may find yourself a lot deeper in debt than you thought.

The bank can get even more interest if it chooses certain methods for calculating the balance on which the interest will be levied. Most banks use the average-daily-balance method. They calculate the balance outstanding on each day of the month, add them, and divide by the number of days in the billing month. That average daily balance is then multiplied by the daily interest rate. This method includes all of the month's

Maximum Credit-Card Rates

18%	APR* (1.5% per month)	All states, except:
18%	(1.5% per month) on first $1,000 and	California, Delaware
12%	(1% per month) on remainder	
18%	(1.5% per month) on first $700 and	New Jersey
12%	(1% per month) on remainder	
18%	(1.5% per month) on first $500 and	Maryland, Massachusetts, Nebraska, New Mexico,
12%	(1% per month) on remainder	New York, Oklahoma, Texas, Vermont, District of Columbia
18%	(1.5% per month) on first $400 and	Missouri
9%	(.75% per month) on remainder	
18%	(1.5% per month) on first $400 and	Ohio
12%	(1% per month) on remainder	
18%	(1.5% per month) on first $300 and	Kansas
12%	(1% per month) on remainder	
18%	(1.5% per month) on first $300 and	Colorado
10%	(.83% per month) on remainder	
15%	(1.25% per month)	Arizona, Pennsylvania
12%	(1% per month)	Connecticut, South Carolina, Washington, Wisconsin
10%	(.83% per month)	Arkansas, Florida
8%	(.67% per month)	Minnesota, South Dakota

*APR = Annual Percentage Rate, or simple interest.

purchases and payments. A modified version of this approach excludes the current month's purchases. This way, an early payment can actually lower the finance cost by covering the cost of recent purchases before they appear.

Retailers have usually favored the previous-balance method, where finance charges are based on what you owed at the end of the past billing month. It takes no account of current payments and purchases.

The adjusted-balance method is best for the consumer. Payments made during the month are deducted from last month's balance and then current purchases are entered.

Another method is the ending balance. Finance charges are levied on the basis of the current month's balance, which reflects all payments and purchases made during the month. The true actuarial average daily balance amounts to the same thing as the ending-balance method, except that even if all purchases are fully paid for by the end of the month, the consumer must pay finance charges on the purchase amounts for any period they were outstanding. It is rarely used.

The difference in cost among these methods can be substantial. Professor E. Ray McAlister of North Texas University found that the average outstanding balance in one retail chain was $91.90 and calculated what the finance charges would be at the same interest rate but applying the various methods:

$1.47   true actuarial—rarely used

$1.41   ending balance

$1.24   previous balance (retailers) and average daily balance (banks)

$1.18   modified average daily balance

$1.09   adjusted balance

That is a differential of 14 percent between the method most beneficial to consumers and the one most often used by banks.

Credits cards may either bear the bank's own imprint or they may be part of a national system. At the outset, banks frequently opted for their own card, but in recent years, two national arrangements, BankAmericard and Master Charge, have come to predominate. Their chief advantage is an interbank clearing system that allows the customer to use the card anywhere in the country. Obviously, the local cards are only accepted by local merchants. By the end of 1972, almost 95 percent of all bank-credit-card systems were affiliated with National BankAmericard, Inc., or with Interbank Card Association (of which Master Charge is a part). The outfits do not themselves issue cards or provide credit; they are clearinghouses among banks, known as interchanges, for transferring charges made in one part of the country to the purchaser's bank in another part of the country. They also centralize information on whether the customer pays his credit-card bills promptly. In 1972, almost one-third of credit-card purchasers benefited from the national interchange service.

Banks may be either principals or agents. About one-fifth of them act as principals, which means that all of the credit drawn by their customers comes from that bank alone. The principal bank may in turn line up other banks as agents. Some are "simple agents," meaning that the principal bank continues to be the source of all the credit, while the agent processes the paperwork and promotes the use of the card. If the bank is a "participating agent," it extends some of the credit, usually no more than 50 percent. Obviously, only principal and participating-agent banks can use the "offset," a procedure that allows them to recover money a customer owes on the credit-card account by dipping into that customer's other accounts. Of the 8,574 banks with credit-card systems, some 1,631 were either principals or participating agents.

Because each credit card is, in fact, issued by a bank, each card holder must establish a relationship with a specific bank, not with BankAmericard or Master Charge.

The card game

When you want a bank credit card, you must apply for it. Although that may seem obvious, when these cards were first launched, they were sent by the hundreds of thousands to people who seemed to have the right profile to become frequent card users. The result was a fiasco. Cards were stolen from the mails, used, and then the bills began to arrive at the addresses of many persons who, in fact, had never used the cards. In Chicago, when mass mailings were made in 1966, children received cards and many people received more than one card from more than one bank. The frauds that resulted cost the banks as much as $6 million. While, obviously, mass mailings were the best way of lining up a large number of card holders, the abuses were serious and eventually unsolicited mailings of credit cards were outlawed.

Even so, it is still possible to obtain a credit card without seeking it. The Federal Reserve, which enforces the Truth-in-Lending Act, has been notably benevolent toward the widest propagation of credit cards and has done nothing to block unsolicited issuance of cards.

But if you fill out an application willingly, be prepared to provide the same kind of information that would be required if you were seeking a consumer loan. While you are expected to reveal a good deal of personal information about your financial condition, the bank may be a good deal less willing to explain the details of the agreement you are making.

You can obtain a copy of the agreement if you ask or manage to pick up the proper brochure. You may be happier not knowing the terms and conditions. One bank lists a number of reasons for default, including "termination of present employment." It matters little that you got a new job. "In any event," the agreement reads, "the Unpaid Balance shall be due and payable . . . all without notice or demand." Elsewhere it states: "Your [the bank's] opinion as to the existence of such failure of performance is conclusive." The bank can then determine the entire balance is due, without being required to inform the card holder. In short, you may innocently change jobs and find the bank claiming you have defaulted. And you have no right, under the contract, to protest that employment was continuous. While the bank may not use this or other provisions of the contract in most cases, it has the right to do so at any time. Another provision of the agreement has the prospective card holder waiving his constitutional right to trial by jury. And it is possible to accept such conditions without even knowing of their existence if you use one of the bank's brochures that does not include any details of the agreement. You cannot negotiate this contract, and after you've read the fine print, you may not want a credit card. In any case, you should know what you are signing.

You will pick up your card at the bank, which does not want to risk its loss in the mail. You can begin using it immediately. If your first purchase is for, say, $100 at a local store that is signed up with the same bank that issues your card, the store will get credit for that amount less the discount, perhaps $3.

So, it will have $97 credited to its account. You may not actual-
ly pay the bank for another forty-five days, at which time you
pay $100. For having lent the store $97 for the forty-five days,
the bank gets 3 percent interest for the period, which works
out to 24 percent on an annual basis.

If the store is affiliated with another bank, its own bank will
skim a fee of about $1.15 for the transaction before passing the
sales slip to your bank. Thus, the merchant's bank will lend the
merchant $97 for about two days and will receive $1.15 or 1.15
percent interest for two days, or 210 percent on an annual
basis. Your bank will get $1.85 for lending the same amount for
forty-five days, which works out to almost 15 percent interest
at an annual rate. The difference in profit to your bank between a merchant that is affiliated with it and one affiliated
with another bank explains why all banks try to sign up as
many merchants as possible or else try to encourage you to
repay only the minimum required. The bank is in business to
lend money, and the more it can lend, the greater its profit.

You will receive a statement monthly, and you may try to
check all of the charges included. But you may find that your
bank does not include a copy of all the charge slips—called
"country-club billing." Instead, the bank may have resorted to
descriptive billing, which reduces mailing weight and allows
the bank to enclose additional brochures for other services.
That saves the bank billing costs, but customers must ask about
any charges they don't understand.

Some statements still place the emphasis on the minimum
payment due rather than the total new balance. That temptation to borrow money is a violation of the Truth-in-Lending
Act.

Holder-in-due-course

Until now, if a card holder was dissatisfied with a purchase
made with a card, he or she was still obliged to pay the monthly bill and then take the matter up with the merchant. In
effect, there was no "stop-payment" provision under a credit-
card agreement. Then, in October 1974, Congress passed the
Fair Credit Billing Act with an effective date one year later.
Now, the credit-card issuer, not the card holder, is liable if the
merchandise is unsatisfactory. However, this provision applies
only to purchases involving more than $50 and made in the
card holder's own state or within 100 miles of his or her billing

address. Hence, the bank card issuer will not help the person who has made small purchases or mail-order or other transactions a long way from home. But this is a major reversal of the "holder-in-due-course doctrine," which provides that you must pay the bank—which in the due course of events holds your debt—and then take your complaint up with the merchant.

Another problem that a card holder might encounter is a monthly statement that arrives so late that the card holder cannot avoid an interest payment. The new law requires the bank to mail the statement at least fourteen days before the due date. The card holder has sixty days to claim a billing error, and the bank must acknowledge such a claim within thirty days. Within an additional ninety days the bank must either correct the error or carry out an investigation and explain why it believes the statement to be correct. Within these time periods, the bank is banned from threatening the card holder's credit rating and from reporting the account as delinquent to any party. Interest is paid on the disputed amount only if the card holder ultimately accepts the bank's explanation. Of course, if he or she is still unhappy, the card holder can take the bank to court.

Yet another feature of the Fair Credit Billing Act bars the use of setoff unless the card holder has expressly authorized use of it at specific intervals. It is also banned whenever the card holder objects because the charge in question is under dispute.

Beware of any statement or contract for a bank credit card that includes a membership fee. Enough banks provide credit cards free of charge that there is no reason to sign up for a plan that involves any membership charges.

In addition to the finance charge—often at the 18-percent annual rate—the statement may reveal other unexpected fees. If the payment of at least the minimum amount due is not made by a date specified on the statement, a late charge may automatically become due. That charge is usually 5 percent of the mimimum payment due, with a minimum of 50 cents and a maximum of $5. While these charges may seem small, they are added to the total balance due and become part of the base figure used for computing interest that is due.

Interest charges that have not been paid are themselves added to the unpaid loan balance and, as a result, the next month's interest is charged not only on the outstanding principal but on outstanding interest. Thus, if the amount owed is $100, the interest at 1.5 percent will add $1.50 to the principal. The following month, interest will be levied on $101.50, not the basic $100.

Merchants price their goods to include the service charge they must pay the bank for the right to accept its credit cards. This charge covers the bank's services as bill collector. In 1974, Consumers Union pressed hard to ensure that if you preferred to pay in cash you would not be obliged to pay this hidden fee. Some credit-card agreements with merchants had actually banned them from giving cash customers a price reduction equal to the merchant's discount paid the issuer. The Consumers Union Washington office brought legal action against several credit-card companies and some agreed to inform their affiliated merchants that they could offer a cash discount. Then, in the Fair Credit Billing Act, Congress specifically banned credit-card companies from preventing cash discounts and provided incentives for merchants to "clearly and conspicuously" disclose that they grant such discounts. While such a provision may encourage purchasers to pay in cash rather than use a credit card, it may also discourage merchants who had urged customers to pay in cash instead of using the credit card because the merchant did not want to give up his "merchant's discount." Now he will have to give it up in either case.

Aces and jokers

The credit card obviously has some real advantages for the consumer. Rather than open a number of charge accounts, a single application can lead to a charge account acceptance by many merchants. Not only can a bank credit card replace charge accounts, it can usually be used in place of a number of special-purpose accounts. Airlines, hotels, and restaurants will often accept bank cards as readily as they will travel and entertainment cards such as American Express, Diner's Club, and Carte Blanche.

Yet another convenience of the bank credit card is the single monthly statement, which enables the consumer to see many if not most monthly purchases at a single glance. This helps in personal budgeting. It usually also means that only one check need be written where it was formerly necessary to write several. That makes for ease and convenience and may even reduce service charges. In fact, if a person can use his bank credit card to cover most of his monthly bills, he may be able to shift to a less expensive type of checking account, based on substantially reduced activity. Finally, the use of bank credit cards usually allows the individual to carry less cash, which may be an important security measure in areas where people fear robberies.

The consumer must weigh such advantages against serious disadvantages. Credit cards can lead individuals to increase their level of purchases beyond what they need, simply because of the relative ease of payment and the notion that the money can be found later.

Whatever the credit-card companies say by way of denial, the fact that the cards are designed to stimulate increased spending is obvious. Merchants would not be willing to give up the discount to the card issuer if they did not believe that the card would attract customers who might make impulse purchases. This is especially obvious when most if not all merchants in a given market area accept credit cards. The issuer must also be counting on increased purchases, which, more than anything else, would stimulate the use of credit.

An even greater danger is that the consumer will go beyond acceptable debt limits into serious overindebtedness and even bankruptcy. As economic conditions worsen, people may find themselves closer to this line sooner than they expected. A look at the charge-off rate, the percentage of accounts that are written off because of failure to pay the balance, is revealing. While, in theory, the longer a credit-card plan is in existence, the lower the charge-off rate as bad risks are eliminated, the overall rate has actually been climbing each year. In 1967, the rate was 1.97 percent; by 1972, it had risen to 2.32 percent. About 15 to 20 percent of the amounts charged off are due to fraud. That means most of the charge-offs occur because account holders simply are unable to pay the bills they have run up and were aware of their inability to pay at the time the charges were incurred.

Other disadvantages include the possibility that record keeping may become more difficult rather than less so with the advent of the descriptive statement. Using this statement, the bank merely sends a list of charges made, not actual copies of the charge receipts. Sometimes it's difficult to recognize a specific item from the cryptic reference on the statement. Another potential problem stems from the loss or theft of a card.

The card holder's liability is now limited to $50 if another person begins using the card. To avoid that exposure, the card holder must notify the issuer as soon as possible, citing the missing card's number. There is no liability from the moment the issuer is notified. That's why it's a good idea for the card holder to keep a record of his or her account number separate from the card itself.

Give yourself some credit

A woman is at an auction and spots a chest she absolutely must have. Sold, for $300. Then, to her shock, her checkbook reveals that she has only $250 left in her account. No matter, she simply writes a check for the full amount, thus activating a loan from her bank. Check-credit, the making of loans by use of a bank checking account, is perhaps the most painless form of credit extension possible.

Some of the check-credit plans are check-overdraft accounts, like this one. The account holder has previously arranged a maximum line of credit with the bank and can at any time overdraw the checking account without any fear of paying penalties. Instead, a loan is automatically extended and this may reach the total amount of the credit line. A variation on this approach allows the customer to make an on-the-spot loan without its becoming an overdraft. In effect, a separate loan account is then automatically activated, even though a regular check has been used to make the payment. Still another wrinkle on the overdraft account is the check-guarantee card, which informs the merchant that the bank will back a check issued on a specific account. That increases the acceptability of the check. Such cards are now issued to preferred customers who may not have any overdraft arrangement.

Another type of check-credit arrangement provides for the use of special checks that are linked with a checking account especially opened for the line of credit. In other words, every check written on such an account causes a loan to be opened. A check-guarantee card may be used in conjunction with such an account. The special checks used under such a plan are, in effect, cashiers' checks, although they are signed by the customer and not the bank. The full credit of the bank stands behind the check.

While a credit-card customer need not have a checking account at the issuing bank, a person using check-credit must open an account. In particular, the overdraft account means that the person must open a demand-deposit account with some of his or her own funds.

Check-credit plans have obvious advantages for the issuing banks as compared with credit cards. There is no need to make special arrangements with merchants to accept the checks. Of course, the merchant's discount is lost, but the bank is more than compensated by the payment of interest by every person who uses the check-credit system. Unlike the credit-card plans, which allow a grace period for repayment without interest, the check-credit schemes involve the immediate activation of a loan on which interest is charged. The bank may designate the use of the check-credit plan for specific groups of customers and design it to fit the needs of each. As a result, the size of the credit line is likely to be a good deal larger than that attached to a credit card. And once somebody has taken the trouble of opening such an account, the activity is likely to be several times higher than for credit-card accounts. All of this makes check-credit plans more attractive to banks than credit cards, and this is especially true for smaller banks that could not hope to operate their own credit-card plan.

By the same token, check-credit is less popular with consumers than is the credit card. The card at least allows the holder the option of not borrowing funds from the bank, and, as indicated earlier, about one-third of card holders avoid borrowing by promptly paying the full outstanding balance. Presumably, check-credit, which absolutely involves debt, is far less attractive, certainly to those who want convenience, not credit.

The cost of money borrowed under a check-credit scheme is high. In California, for example, the monthly rate is 1.5 percent, which works out to 18 percent annually. That rate is permitted in many other states and, as in California, a transaction fee may also be levied, which, in effect, pushes interest even higher. The banks that begin charging interest immediately stay away from using such fees. But if interest is not levied until a month after the credit line is activated, fees of either 1 or 2 percent or flat charges ranging from $1 to $2 are levied. A $2 fee on a $100 overdraft amounts to interest at an annual rate of 24 percent.

Just as with credit cards, banks use at least two different methods to determine the balance. Some use the average daily balance and charge interest immediately. Others charge a flat fee for the transaction and delay the start of interest payments until sometime after the loan is made. They use the unpaid balance after the delay period. If the loan is repaid quickly, the daily charge is likely to be less costly than the transaction fee associated with the delayed-action accounts. Over a longer period, the interest cost would be higher on the average-balance account than on the unpaid-balance account.

Perhaps the most serious drawback of the overdraft account is the amount of the loan that is created when the account is activated. In some accounts, you incur a debt only in the exact amount of the overdraft. But in many others, banks require that the loan be made in multiples of $50 or $100. The customer should assume there *is* a multiple and ask what it is. In some places the customer can avoid the minimum by filing a specific written request for a loan in the exact amount desired.

Another hidden problem for the account holder may be in the repayment rules. Customers run into trouble if they assume that deposits are automatically credited against loans from their check-credit accounts. Quoting one customer:

> When my daughter got sick a few months ago, I overdrew my Checking Plus account by $100.00 in order to pay the doctor's bill. When I deposited my paycheck in the account, I assumed that the loan was repaid. When my first monthly statement arrived and indicated that I was still paying interest on the loan, I assumed that it was due to a lag between the time I deposited the money and the time the bank gave me credit for repaying the loan. When the next statement still showed the loan had not been repaid, I went into the branch and was told for the first time that Checking Plus loans must be repaid separately from normal deposits in the account.

Chase Manhattan, which always includes the terms of the agreement on the back of its applications for Cash Reserve loans, is explicit: "All deposits to the Account when there is any amount owing shall be deemed payments or prepayments of the amount owing until paid in full with interest." In the absence of such a clear statement, the account holder may easily find that loan charges keep mounting while deposits are being made. Occasionally, the only difference between deposits is that a special form must be used for those deposits which are supposed to reduce the loans.

A Credit Checklist

Welcome to the wonderful world of credit. But remember that the bank is in business to lend you money and that it derives its profits from the interest and fees you pay for the use of that money:

1. A credit card and a check-credit plan are loan programs designed to encourage you to borrow money. Only one-third of those who have bank credit cards refrain from using the credit facilities made available.

2. Get a copy of the rules and regulations governing the account, take them away from the bank and read them, and then return to open the account when you want. This procedure has several advantages. You get a copy of the rules, often difficult to accomplish without persistence; you have the chance to learn about all or most of the charges and penalties; you can compare the terms of plans offered by several banks. Just because two banks offer the same national credit card is no assurance that the terms they use are the same. Do not feel obliged to open a credit-card account at a bank where you already have checking or savings accounts. In fact, the offset rule should discourage you from putting all of your eggs in one basket.

3. Analyze your own needs and then compare the cost of borrowing by credit card, check-credit, or cash advance. Even in the same bank the charges will vary considerably.

4. It is still possible for you to receive an unsolicited credit card. Do not accept it. If you have shopped around and want a card, you need not pay a membership fee. Try to select a plan in which other fees are as minimal as possible. Ask if the statement is merely descriptive or provides copies of charges. According to the ABA, descriptive statements are still fairly new and issuers are especially sensitive to customer reaction. If the bank refuses to provide copies of charge slips, you should keep sales slips to compare with the statements.

5. Because bank plans differ, you should ask how the balance is calculated and give preference to the system that uses last month's unpaid balance less the current month's payments and credits.

6. Try to use the credit card as a budgeting and payment method. Pay the full amount of the outstanding balance unless you have decided that you wish

to borrow money. Then, the credit card may be the preferable method because it allows you to borrow just the amount you want while avoiding some of the fees associated with check-credit.

7. Take advantage of the provisions of the Fair Credit Billing Act that allow you to protest charges appearing on your statement without being harassed. It may also relieve you of liability for payment for certain purchases when the merchandise was unsatisfactory. Also, check state consumer credit codes that may provide additional coverage.

8. If you use check-credit, use it sparingly. To avoid impulse buying, it is preferable to open a separate account instead of tacking check-credit on in the form of an overdraft provision. In that way, there is no possibility of inadvertently drawing down part of the credit line.

9. Determine all of the fees and conditions of check-credit and pay special attention to the amount of the loan that is activated. You should only use a plan that allows you to borrow the amount you want. The plan should also make repayment as easy as possible and not permit situations where deposits are not credited against outstanding loans. Finally, the best plan will not begin charging interest immediately, thus allowing time for repayment as with a credit card. In such a case, determine if there is a transaction fee and its amount.

10. When using a cash advance, determine if it is activated in minimum multiple amounts and is subject to transaction fees. Evaluate the relative utility of cash as compared with using a credit card to make specific purchases. You should also carefully consider whether the cash-advance feature of travel and entertainment credit cards offers you a service you may already have obtained under a bank credit card plan.

11. All of these forms of borrowing are what's known as open-end credit. That means the bank wants you to take as long as you want, within few limits, in order to pay back a loan. It's in your interest to cut repayment time as short as possible. If you need to borrow relatively small sums over longer periods, you would probably do better to take an installment loan from the bank or credit union and handle your short-term debts out of those funds. Otherwise the shark may have caught you.

Other drawbacks of overdraft checking are similar to credit-card plans. The offset is almost always used and applies to all property in possession or under control of the bank. That could be construed to include even the contents of a safe-deposit box. In the event of what the bank determines to be a default, the account holder is also liable for a charge of 15 percent of the amount owed to cover the bank's legal expenses. Finally, the bank may charge a 4-percent late fee each time an installment is more than ten days overdue. The account holder must keep a sharp watch on the bank's monthly statement for due dates and amounts repayable.

A little something in advance

The hybrid of the bank credit card and the check-credit plan is the cash advance. The credit card is used to purchase a product from a merchant, only this time the product is money and the merchant is the bank itself. The card is brought to the bank and a cash advance is applied for. The total amount cannot exceed the line of credit that was made available to you when you opened the credit-card account. In other words, the line of credit can be used either to cover purchases or in the form of cash paid directly to the account holder.

The cash advance is actually nothing more than a small personal loan. But the interest rate is high—18 percent in many places and 12 percent in New York. In California a one-time transaction fee may also be charged, perhaps as high as 4 percent of the loan. A few banks advance cash in multiples, which may mean that you have to borrow more than you want. Interest is not likely to begin on any advance where a transaction fee is levied if the loan is repaid within a month.

Some banks will provide blank checks for use in paying taxes, insurance premiums, doctors, and others who won't accept payment by credit card. But these checks are, in fact, portable cash advances with the same high interest. You automatically borrow money when the check is presented to the bank for payment. This is simply a variation on check-credit.

Another variation on the theme is the plan linking banks and travel and entertainment credit cards. Such cards, as well as airline, oil company, and retail store cards, have nothing to do with banks. But through a plan like American Express Executive Credit, a link is forged. American Express, not the bank, lines up and recruits customers. The card is, in the first instance, a normal American Express credit card, accepted by airlines, restaurants, and hotels. In addition, the card provides a minimum of $2,000 in a credit line, provided by the bank, which can be used to pay the monthly Amex bill (over $100), to buy travelers' checks, and to take a loan from the bank, in line with its own procedures. In addition, check-cashing privileges, already available under American Express, are expanded. In short, this is just another bank credit card, although it is accepted by those who may not normally accept the bank's own card.

It's in the cards

The bank credit card and its cousin, the check-credit account, have come to play a major role in the dispensing of consumer credit.

For many people who extend their relationship with a commercial bank beyond the simple checking account, the next step will be establishing a credit arrangement through one of these two plans. They are both designed to be so simple for the customer to use that he or she can be led easily from simply having a checking account to opening a more profitable (for the bank) loan relationship. Although banks' accounting tends to underrate the contribution of credit-card loans to profits, they constitute about 1 percent of the assets of commercial banks.

Even more important, of course, is that they may lead to more extended credit arrangements between the account holder and the bank.

Because of their ease and convenience and the relative freedom with which they are issued, they are subject to high interest rates. In late 1974, for example, the average rate for credit-card plans operated by banks was 17.15 percent annually, as compared with 13.47 percent for 12-month personal loans at the same banks and 20.93 percent for personal loans from finance companies, which are expected to take on the highest-risk customers.

The credit-card rate is just below the highest rates allowed nationally—18 percent. The banks are taking the maximum the law will allow. Like the loan shark, they seem to be immune from competitive pressure.

The growth of the bank credit card and check-credit has been substantially greater than the increase in other forms of credit. In the period between 1968 and 1974, these gains were registered in the amount of credit outstanding:

Bank credit cards	500%
Check-credit	196%
Credit unions	113%
All consumer credit	82%
All credit	70%
Bank personal loans	60%
Retail credit	53%
Finance companies	49%

Credit cards and check-credit have grown a lot faster than credit extended by retail outlets, finance companies, and the banks' own personal loan departments. Of course, the banks have consciously tried to divert small borrowers from their loan departments to credit cards.

Many banks have forced the shift away from personal loans by refusing to make installment loans of less than $1,000, or even $2,000. That means the cheapest way to make a personal loan of that amount or less is by using the credit card. It costs the bank almost $40 to process an installment loan, while the credit-card loan may cost only a fifth that much. The average size of an installment loan in a large bank is $1,738, while a credit-card loan in the same bank averages $33. While an installment loan would be less costly to the customer, the bank in effect raises the cost when the customer wants to borrow only a small amount.

Like just about all other forms of installment credit, but with a great deal more flexibility than most, credit-card loans reflect consumer reactions to economic conditions. When inflation was soaring in 1974, people made increased use of card-credit in order to maintain their standard of living. The continued expansion of credit-card use took place even as borrowing for automobile purchases and at the personal loan department, finance companies, and thrifts all declined. Then, in early 1975, recession cut their use as people could no longer look forward to receiving income later that would cover their current expenditures.

CHAPTER 5

We Give You a Lot of Credit

There is one four-letter word that is music to the ears of most bankers. The word is "loan."

Banks are in business to make a profit, and loans produce the largest profits. So, banks make loans of all varieties available to individual customers. Of course, a major part of banking operations is devoted to loans to business, but the consumer, or personal, loan is, nonetheless, the most important link a bank can establish with its individual customers.

Through extensive marketing efforts, banks try to induce people to borrow money. Indeed, the credit-card and check-overdraft account are, in some respects, a painless introduction to bank credit. The customer may move from this do-it-yourself loan on a small scale to a larger loan from the bank. At the other end of the spectrum is perhaps the largest loan that a person will make, a mortgage loan for the purchase of a home.

Credit-card borrowing is what is known as an open-end loan

because there is no fixed deadline for repayment. Through a revolving account where new charges and new payments may be made every month, there may always be a loan balance. Other consumer loans that a bank may make are called "closed-end," because they are for a fixed term.

Commercial banks provide about 44 percent of all consumer credit directly and a substantial additional amount indirectly. For example, finance companies account for 20 percent of consumer credit, and they draw a large part of their funds from the banks. Other major sources of consumer credit are credit unions, which represent about 12 percent, and merchants, who account for much of what remains. The total amount of money borrowed by consumers at the end of 1974 was $190 billion.

Most often, people make consumer loans in order to purchase an automobile. Other consumer goods purchases, including mobile homes, are almost as frequently cited as the reason for making a loan. The third major area is the personal loan, which may not be associated with any specific major purchase and which may, in fact, be used to consolidate outstanding debts.

Shopping for interest rates

Many people believe that they are at the mercy of the banks when it comes to determining how much they will have to pay for the money they want to borrow. In fact, they have a good deal more discretion than they may realize.

At one extreme, of course, is not borrowing money at all, but waiting until enough has been saved. There is no interest cost at all, and the bank or thrift will contribute interest to the amount you deposit to bring you closer to the sum needed. But there may be an "opportunity cost." Perhaps the price of the item you wish to buy is actually increasing due to inflation. By waiting for a few months, you may end up having to pay more than you have saved by not paying interest. In addition, the interest the bank pays you is taxable income, while interest you pay on a loan is deductible from your income for tax purposes. The best interest rates are usually available on passbook loans from thrift institutions and on loans from credit unions.

Savings and loans and savings banks will usually lend an amount almost equal to the full balance in the account you have with them. This loan is easy to contract because it does not have to be reviewed by any loan officer or committee, beyond a verification that the account does, indeed, exist. The rate charged is likely to reflect only a relatively small margin of profit for the thrift above what it pays on savings. Consumers Union has found that thrifts usually charge about 2 percent more than they pay in interest.

A thrift will take possession of the passbook as a simple precaution against withdrawal while the loan is outstanding. But the interest earned by the money on deposit will continue to be credited to your account and entered into the passbook. The depositor should be able to withdraw this interest and that part of the principal which is not needed to back the loan. Some thrifts do not allow the depositor to touch the funds in the account throughout the life of the loan. The borrower should talk with the loan officer about this rule and ask to have it waived if it does apply. If the thrift institution is intransigent and there is sufficient time to transfer funds without losing interest, you may want to change to another thrift. In any case, you certainly should not deposit any more money in an account at that thrift so long as you have an outstanding loan.

Commercial banks usually do not offer low-interest passbook loans on their savings accounts. That's one good reason not to open a savings account in a commercial bank.

Credit unions will let their members take loans against the value of their shares on almost the same terms. Again, the chief attraction of such loans is their low interest rate and the ease in obtaining the money.

The rates that credit unions offer on loans that are not secured by deposits may also be quite attractive. The most that federal credit unions may charge is 12 percent a year, and in 1973, a year of relatively high rates, 76 percent of loans were made at this rate. But some 17 percent were made at a rate of 9 percent or lower. Because credit unions may have a relatively close relationship with their members, they charge about one percentage point less than commercial banks on personal loans. Some credit unions even refund a part of the interest they have collected during the year to borrowers who had loan balances outstanding during that same year. This is a form of profit-sharing and is designed to encourage members to borrow from the credit union rather than elsewhere.

Because credit unions are often sponsored by employers, they may have a unique relationship with them. One disadvantage is that the credit union can obtain a wage assignment from the borrower as a condition of making the loan and then be able to tap his or her wages directly in case of late payment or nonpayment on a loan not secured by deposits.

Next up the ladder of interest rates are loans obtained from banks and credit unions that are secured by assets other than passbook deposits. Often these are stocks and bonds that the borrower does not plan to sell. Just how much the banks will lend depends on the nature of the security offered. Some are traded on securities exchanges and have a price that can be determined easily each day. Others, which are less attractive, are traded over-the-counter and not on any exchange. The least attractive are shares of closely held corporations, whose shares are held by a few people and are not generally traded. Their price can be determined only by what a purchaser is willing to pay for them at the time they are offered. Outside of this scale are government securities, which are very good backing for a loan and will bring almost full value. Depending on the economic situation and the volatility of the market, the bank may offer 60 to 80 percent of a recognized and listed stock, or 40 to 50 percent of an unlisted stock. If prices fall, the bank may ask for additional collateral. Finally, if you are pledging stock to borrow money to buy more stock, the Federal Reserve Board sets limits on how much can be borrowed.

The cash value of whole-life insurance policies may also be a suitable security for a consumer loan. Of course, the policyholder can borrow directly from the insurance company up to the cash value and is almost certain to pay only a low interest rate. Chances are that the older the policies, the lower that rate will be. In addition, the principal does not actually have to be repaid as long as interest is either paid regularly or added to the loan amount. The chief drawback in borrowing against the insurance policy from the issuing company itself is that in the event of death the payment will be reduced by the amount of the loan outstanding. As an alternative, the cash value of the policy can be pledged as security at the bank, which in no way affects the amount of insurance. Usually, it will be a good idea to have the beneficiary of the policy also agree to the assignment of the cash value to the bank. In the event of default on the loan, the bank will cash in the policy. That not only reduces insurance, it eliminates it. Thus, a great deal of care should be used in borrowing against a life insurance policy.

The next and probably the most likely step is to turn to a commercial bank or a thrift for an unsecured loan. There are significant differences even among banks in the same market. And it is likely that you will have to borrow money in your home market; banks seldom lend to individuals who come to them from another market without a sound reason.

Surveys conducted by Consumers Union and the Federal Reserve Board indicate that small commercial banks usually charge about 1 to 1.5 percent less than large banks for consumer loans. However, this generalization may not apply in every market and even in each bank in relation to loans for various purposes.

It is wise to shop around on rates. Do not sign any papers until you have accumulated comparative data from several banks. Each month, the Federal Reserve publishes national averages of rates for five categories of installment credit. Here are the figures for December 1974 expressed in annual percentage rates:

New automobiles (36 months)	11.62%
Mobile homes (84 months)	11.71%
Other consumer goods (24 months)	13.27%
Personal loans (12 months)	13.60%
Credit-card plans	17.21%

Of course, these rates change continually, but these figures are useful as an indication of the relationship among rates for various purposes.

It is impossible for the consumer to go to any single source to determine interest information for a specific market. The Federal Reserve figures are based on monthly information provided by some 350 commercial banks throughout the United States. Consumers Union has sued to make this information public, but the Federal Reserve insists that banks would not be willing to provide information if they could not be confident that it would not be released. In March 1975, Consumers Union obtained and published the interest-rate data submitted by ninety-five banks in eleven major markets.

The data that Consumers Union made public showed major rate differences even within a single market. In the New York City area, a $2,000 personal loan for a year from Chemical Bank Hudson Valley would cost $130, while the same loan would cost only $109.09 at Irving Trust. In Chicago, the gap was $41.27 between Main Bank's low and Northern Trust's high. The biggest gap in a single market occurred in the Dallas-Fort Worth area, with a low of $108.33 at Republic National Bank and a high of $194.68 at First National Bank of Dallas—a difference of $86.35. The widest national disparity was between First National Bank of New Jersey at the low end and Valley National Bank of Glendale, California, at the high end; the difference worked out to $134.98. Valley National was 238 percent more expensive. Incidentally, the Federal Reserve's composite national figure worked out to $145.92, higher than any of the New York or Chicago banks.

Obviously, this is the kind of information that local consumer groups or consumer bureaus in state and local government could compile. The net result of full disclosure of rate information will inevitably be lower interest rates because of open competition.

Not only is it worthwhile to shop around among banks to find the lowest interest rate, but the consumer should also be prepared to bargain with the bank over the specific rate. Remember that the rates quoted to the Federal Reserve are merely the most common, not the only rates charged. If you argue that you should be charged less than the original amount the bank quotes, you may succeed in bringing the rate down. The loan officer may be impressed by your other accounts in the bank, your income, your past loan record, and the security you offer. Your willingness to shop around at other banks is also bound to make an impression. The loan officer wants to give you the money as long as he or she feels confident that you won't default.

If you ask, you may find advantageous rates for certain customers. For example, one bank cuts the interest on unsecured personal loans of as much as $10,000 by 1.2 percent for those who have $2,000 (or less, depending upon the loan) in a savings account.

Beyond the commercial banks, in the stratosphere of interest rates you will find automobile dealers and, above all, finance companies. The automobile dealer will probably save you a lot of trouble by offering to take care of financing, but you will pay more than if you went directly to the bank yourself. The finance company exists mainly to lend money to people who cannot get money at the bank. It charges a much higher rate of interest to enable those who pay their loans to help subsidize the finance company for those who default. In addition, the finance company has to charge more because it pays more than does the bank for the money it lends.

While thrift institutions write loans that are secured, in many places they are forbidden to make unsecured personal loans. They are banned from doing so because they might make personal loans in preference to mortgage loans, thus defeating one of their major purposes. A strict limit could be placed on the share of the thrift's assets that could be allocated to personal loans. Chances are that the interest rate charged would be lower than at a commercial bank.

Apply yourself

Whether or not you get a loan depends quite a bit on what may seem a subjective judgment of you and your ability to repay. The bank will want to evaluate your character, your job security, your financial condition, your personal qualifications (including marital status and family background), and your past loan history. Inevitably, as part of gathering this information, a loan officer will interview you. The American Institute of Banking teaches new bankers that there are no less than sixteen danger signals to watch for during a loan interview. Among them are:

1. The applicant applies at a bank far removed from his home or work.

2. The applicant resides in a rooming house . . . a slum area . . . or he uses a post-office box as his address.

3. The applicant is suspected of being a heavy drinker.

4. The applicant does not have an established place of business . . . operates out of his home or has a telephone answering service.

5. The individual enjoys diplomatic immunity.

Of course, many of the warning signs are quite legitimate. But some of those cited above make it difficult if not impossible for diplomats, writers and artists, newcomers to town, or some minority group members to obtain a loan. Of course, the personal preferences of the loan officer may enter into the decision, so that's why some people have a haircut before they go to the bank.

Not only will this evaluation determine if you get the loan, it may also determine the interest rate to be charged. Other determinants of the interest rate are the amount and nature of the loan. Rates can actually change as the loan amount increases. Well-secured loans, where the items being purchased can serve as collateral, will bring the rate down.

You simply won't be able to get certain personal installment loans because they are too small. You will be obliged to borrow by means of a bank credit card or a check-overdraft account. If you are borrowing a small amount—say, less than $500—for a short period—say, six months or less—you will probably do better to borrow in one of these other ways. You thus avoid paying any minimum fee that the bank may charge for making the loan in case the interest paid doesn't cover its costs, and the prepayment penalty that is levied as part of a closed-end loan if you wish to pay off the loan early. Otherwise, the personal loan will be preferable, because the interest rate is almost certain to be lower than the rate on the credit-card loan.

You have to be calculating

Perhaps the most difficult problem in making a loan is figuring out how much interest you have to pay. In an effort to make it easy for borrowers to compare interest rates asked by various lenders and to get a better idea of the real rate they would pay, the Truth-in-Lending Act requires that the loan be quoted at the annual percentage rate (APR). The APR is calculated on the basis of the amount of the loan principal outstanding at the time of each payment. This is then converted to an annual rate of interest. The APR is also called the simple rate of interest, but figuring it out is by no means simple and the consumer cannot ordinarily handle the computation. The lender will provide the dollar amount of interest to be paid, if you ask. That's why the APR must be regarded as an abstract figure, not as the real price tag.

Before the requirement to use the APR, many lenders gave the so-called add-on rate. An add-on of 6 percent meant that it cost $6 to borrow $100 for a year. If payments were made monthly, the total amount to be repaid was $106, or $8.83 per month. That was easy enough for the borrower to calculate. The drawback was that the 6 percent substantially misrepresented the actual interest paid. With each monthly payment, a part of the $100 principal was repaid, so the borrower did not have use of the money for the full year. Yet interest of $6 was calculated as though the $100 were not repaid until the full year had elapsed. Because the amount of principal outstanding actually diminished each month, the $6 fee (supposed 6 percent rate) amounted to a real interest charge of 11.4 percent of the amount of principal that the borrower actually had over the entire course of the year. That 11.4 percent is the APR.

Obviously, consumer activists wanted the standard use of the APR because it is more accurate.

If you are shopping for a loan and are cited what seems to be a surprisingly low rate, ask the prospective lender if that is the APR. It almost certainly isn't. Some lenders persist in citing the add-on or discount rates on the grounds that they are more comprehensible to the borrower. With the widespread use of the APR these days, these old rates merely serve to confuse matters.

The APR is supposed to include not only the basic finance charge but any other fees. If the lender is paid an extra percentage point during the first year as a fee for administrative costs of the loan or if a charge is made to cover an investigation of your credit standing, both should be included in the APR. When the add-on rate was used, such charges were often levied separately.

Usually a loan is repaid by level, monthly payments. Some lenders offer loans on which interest or perhaps a small portion of principal is repaid in each regular payment. The bulk of the principal is left for the final payment. This kind of loan, not too frequent now, is an open invitation, if not a requirement, to refinance the loan and start all over again. This loan is likely to be much more in the interest of the lender than the borrower.

The costs of prepaying

Because consumer loans are generally small, a change in the borrower's circumstances may well lead to an attempt to prepay the loan. While it may seem fair and even obvious that full repayment of the loan should mean the end of interest payments, the penalties for prepayment may be considerable.

The penalty may come either in the form of a flat fee or as a result of the computation method used by the bank. In theory, a flat fee should be charged only when a loan is prepaid in the first month or two. In such a case, the bank has probably not received enough interest income to cover its costs in setting up the loan. But some banks may insist on a prepayment penalty fee at any time the loan is paid off before its term.

You may recall that both the add-on and discount methods of calculating interest do not accurately reflect the amount of interest you may owe at any particular moment during the life of a loan. If you decide to prepay, how does the bank know how much interest you have paid to that point? Chances are, the bank uses a method called the "Rule of 78s."

The Rule of 78s is based on the notion of a loan paid off in twelve equal monthly payments. The loan is deemed to be composed of twelve principal parts in the first month. Twelve installment units are payable that month, one for each part. In the second month, when one-twelfth of the principal has been repaid, eleven principal parts and eleven installment units remain. Each month, the number of installment units decreases by one. Over the twelve months there are a total of seventy-eight installment units. (The "Rule" can be extended to any number of months.)

If a loan is prepaid at the end of the first month, the borrower is considered to have used twelve installment units. Therefore, he or she must pay 12/78s of the total finance charge. That means that more than 15 percent of all the interest that must be paid on the loan is due for just a little more than 8 percent of the time the loan was outstanding. In the second month, 11/78s must be paid in addition to the 12/78s paid as interest in the first month.

Obviously, the Rule of 78s is not exact. It dates from precomputer days when it was just about the best a bank could do. It is roughly fair when used in conjunction with the add-on or discount methods of computing interest. It is most unfair in the early stages of a loan. At those stages, the bank is paid more interest than it has actually earned. The Rule of 78s is not illegal, but lenders are now required to inform borrowers in advance just how much of a penalty is built into the loan in case of prepayment. San Francisco Consumer Action calculates that "with a $3,000, thirty-six-month loan and a total finance charge of $585.00 (APR 11.96 percent), the penalty under the Rule of 78s for prepayment after three months would be about $7.00." As loans get larger, the prepayment penalty using this method can be substantial.

The best prepayment method for the consumer and the one most likely to be used if the loan is actually calculated using the APR is the "actuarial" method. The bank can calculate exactly how much interest is due at the time of any given payment. If the borrower pays the interest on the loan for the period he or she has actually held the loan, plus whatever remains outstanding of the principal, there are no additional interest payments. That amounts to making a payment when it is due and then returning the rest of the principal.

As banks have begun shifting over to actual calculation by the APR method, they have begun dropping prepayment penalties.

Truth or consequences

The Truth-in-Lending law was designed to ensure that borrowers could compare the cost of loans and, in general, know what they were getting themselves into.

Banks and other lenders are forbidden to quote add-on or discount rates that give the inaccurate impression of a low rate of interest. They are required to give the APR, or simple interest rate. In many cases, however, the same "low" rates are quoted as previously, thus putting the honest lenders at a great disadvantage because they quote the "higher" annual percentage rate.

The potential borrower should ask specifically if the rate quoted is the APR and accept nothing other than a direct affirmative answer. If you don't get the proper answer, the bank should be reported to the Federal Reserve Board, which is responsible for national enforcement of the Truth-in-Lending law.

In some states, the law is under the administration of the state, and you should be on the safe side by submitting a complaint to the state banking department as well as to the Federal Reserve.

For nonbank lenders, complaints should go to the Federal Trade Commission. Failure to provide you with APR information is a violation of the law, and almost all banks will provide the proper information if they see that you know exactly what you want.

Another requirement of the law is that all charges in addition to the principal be figured into the APR. That means that you need not pay any amount that the lender claims in addition to the finance charges. Such charges would actually push up the effective interest rate, which is not permitted.

Information on prepayment penalties is also supposed to be provided by the lender before the loan is made. San Francisco

Consumer Action has found that a typical disclosure statement reads:

> If the loan is paid in full prior to maturity, borrower shall receive a rebate of any precomputed interest in the finance charge according to the Rule of 78s; provided, however, that there will first be deducted therefrom the sum of $25.

The borrower has to pick his or her way through this jargon in order to understand the prepayment clause. "Precomputed interest" refers to the finance charge that is added to the principal at the initiation of the loan. In short, if the principal is $1,000 and the finance charge is $200, thus requiring repayment of $1,200, the $200 constitutes precomputed interest.

The "rebate" is not actually paid to the borrower. Instead, the credit or interest that is due as a result of prepayment is applied against the outstanding amount of the loan. That may mean that the borrower has to return less to the lender.

If, for example, the $1,000 loan is paid back in one month, by the Rule of 78s the amount of interest due is 12/78 of $200, or $30.77. That leaves a rebate of $169.23. At the end of the first month, the borrower must thus pay $1,030.77. There is no actual cash return to him. This amount is increased by the flat fee of $25, making the total payment $1,055.77. Interest of 5.6 percent will have been paid for the month—67 percent annual interest. Only the existence of interest-rate ceilings in the law prevents the interest rate from reaching this point. Yet this example indicates just how prepayment penalties can push effective interest more than three times as high as the apparent rate. That's why it's important for the borrower to know exactly what the prepayment penalties are.

The high cost of money

In addition to interest rates and the methods of calculating them, a number of other factors push up the cost of borrowed money.

Many lenders charge a late fee if any specific installment payment is more than ten or fifteen days late. The charge is often 5 percent of the amount of the overdue monthly payment, including both principal and interest. This late charge is added to the monthly installment and can obviously drive the cost of the loan up. If it is not paid, it may hasten the moment when the loan goes into default.

In the case of APR or simple-interest loans as they may be called, the bank should calculate the interest due on the basis of the actual period of time the money was on loan. Thus, if the payments are made late, that will drive up interest costs because the principal has been held longer. Some banks will charge a late fee as well, but there is no justification for such a charge. The bank is assured of full compensation for the money it has lent, because it charges interest for each day the loan is outstanding.

By the same token, if you make payments ahead of the agreed schedule, you should be charged less interest. Whatever you do, the amount of the installment payments should be level, unless you make a special deal. Only the last payment, which will take care of remaining interest, may differ.

Some banks require people to whom they lend money to have an account with them. While they claim that such an account establishes a relationship with the borrower, making him or her a customer of the bank and hence a favored loan client, these tie-ins boost the interest rate. Of course, such a request is normal for a credit union, which is generally permitted to do business only with its members. In addition, if you have actually banked at the same place for some time, you may be better known as a loan client and eligible for better treatment than a person off the street.

By depositing some of your money in an account at a bank where you borrow money as a result of a tie-in, you do not actually take from the bank all of the principal you have borrowed. In effect, the loan principal is deposited with the bank until it is used. Even if the loan is used immediately, the total amount is reduced, from the bank's point of view, by the balance in your new account. If, for example, you borrow $1,000 at 14.8 percent APR, you might be required to open a checking account with an average balance of $100. The actual net amount that you would have taken from the bank would be only $900. But you are paying interest on $1,000. That would make the actual APR about 16.4 percent.

What's more, checking or savings accounts in the same bank where a loan was made may create the right of offset. The bank can withdraw from that account any amount due on a loan without recourse either to a court or to the borrower. The failure to notify the account holder may put him or her in an embarrassing situation from inadvertently overdrawing the account. This right can create actual added costs and a lot of anguish for the borrower.

If property is pledged as security for a loan, it may be possible for the bank to repossess it without any court action or notice to the borrower. In particular, cars purchased with auto loans are natural targets for such bank action, since they can be picked up right on the street.

The bank may also require that property used as security be insured, and will provide the insurance, with payments as part of the finance charge. These premiums can be high and certainly they profit the lender who gets a cut of them. It's wise for the borrower to shop around for the lowest-cost insurance. The bank cannot require that the insurance be purchased under its auspices.

Your money or your life

The bank can require that the borrower purchase insurance that will guarantee repayment in case he or she is disabled or dies. Credit life insurance fees, if they are paid through the bank, must be included in the APR. Because this pushes up the rate the bank must quote, some have dropped their insistence that credit life insurance be obtained through them.

When banks have sold such insurance, the premiums have often been unusually high. A rate of 50 to 75 cents per $100 of initial indebtedness is common. And federal statistics indicate that as many as 95 percent of borrowers do purchase credit life insurance from the lender—finance company or bank.

Perhaps the greatest abuse of credit life insurance is that the borrower is required to buy a lot of unnecessary coverage. The face value of the insurance may be the sum of the principal and all of the finance charges over the life of the loan. Yet were the borrower to die before the loan was fully repaid, all of the principal but only a part of the finance charges would actually be due. Admittedly, the amount of insurance declines as the amount of the outstanding balance declines, but it still covers all of the finance charges at any one time.

Most credit life insurance covers the principal amount of the loan, all interest to be paid, the single premium to be paid for insurance, and any other elements of the finance charges. In case of death, any overpayment on the single premium is not refunded. Thus, if the borrower dies early in the life of the loan, the insurance premium is astronomical.

Although credit life insurance offerings are approved and rates are set by state statute or by state insurance department regulations, the actual premium rates and coverage vary. For example, some companies offer an extended benefit period so that if you fall somewhat behind in your loan payments before the loan term draws to a close, you have a better chance of remaining insured.

You may always go to an insurance company and request exactly the insurance policy you need to cover the bank's specifications. Comparison shopping among insurance companies is advisable. In any case, you should always carry sufficient life insurance coverage to protect your survivors from a burden of debt.

If you purchase a policy from an insurance company, you will gain advantages further reducing the cost that are not available with credit life insurance bought through a bank. The premium for credit life insurance is set in terms of the amount being financed and does not take into consideration the age or health of the borrower (credit life insurance is not available for borrowers over age sixty-five). Commercial life insurance always takes age into account and may also require a physical examination. Because such flexibility is absent in credit life policies, the younger subsidize the older borrowers.

Unlike mutual life and savings bank life policies, credit life pays no dividend based on the experience of all those insured. Thus, if there is a particularly low payout by credit life, that simply means more profit for the insurer. Indeed, credit life insurers often share their gains with the banks that have sold such profitable insurance.

Get a horse

Perhaps the most frequent purpose of a consumer loan is for the purchase of an automobile. Banks like to make this kind of loan because it will be secured by the car itself. Even if you borrow the money directly from the automobile dealer, he will probably transfer your debt to the bank, making you ultimately the bank's customer.

If you borrow from the dealer and he's sold you a clinker, you may be able to use the threat of nonpayment as a weapon for getting him to fulfill his part of the bargain. In some arrangements that the dealer makes with banks, he must re-purchase all loan contracts in default. To avoid this situation, he may be willing to meet your demands to repair the buggy. But in many arrangements, the dealer sells the note to the bank, which will have to repossess in case of default.

If you borrow the necessary funds from a bank, you cannot use the withholding of payments as a way of influencing the dealer. You should weigh this disadvantage against a major advantage in borrowing from the bank: If you eliminate the dealer as a middleman when you borrow, the finance charges are likely to be considerably lower. It's always wise to acquire competitive information from the dealer where you may purchase a car and from the bank where you may borrow the money. Both should be willing to provide you the information without your being obligated. If they insist on your making a commitment before they provide the information, go elsewhere.

Until recently, the maximum term for automobile loans was thirty-six months. Because of inflation, which pushes auto prices up, and recession, which limited purchasers' ability to pay, such loans may now run as long as forty-eight months. The longer the loan, the greater the total interest paid, and with high rates the difference can be substantial.

Education loans: a good deal

A wide variety of education loans and grants are available, many of them administered directly by the college or university. But banks also participate in a loan program that offers the borrower a good deal.

The program was initiated by New York State in 1958 and was later adopted by the U.S. Department of Health, Education and Welfare (HEW). Loans are made to the residents of the state where the bank is located for use at any regionally accredited institution anywhere. In New York, loans used for vocational training must be used in-state.

If a family's total income minus an allowance of 10 percent is less than $15,000 a year, the federal government will pay all finance charges until nine months after graduation. At that point, the borrower must begin to repay the loan at an annual rate of 7 percent. When the adjusted family income is between $15,000 and $30,000, the state pays 4 percent of the interest and the borrower's family pays 3 percent. Repayment begins immediately, even while the student is still in school.

The 7-percent rate is obviously well below the recent commercial rates. That's because of the government repayment guarantees. For college loans, 80 percent of any bank loss on a loan would be paid by HEW and 20 percent by the state.

Tne New York experience shows a loan loss of 4.6 percent of the dollar value. A spokesman for Chase Manhattan Bank, which is an active participant in the program, said that their defaults have risen during the last five years. New York State officials maintain that the delinquency rate has not increased significantly. The Chase officer reported that the terms for making loans have been liberalized. He also noted that students' families appear to regard the loans as something of a grant and make inadequate preparations to make the monthly loan payments. The potential borrower should inquire at the bank about such a loan well in advance of the time it would be needed. And watch out for education loans that amount to nothing more than personal loans.

The discriminating lender

Some people have no trouble with loans because they simply cannot obtain them. Whatever the guarantees of the Constitution and laws, members of minority groups, young people, and women may well find themselves the victims of discrimination. Supposedly, loan officers base their rejection of such people on an appraisal that they probably will be unable to repay. But that appraisal itself may be based on outmoded prejudices about the financial responsibility of such people.

While general provisions of the law are designed to ensure fair treatment of all groups, there is little specific protection built into the law. Lenders will often go to considerable lengths to disguise the grounds of their discrimination against minority group members and young people. But they have been amazingly frank in their refusal to grant credit to women on equal terms with men.

The Equal Credit Opportunity Act, entered into effect in October 1975, is designed to abolish this outmoded discrimination on the basis of sex. The new law specifically bans discrimination on the basis of sex or marital status in all kinds of credit transactions. As for banks and thrifts, the only institutions not covered are the few state banks that are neither federally insured nor members of the Federal Reserve System.

In the past, single women have sometimes been required to

have a cosigner on a loan when a single man faced no such requirement. A married woman frequently could not take out a loan without her husband's permission, although the husband was not asked for similar authorization. When making mortgage loans, some banks have refused to consider the income of both husband and wife on the grounds that the wife's income might suddenly be halted. Women would find themselves rejected for loans on the basis of adverse reports from credit bureaus, based not on financial condition but on sex, race, or age.

The Equal Credit Opportunity Act rules out all of these forms of discrimination. If they are encountered, the borrower should take the matter up with the appropriate federal regulatory agency (see chapter 8). The Federal Reserve has the ultimate rule-making authority.

Women have used credit less often than men, so they may not have established credit records. For a married couple, the husband may simply have signed for all of the loans. Generally, maintaining checking or savings accounts or a credit-card account should be sufficient to satisfy most banks. Consumers Union suggests that women take out a loan that they don't need and then repay it as a way of creating a credit record. Yet this is both unreasonable and wasteful and will tend only to accentuate the arbitrary standards maintained by some banks. Indeed, a woman should need to prove only that she has no adverse credit experience and that she has the capacity to repay. Any other requirement for obtaining credit is not in the consumer's interest and may be against the law.

Discrimination on the basis of race and age is not so specifically covered. Both expanded coverage and serious enforcement are obviously needed.

To have and to hold

Banks may become involved in credit transactions without the consumer's being immediately aware of their role. If the consumer makes a purchase and finances it on credit extended by the merchant, the note may be "discounted" by a bank. That means that the bank pays the merchant less than the amount of the loan but relieves him of the further need of trying to collect what's due.

As a result, the consumer will actually be paying the bank even though the original deal was made with the merchant. If the goods purchased prove to be defective or even worthless, the bank will still want to be paid and will take action to get you to make the required payments.

The bank cannot be held responsible for the merchant's failure to sell a good product, because it is the holder-in-due-course of the loan. The law presumes that the bank cannot be aware of the merchant's failure to perform his part of the deal and is once removed from him. In effect, the law requires you to pay for a product that may never have been delivered. In case of difficulty, the purchaser must have direct recourse to the merchant. Only with regard to credit-card sales does federal law sweep aside the holder-in-due-course doctrine.

The lesson is not to believe that if you are dissatisfied with a product, you can have the matter taken care of by withholding payment on the loan. That may only complicate the situation further.

Just as banks sometimes discriminate against people who are fully qualified to borrow, they also make it too easy for people who should not go deeply into debt. Loan officers get ahead by making loans, and it is often easiest to "sell" a loan to a person in tight financial straits. The prospect of a loan to consolidate debts may be irresistible. The loan officer may give very little thought to the sacrifices the borrower will have to make in order to repay the loan, or, more seriously, to the real possibility of default.

The friendly finance company

The borrower's last resort is the finance company. It will provide a loan to a person who expected to have a hard time getting one from the bank. In return, the finance company will charge the maximum interest the law will allow.

The finance company is, in many cases, merely an extension of the bank itself. Because finance companies do not have depositors, they turn to the bank for their funds. They must pay whatever rate the bank may require, which can drive up the cost of their funds. Actually, such giants as Household Finance or Beneficial Finance have good standing with the banks because they repay their loans.

Finance-company rates are kept in check by legal limits. They may go as high as 45 per cent on loans of less than $300. At the end of 1974, the national average rate for personal loans by finance companies was 21.11 percent, more than half again

A Loan Checklist

Most people have an immediate need for the money they seek to borrow. All too often, they fail to recognize that most financial institutions eagerly solicit their business because it means profits. But even though a bank is eager to lend you money, you should be careful to investigate any loan:

1. It may be preferable to save in advance rather than to borrow. Consider the alternatives.

2. Shop around for interest rates. Investigate the charges and conditions of commercial banks not only as compared with thrifts and other institutions, but even among the commercial banks themselves.

3. Join a credit union if you are eligible. Not only will you receive a reasonably good return on your savings, but you will be able to obtain loans easily and on good terms. As an essentially cooperative undertaking, a credit union may even rebate a part of your interest charges.

4. When applying for a loan, prepare the answers to all obvious questions in advance. Do not hesitate to volunteer all relevant facts when answering a question orally or in writing.

5. Insist on knowing the APR for the loan. You should also inquire as to the amount of the monthly payments.

6. You should be informed about any prepayment penalty in whatever form it is levied.

7. Check on all other fees and make sure they are included in the calculation of the APR. Watch out also for tie-in arrangements such as the requirement to open a checking or savings account. Inquire if the bank uses an offset that allows it to take money out of your account to meet a loan charge. If there is both a tie-in and an offset, keep shopping.

8. Avoid the purchase of credit life insurance if it is possible.

9. If you take a loan to purchase an automobile, be sure to compare the various dealer plans

and what you can obtain at a bank or thrift institution.

10. If you feel you are the victim of discrimination with a loan, tell the lender directly and let him know you intend to take further action.That may be enough to bring about a change in his attitude. If not, write him formally, with a copy to your local or state consumer department, the state attorney general, the state banking department, and the Federal Reserve Board. That may bring results.

11. Beware of the holder-in-due-course doctrine. Do not count on being able to settle your differences with a merchant by withholding payments from the bank or other institution where you borrowed the money to make a purchase.

12. Don't take a loan unless you can afford it. The guideline of not taking on a total debt, exclusive of mortgage, of more than 20 per cent of income is absolutely sound.

13. If it's at all possible, avoid using a finance company. If you decide to go ahead with one, ask questions about rates, duration, amount of payments, prepayments, and all of the other matters peculiar to a loan.

14. If you find yourself over your head in debt, you may be advised to seek help from a credit counselor. Consumers Union suggests contacting the National Foundation for Consumer Credit in Washington, D.C., which maintains a list of 167 nonprofit credit-counseling centers.

It's worth asking what relationship, if any, a credit counselor has with banks and other lenders. If the counselor is supported by banks, he or she will want to devise a way for you to repay your debt fully. Bankruptcy may be the only way to get your personal financial affairs on a sound footing again. You would have to consult a lawyer if you wanted to consider this course.

higher than the rates charged by commercial banks. With the need for the companies themselves to borrow from a bank, and a default rate about double that at banks, such high rates are not surprising.

What may be surprising is the number of people who are willing to pay those rates. About 25 percent of all installment credit is obtained from finance companies. People are driven to use the finance companies by banks that do not want to assume the risk of loans but are willing to provide the capital.

In addition to those whom the banks would consider marginal borrowers, many middle- and upper-income people feel more comfortable with a loan company. Maybe they fear that a credit check by the bank would reveal a past event they would just as soon keep quiet. Perhaps they believe that they will simply not have to bare as much of their financial history to a loan company as to a bank. Possibly they believe they have already borrowed all the bank will give them. Or they simply prefer the atmosphere of a loan company. Finally, in many cases, borrowers believe the banks would refuse them when, in fact, they would not.

Finance companies are often criticized as harmful to the consumer interest because of their high rates and their ready willingness to extend loans even if their borrowers are unable to repay. They merit such criticism when they willfully disguise the high interest payments instead of honestly stating the rate.

In some places finance companies have been driven out of the market because of the alleged harm they do consumers. This has been accomplished by denying them the right to charge sufficiently high interest to cover their losses on defaulted loans. Banks may actually have given their quiet support to the antifinance-company movement in these places. They will then pick up those customers who would, in any case, have been eligible for bank loans. What happens to the others? Some will travel considerable distances to patronize finance companies in neighboring states. Others will turn to the illegal loan market—to the loan sharks who can charge rates that are totally uncontrolled by law. Finally, some, who would have been able to repay a finance company loan, will simply be unable to obtain credit.

In short, the consumer-oriented push to shut down finance companies can result in some people having to pay higher rates, others having their freedom of choice limited, and still others being prevented from having any chance at all for a loan.

There is nothing illegal about the way many reputable finance companies operate. They have evolved as a part of the credit system to meet a real need.

On the basis of rates alone, you should try a bank before turning to a finance company. If you do seek a loan from a finance company, remember that the rates will be high, particularly for a small loan. In any case, insist on knowing the APR. The finance company may prefer to cite only the amount of each installment payment. That's useful to know in calculating whether you can afford the loan according to the 20-percent guideline, but it will not allow you to compare the cost of the loan with that of another finance company or other credit source.

Some finance companies can be unscrupulous—charging too much and disclosing too little. And some are relentless in their harassment of slow payers or "deadbeats." Some try to pressure customers to get deeper into debt, and thus extend the loan-repayment period, or to take a new loan. Such tactics may result in the borrower's permanent financial bondage. Thus, most states supervise finance company operations closely.

In short, try to avoid using a finance company, but if you do, handle with care. In case of any difficulty with one, contact your state or local consumer affairs office, the state attorney general, or the state banking department.

6

Mortgaging Your Future

A mortgage loan is almost certainly the largest loan you'll ever take. While you may borrow money to buy a home from another member of the family or from a credit union or even from a life insurance company, you are most likely to obtain the mortgage from a bank or a thrift institution. Well over three-quarters of all mortgages on one- to four-family dwellings and on farms were held, on September 30, 1974, by these financial institutions and life insurance companies. Among these, the savings and loans held the lion's share:

Savings and loans	56.9%
Commercial banks	22.5%
Mutual savings banks	12.6%
Life insurance companies	8.0%

This means that in most parts of the country you are most

likely to obtain your mortgage from either a savings and loan or a commercial bank.

The savings and loans have virtually exploded on the scene within the past thirty years to meet the need for mortgage money to service the post-World War II housing boom. The expansion of savings and loans was directly tied to the increased demand for housing because they are, in fact, highly specialized in the mortgage business. Mortgages represent some 84 percent of their total assets.

Historically, although not now, savings and loans have been able to pay more for their deposits—the money they need to lend for mortgages. Their ability to pay more for their money resulted from their mortgage loan charges, which are somewhat higher than those of other institutions.

They specialize in so-called conventional mortgages, those which do not benefit from any federal government guarantee. Government-backed mortgages are subject to interest ceilings imposed by the agency making the guarantee. Conventional mortgages are limited only by state law.

Another factor that has made savings and loans popular is their close relationship to their community. Not only are they in a good position to evaluate risk, but they remain involved in the mortgage-making and -servicing business throughout the life of the loan.

Commercial banks were attracted increasingly into the mortgage business by the expansion of government guarantees. The Federal Housing Administration (FHA) program began in 1934, and the Veterans Administration (VA) guarantees after World War II enabled banks to make mortages secure in the knowledge that they could be bailed out in case of bad judgment. In addition, the rate of return on mortgages was better than on other possible investments. Such loans are now a major profit line for commercial banks. In 1973, for example, large banks reported that money cost them only a 4.6-percent interest rate but that they received 8.1 percent on mortgage notes. (Of course, banks obtained much of their funds from low-interest savings accounts, and those mortgages include commercial properties in which the banks specialize.) Finally, with increased acceptance of the idea of one-stop banking, more people have put their funds into savings accounts at commercial banks, thus providing more mortgage money.

Not all commercial banks are interested in making residential loans, and even fewer back multifamily dwellings. About 9 percent of the assets of all commercial banks are made up of farm and small-family residence loans. Obviously, commercial banks prefer to concentrate on commercial properties. For those residential mortgage loans they do make, commercial banks usually ask for bigger down payments than do the thrifts.

Mutual savings banks date from the early nineteenth century. Savings banks developed to meet the need for a safe place to deposit funds. They did not spread far off the Eastern seaboard as the nation developed, but those banks which were formed have become a major part of the mortgage scene.

Conservative in their lending policies, they fared better during the Great Depression than did other institutions holding mortgages. Mutual savings banks not only operate on their home turf, but also act to allocate mortgage money to high-need areas. Their officers actively search for such places to invest their banks' funds.

Life insurance companies generally purchase mortgages from banks, so the individual is unlikely to come in contact with one in connection with the purchase of a house.

The choice of an institution for obtaining a mortgage may, of course, be limited. In many areas, there are no savings banks. In others, commercial banks are more interested in mortgage loans. On an existing house, the mortgage may be held at a thrift that knows the property and is willing to continue the mortgage or originate a new one with the purchaser. But you should check the market whenever you make a real-estate purchase, because loan rates and other conditions may vary. When dealing with loans of this magnitude, small interest-rate differences can amount to thousands of dollars over the life of the mortgage. With a long relationship ahead, the individual will want to seek an institution that is interested in its mortgage business and has experience in handling the kinds of problems that may arise.

Yes, we have no money

In the mortgage area, the notion of the financial intermediary, so dear to economists in explaining the banking system, is the most clear. If people have money to save and if they put it in the bank or a thrift, more money will be available for underwriting mortgages. If the economy is prosperous and inflation is moderate, people are likely to have funds available to save. That means "easy money," with the interest rates that banks must pay to attract savings being allowed to slip down. Because they must pay less for funds, they can charge less for mortgages, and there is generally enough money available to finance all mortgage requests.

In recent years, this state of affairs has become a fading memory. First, inflation began to eat into the share of personal income that could be allocated to savings. In addition, the Federal Reserve raised interest rates in an effort to draw some funds into savings. Inflation often means that too much money is seeking to buy too few goods. The Federal Reserve's action was designed to ease the inflationary pressure by drawing away some of the money. Unfortunately, that "tight-money" policy is in itself inflationary. Because banks and thrifts have to pay more for the money they attract, they must charge more for the money they lend. The interest rate on mortgages has skyrocketed in the past ten years from less than 5 percent to more than 9 percent. State usury laws, which set a limit on the interest rate for mortgages lower than for other loans, did not rise as fast as the cost of money. When the going rate hit state ceilings, banks ceased issuing mortgages because they could not operate in the black under the ceiling. With less money available, the banks and thrifts had to increase the qualifications they set for mortgage borrowers. In particular, they required that the home purchaser put up a larger share of the cost as a down payment.

Added to inflation were the effects of recession. Individuals simply had less money to spend as production was cut back and they either worked less or were laid off. Obviously, that put a further crimp on savings available to finance mortgages, to say nothing of the problem faced by the unemployed in buying or keeping a home.

While these obvious developments were taking place, thrifts were running into other problems. Higher interest rates meant that thrifts, in particular, had to face competition for the saver's dollar. Even the federal government itself offered higher interest rates on Treasury bills than the thrifts were allowed. When people took their funds from the thrifts in order to gain the higher interest paid elsewhere to keep pace with inflation, the savings bank and savings and loan faced serious problems in finding deposits to finance mortgage loans.

Banks traditionally borrow short and lend long—they accept deposits for short periods but lend out those funds for long periods. Thus, when people wanted to withdraw funds from the thrifts, it meant that the thrifts had to liquidate some of their mortgages that were bringing in a low rate of return because they had begun years earlier.

Toward the end of 1974, banks and thrifts began to give borrowers big discounts on interest in return for full or partial repayment of low-interest mortgages. For example, Lincoln Savings Bank in Brooklyn reportedly told a customer that it would take $12,831.40 in full payment of the $15,073.07 outstanding on his loan. On a monthly basis, the bank said it would count each $100 above the regular payment as $117.47. Chicago's First Federal Savings and Loan said it would negotiate individual deals. This approach has some benefit for the borrower nearing the end of the loan. Most of each payment is likely to be principal and not interest, which is deductible. As a result, it may be worthwhile to take advantage of the savings possible by advance payment. But some banks will act only if the borrower takes the first step and makes a cut-rate repayment offer.

In short, perhaps more than any other aspect of an individual's relationship with a bank or thrift institution, mortgage loans are directly affected by what's happening in the national economy. As inflation pushes up the purchase price of housing, it also makes it difficult to meet higher down-payment and interest charges. As a result, potential home buyers should seek to avoid finding themselves in a situation where they must purchase a home at a specific time. Although the maxim seems correct that over the long run, interest rates do not decline, recent history indicates that rates reflect the economic situation. In 1972, a year when inflation dropped below 4 percent, the general interest-rate level was almost 1 percent below the 1970 standard and more than 1.5 percent below the level that would be reached toward the end of 1974, when double-digit inflation prevailed.

Conventional and unconventional

A mortgage loan is, in most cases, like any other loan, but a lot bigger. Such a loan is called conventional. Where the government steps in to insure or to guarantee the loan, it assumes a special character. In general, the government does not back loans. But it does stand behind certain housing loans as a way of encouraging banks and thrifts to put money into mortgages in order to stimulate the housing market.

For a person who seeks a mortgage, one backed by the government is almost certainly going to be a better deal than a conventional mortgage. It's important to determine eligibility for either FHA or VA mortgages.

The FHA does not make loans or build houses; it insures mortgages extended by banks and thrifts to certain individuals. Just how much is available to back mortgages is determined by appropriations of the United States Congress.

The basic requirements for obtaining FHA backing are similar to those a responsible bank or thrift will impose: a good credit record, sufficient cash for a down payment, a regular income sufficient to cover mortgage payments. The FHA also determines if the property is satisfactory and if the price is fair.

The FHA gets involved at the request of the lender; the home buyer may never have direct contact with the government agency.

The maximum interest rate that can be charged by the institution making the mortgage loan is limited by the federal government. Often, the FHA interest rate will be lower than the conventional rate by perhaps ¼ or ½ of 1 percent. But in addition to the interest, the borrower pays ½ of 1 percent as a mortgage insurance premium. And the bank or thrift may charge an extra fee to bring the interest on an FHA-backed mortgage up to that of the commercial mortgage. In most cases, however, the person selling the house rather than the buyer must pay these "discount points."

The purchaser may have to make a number of other payments. If the price of the house is higher than the FHA evaluation, the FHA guarantee, and thus presumably the mortgage itself, will cover only the amount the FHA certifies. This, in effect, pushes the amount of the down payment that must be made. There is also an FHA application fee, and under the terms of all FHA-backed mortgages, the monthly mortgage payment must also include a prorated share of fire insurance and other premiums and of local taxes.

The FHA has two plans for insuring mortgages. Mutual mortgage insurance, known as Section 203 insurance, covers mortgages up to $45,000 for a one-family house. The FHA will not insure the full estimated value of the property, the percentage covered decreasing as the value of the house increases. Unless the purchaser is over sixty-two or purchasing a very low-cost, owner-occupied dwelling, he or she must make the down payment in cash. For buyers over sixty or those purchasing homes in remote areas, the down payment can itself be borrowed. Loans are to be repaid in periods of ten, fifteen, twenty, twenty-five, thirty, or, in the case of mortgages made before construction, thirty-five years.

So-called Section 221 insurance is designed for low- and moderate-income families and for those forced to move because of urban renewal or other government action. The terms of such mortgages are generally far more liberal than Section 203-insured loans, with the down payment set as low as $200 and thirty years to repay.

In general, banks and thrifts like FHA loans because they lend a major element of certainty to mortgage loans that are, in other respects, conventional. In addition, banks can sell FHA mortgages to others easily because they are certain of repayment. That means the bank can obtain needed cash more easily with such mortgages than when it has to try to sell its own conventional loans to other financial institutions.

The VA program is a government guarantee or insurance of a mortgage obtained by an eligible veteran. Eligibility varies over the years as Congress acts to determine just who is classified as a veteran. In addition, entitlement extends for varying periods beyond the end of active duty, depending in part on the nature of the service. Any former member of any of the armed forces can apply to the Veterans Administration, submitting discharge records, to obtain a determination of eligibility and length of entitlement. This application need not be done just at the moment when a house purchase is planned. It may be done at any time and actually facilitates the purchase because the veteran has immediate proof that a VA guarantee can be expected.

The guarantee covers $17,500 or 60 percent of a loan, whichever is smaller. Even if the actual mortgage loan is substantially higher, it is considered to be a VA loan. There is no required down payment so long as the sales price does not exceed a price the VA determines to be fair. The veteran must actually live in the house that is purchased with the VA guarantee. The maximum length of the mortgage is thirty years, and the federal government imposes a ceiling on the interest rate. As with the FHA-insured loans, VA loans generally have a somewhat lower interest rate than is charged on conventional mortgages. Other conditions require that the veteran have fire and other damage insurance and that if the loan extends beyond five years, there be adequate provision for regular repayment of the principal.

About 25 percent of mortgage loans for residences and farms are backed by FHA or VA plans. The percentage is higher in both savings and loans and mutual savings banks than in commercial banks and other financial institutions.

The VA also makes some direct loans to eligible veterans. For those in small towns and rural areas where there is a shortage of housing credit, and particularly where VA-backed loans have not been made recently, direct VA loans can be made. The maximum loan is $25,000. If the cost of the property is below this, the VA may require no down payment.

Either before a mortgage is sought or when you begin talking with a bank or thrift, you or the lender should contact both the FHA and VA to determine possible eligibility. That small amount of effort could be worth thousands of dollars later on.

Mortgage shopping

Most home purchasers are completely unaware of the variety of mortgage arrangements that is possible. Instead, they accept what the bank suggests, as long as it meets the general goals they have set. Of course, one bank may use only a limited number of approaches, but it may be worth the purchaser's effort to ask the bank to examine other possibilities or to comparison-shop at other banks or thrifts.

The one rule that is pretty generally part of every mortgage is amortization. That means that the principal of the loan will be fully repaid by a certain deadline through periodic installment payments. While repayment of the principal as well as interest may seem obvious, such a provision was not included in many pre-depression mortgages. Some home buyers who had faithfully made their interest payments were faced with foreclosure when the bank asked for large repayments of principal.

The most common payment plan, used in all FHA and most VA loans, provides for level payments. Also known as the direct-reduction plan, it provides that each month, for the life of the loan, you pay exactly the same amount. That payment is used to pay the interest due on the loan, and whatever is left goes toward reducing the principal. Because the amount of the principal debt is thus decreased each month, the amount of interest due the following month is also reduced. As a result, in each successive monthly payment, a larger share goes to pay off the principal and a smaller share goes to pay interest due.

By a limited-reduction plan, the bank can provide for partial amortization of the debt during the loan's life with a lump-sum payment due at the end of the loan. For example, a borrower could contract for a ten-year loan for $20,000 with annual amortization payments of $1,000. Then, at the end of the loan period, the borrower would be expected to pay the remaining $10,000. Of course, the bank or thrift could arrange for the refinancing of the mortgage loan.

These loans are popularly called "balloon" mortgages. For the life of the loan, payments are just like those of any other mortgage. The major difference is the relatively short life of the loan. In part because the VA requires that any loan for more than five years include an amortization feature for the repayment of principal, balloon mortgages, on which the principal is repaid at the end of the period, often run no longer.

The obvious advantage of the balloon mortgage for the bank or thrift is that the interest rate can be adjusted to reflect changing economic conditions, and the institution is thus not forced to accept too low an interest rate for as long as thirty years. For the purchaser, there is always the chance, but a slight one, that interest rates will fall.

When the balloon mortgage comes due, the bank may require full payment, although this is not likely, because it recognizes that you will have to obtain a mortgage elsewhere. Instead, a new agreement may be made for another balloon mortgage or perhaps for a long-term mortgage, which is, in effect, payable on demand after the fixed termination date. In practice, the bank does not call in the loan except in case of default. But there is an element of risk. Amortization may not be required under such a mortgage.

Yet another amortization plan calls for each payment to cover a fixed portion of the principal and the interest due on the outstanding balance. Monthly payments are largest at the beginning and gradually decline until the last payment, which is the remaining installment of the principal. This "straight-reduction" plan is not useful to young homeowners with limited incomes. But because the straight-reduction plan is used with well-secured loans due quarterly or semiannually, it may be attractive to professionals such as doctors, lawyers, and architects, whose income comes from fees rather than from a regular paycheck. The longer payment frequencies allow them to take into account wide swings in their income.

Three other specialized forms of mortgage loans have been developed. The "package" mortgage allows the borrower to include the cost of basic household appliances in the amount of the loan. The "open-end" mortgage allows the bank to lend additional amounts on the same mortgage. In general, the additional borrowing cannot exceed the amount of principal already repaid. Finally, a "demand" mortgage is used for houses under construction. It contains neither a fixed maturity nor a plan for repaying the principal. Once construction is completed, the demand mortgage—actually a construction loan—is liquidated and replaced by a standard long-term loan.

Many people believe that the only mortgage is the long-term, level-payment, amortized loan. Unless the potential borrower asks questions, the lending institution is likely to offer the plan that best suits its interests, given prevailing conditions in the mortgage market.

A matter of great interest

Three principal factors determine the cost of a mortgage loan: the interest rate, the duration of the loan, and the down payment. The lower the rate, the shorter the length of the mortgage; and the smaller the amount borrowed, the lower the cost of borrowing money. Obviously, the reverse is also true.

Carried to its logical extreme, this rule would say that if you didn't borrow any money at all, the charges would be zero. But that may not be as desirable as it sounds. First, you might have to wait quite a long time before you'd saved up enough to buy a house. Second, you would probably be paying rent in the meantime, which could, in fact, all be going toward a mortgage loan. Third, tax laws favor home purchases by providing deductions for the interest paid on the mortgage loan and for the local property taxes. There is no tax deduction for rent. Finally, with the virtual certainty of permanent inflation, the value of the dollar can be expected to decrease over the years. As a result, by promising now to pay back much later, you will be able to make repayment with dollars that are substantially less valuable. Chances are your income will have been keeping pace with inflation, so the portion of your income devoted to mortgage repayment will have decreased over the years. What's more, inflation will probably have boosted the value of your house quite a bit during the life of the mortgage. For all these reasons, it may, in fact, be more desirable to seek a longer-term mortgage.

To give an idea of the effect of the length of a mortgage on the total amount of interest paid, let's take a $30,000 loan at 7 percent for varying intervals:

5 years	$ 5,643 interest
10 years	$11,800 interest
15 years	$18,537 interest
20 years	$25,822 interest
25 years	$33,612 interest
30 years	$41,852 interest

Thus, to borrow $30,000 for thirty years costs $8,240 more than for twenty-five years. The monthly payment for a level-repayment mortgage over twenty-five years would be $212.04; over a thirty-year period it would be $199.59.

The chief immediate factor that you will have in mind in seeking a mortgage loan is the size of the monthly payment. Most experts say it should be no more than 20 percent of your take-home, not gross, income. It certainly should go no higher than 25 percent. As a result, selecting the length of the loan, on which the bank may accord you some flexibility, can be determined only after you know the interest rate. Look at the impact of rate differences alone on a twenty-five-year, level-repayment mortgage (facing page). The payments include both principal and interest.

The difference over twenty-five years resulting from an increase of one-half a percentage point in interest on a $30,000 loan amounts to $3,105. And if interest were 9 percent instead of 8 percent, you might well find it necessary to extend the mortgage by five years, if you could. The added point would cost you $20.21 each month. The extension would reduce monthly payments by only $10.37, and of course, payments would extend over five more years.

The impact of higher interest rates on the eventual cost of

How Interest Rates Affect Mortgage Payments

Rate	$20,000		$30,000		$40,000	
	Monthly	Total	Monthly	Total	Monthly	Total
.05%	$116.92	$35,076	$175.38	$52,614	$233.84	$ 70,152
.06	128.86	38,658	193.29	57,987	257.72	77,316
.07	141.36	42,408	212.04	63,612	282.72	84,816
.08	154.37	46,311	231.55	69,465	308.73	92,619
.09	167.40	50,220	251.76	75,528	335.68	100,704
.095	174.74	52,422	262.11	78,633	349.48	104,844

purchasing a home is greatly significant. Only on mortgages bearing relatively low interest and extending no longer than twenty years can you expect to avoid paying twice the amount of the principal borrowed. To this must be added the down payment. In short, shopping for interest rates is worth the effort; but, far more important, waiting awhile until high rates come down is advisable if at all possible. By the same token, a mortgage at a bargain rate, which may be possible if the bank allows you simply to assume an existing mortgage, is definitely worthwhile.

If you want to know how your own prospective purchase compares with others, the Federal Reserve compiles a national average. The average purchase price for a house financed by a conventional mortgage begun in November 1974 was $42,800, with a down payment of 24.1 percent, or $10,315. The mortgage loan, for $31,800, ran for 27.3 years at an interest rate of 9.07 percent. Fees and charges amounting to 1.51 percent of the loan, or $480, were levied. Those charges were mostly accounted for by the bank's fees for making a loan.

Let's make a deal

When you are ready to make a purchase requiring a mortgage, it's time to shop for a bank or thrift that will provide the loan. Especially in times of tight money, that institution is quite likely to be located in the same community as the new house. As the amount of money available for loans is reduced, banks tend to provide mortgages increasingly as part of their obligation to the local community from which they draw deposits. Having an account at a bank where you seek a mortgage can be an advantage.

The bank or thrift should provide you with a disclosure statement as required by the Truth-in-Lending Act. You should always get one at the time a mortgage loan is made, but when shopping for a mortgage, it is wise to ask for such forms from each lending institution you visit.

The disclosure form will indicate the type of mortgage, the amount of the note, the term, and the interest rate. It will also include the amount of each monthly payment, including a balloon payment, if appropriate. Most important, it will include the total of all payments of interest and principal. In addition, data on fire insurance and life insurance may be included. The bank or thrift cannot require you to purchase either through a company they suggest, but it is virtually certain that they will demand that you obtain fire insurance satisfactory to them.

On the disclosure form, the bank or thrift must indicate all finance charges such as their own service and origination fees and title search and all other expenditures relating to the recording of the agreement. In the event the fees included a special interest charge during the first year—designed to cover the administrative costs of making the loan—that must be included in the annual percentage rate indicated on the form. The form will also include the security offered for the loan— presumably the house itself—and information on prepayment and late-payment charges.

In June 1975, the Real Estate Settlement Procedures Act (RESPA) went into effect. Designed to help home buyers shop around, RESPA requires that the lender inform the buyer of as many as fifty separate charges at least twelve days before final papers are signed. The law also bans referral fees for the lender's help in lining up insurance or other services. Savings and loans say RESPA involves too much paper work and that customers complain of delays. But consumers benefit from being able to shop. Perhaps they should be given the right to shorten the waiting period.

"Points" are a not-too-hidden device for increasing the interest payment. This device is like a balloon-in-reverse, because the special lump-sum interest payment comes at the start of the loan. Points go by a variety of names but can generally be found on the disclosure statement as a fee payable to the bank for its trouble in making the loan. The term itself refers to a percentage of the amount of the loan itself. A single point refers to 1 percent of the loan amount. Thus, on an 8-percent loan, one point pushes the interest for the first year to 9 percent. Banks and thrifts have no statutory right to charge points. Their presence usually reflects competitive conditions in the local market. The purchaser should try to bargain on points as much as market conditions permit.

Frequently, banks and thrifts charge prepayment penalties. With the mortgage running for twenty-five or thirty years, the possibility that you will pay it off in advance is relatively high. So is the amount of the penalty. It may be as much as six months' interest or a percentage of the balance due on the principal—in effect, more points.

Like points, prepayment charges may be negotiable. The bank or thrift may give up the right to make such a charge if the borrower is selling another house to a person who will continue to mortgage it at the same institution. That way, the lender keeps the old house on the books and adds one. In fact, perhaps neither purchaser will have to accept a prepayment penalty. Obviously, banks may waive the prepayment penalty at the time of repayment if prevailing interest rates at that time are higher than the rate on the existing mortgage. The bank or thrift wants to dispose of lower-rate mortgages when it can. Finally, good customers of the bank or thrift are generally in a sound position to negotiate on this point. It's important to bargain about the prepayment penalty at the time the mortgage loan is made, and then, if it has been included in the terms, at the time of prepayment itself. While the penalty supposedly indemnifies the bank for a prepayment that may disturb their financial planning, from the borrower's viewpoint there is no reason why any penalty should be due for simply exceeding the requirements of the loan agreement.

Some mortgages contain clauses stating that they are "due on encumbrance," which means that if the property is pledged as security on any other loan, including a second mortgage, the first mortgage is immediately due in full. While this is not legal in some places and usually not enforced when it is legal, the purchaser should watch for it and request that it be deleted. In general, banks and thrifts are wary about any encumbrances that might be on a piece of property before the loan is made, but their priority of interest is usually reassuring enough to allow them to maintain the loan even if a second mortgage is taken later.

Mortgages frequently contain "due-on-sale" clauses. The loan must be paid in full when the property is sold. While the bank may extend the mortgage to the new owner, it is not obligated to do so. In addition, the prepayment penalty may be levied. San Francisco Consumer Action reports that this provision is being tested in court.

If the borrower fails to make the regular mortgage payment within a certain allowed period beyond the due date, he or she will probably have to pay a late charge. The charge may be levied either on the payment itself—perhaps as much as 4 percent—or it may be calculated on the basis of the entire outstanding balance. The California Supreme Court has ruled against a late penalty based on the entire balance, since it is entirely unrelated to the damage to the bank resulting from late payment. But the late penalty itself is perfectly legal.

Beyond security of the house, the bank may seek additional backing for the loan. The disclosure statement will indicate such added security, which may include property later added to the mortgaged premises and any deposits the borrower has with the lending institution. Recourse to such deposits is the offset and may discourage the borrower from leaving significant sums in the lending institution. In any case, given rising real-estate prices, the borrower should not need to put up additional collateral and should not provide the bank with such security.

Above all, watch out for escrow payments. The bank or thrift can and, in the case of FHA loans, must, require that the regular mortgage payments also include a prorated share of local taxes and insurance premiums. This money is not paid out as soon as it is received. The bank keeps it in "escrow" or in an "impound" account. Because property taxes may be due only once or twice a year and insurance can be paid by annual premiums, the regular monthly payments amount to forced savings.

The logic behind the escrow payments is obvious. The lender does not want to see the house attached for failure to pay taxes or lost through fire because it was uninsured. Of course, the bank or thrift can easily determine if taxes are paid and require proof of continuous insurance without actually han-

A Mortgage Checklist

While the mortgage loan is only a part of the arrangement required to purchase a new house, it is an essential element in making the deal possible. Thus, the borrower should be as careful as possible in settling on a mortgage:

1. Get a lawyer's help. There's a lot of paperwork and filing of legal documents, all of which can be handled far more efficiently by a lawyer than by yourself.

2. Figure out in advance what you want in the way of a mortgage. It's desirable to begin negotiating with your interests firmly in mind. Most important, you should determine how much you can afford in the way of monthly payments. The 20-percent rule is a sound one.

3. Determine your eligibility for an FHA or VA loan.

4. Shop around among institutions and ask for Truth-in-Lending and RESPA disclosure forms from those from which you might obtain the mortgage.

5. Investigate the various kinds of mortgage plans to determine which might best suit your special needs. Negotiate with the lender on the type of plan.

6. Remember that the longer you take to pay off the mortgage, the more it will cost in interest.

7. Unless you have to buy right away, or mortgage market conditions are particularly favorable, don't buy when interest rates are at their peak. A small increment in the interest rate can cost thousands of dollars over the years.

8. Be prepared to negotiate with the lender about special terms of the mortgage agreement. Try to avoid paying "points." Ask for the deletion of prepayment penalties and "due-on-encumbrance" or "due-on-sale" clauses. Above all, seek the elimination of the escrow clause. If that fails, ask for interest on the funds you are to pay the bank.

dling the payment themselves. Only for those people who will find it difficult to save the funds for the required payment is the escrow account an advantage.

In almost all cases, lenders refuse to pay interest on escrow accounts, although they themselves are earning interest on them. The California bank survey calculated that the borrower may lose over $750 on a thirty-year loan, using a 5-percent interest rate, when the amount in escrow averages $500 a year.

Along with the recent trend to require interest payments on security deposits with telephone and other utility companies, efforts are being made to require payment of interest on escrow accounts. In New York, Massachusetts, Connecticut, and Maryland, the law requires the payment of interest on escrow accounts.

Borrowers should insist that they do not want an escrow account, except where the FHA leaves them no choice. In fact, all property tax payers should be opposed to the money's being held in escrow instead of going directly to the local government.

As matters stand now, the bank holds the escrow money until the date it is due. In the meantime, the localities must make tax-anticipation loans, perhaps from the selfsame banks. Because local expenditures continue all year, the towns and cities borrow funds to operate until the bank turns over to them the funds in escrow accounts. The interest costs paid by the local government are, of course, passed on to the property owners in that locality. Thus, the escrow system not only denies them interest but actually forces them to share in the interest paid to the bank by the local government. Yet those who favor escrow accounts say that local governments are the chief beneficiaries because their collection costs are held down.

Some institutions offer alternatives to escrow. Under the capitalization method, monthly tax and insurance payments are credited against the outstanding mortgage principal until they must be paid to the local government or insurance company. As a result, the amount of mortgage interest is lowered. In effect, the thrift using the capitalization method is paying interest on the escrow funds.

Other savings institutions waive escrow if the purchaser opens an interest-bearing savings account in the amount of the annual tax bill. While the principal cannot be withdrawn from the account even to pay taxes, the interest is available.

Still another alternative provides for giving the purchaser the option of closing out the escrow account when his or her equity in the property reaches 40 percent. At that point, the bank figures, equity interest will be a powerful incentive to the borrower to keep up tax payments.

Redlining

Some prospective homeowners have found that they simply cannot obtain a mortgage because the house they want to buy is located in the wrong part of town. Banks rule out entire neighborhoods on the grounds their future prospects are either marginal or poor. They believe that even solid citizens may want to get rid of their homes at a later date and won't be able to find buyers. As a result, the banks would be stuck with defaulted mortgage loans.

This system of ruling certain areas off the mortgage map is called "redlining." Bankers object to the use of the term in a negative sense, but they admit that such a practice seems eminently sensible to them.

Without incentives or direct government financial intervention in the form of housing subsidies or loan guarantees, redlining can be expected to continue. As a result, it can perpetuate the decay of neighborhoods, because it would deny loans to those very middle-class people whose presence could help begin the reconstruction of an area.

The Home Mortgage Disclosure Act of 1975 would, if adopted, require disclosure of where banks make mortgage loans by zip code area. That probably wouldn't end redlining, but it might discourage banks that wanted to avoid the image of being the cause of slums.

7

Do You
Trust
Your
Bank?

Ask a banker how his trust department is operated and he will, without blinking, cite the dictum of Justice Benjamin Cardozo in *Meinhard v. Salmon*: "A trustee is held to something stricter than the morals of the marketplace. Not honesty alone, but the punctilio of an honor most sensitive, is thus the standard of behavior." But he may well be thinking more in terms of Oliver Wendell Holmes's blunt homily in *The Autocrat of the Breakfast Table*: "Put not your trust in money, but put your money in trust."

To many people, the trust department is reserved for rich folks and of little interest to the rest of us. Yet, millions of people are beneficiaries of trusts operated by banks and are completely ignorant of that fact. They are participants in pension funds whose assets are managed by trust departments of commercial banks.

Of course, many large personal trusts have been established

by wealthy people who have demonstrated their ability to watch out for their own financial interests. The same cannot be said for their beneficiaries, who, though they may be wealthy, are generally at the mercy of the bank that is trustee. Merely by being wealthy, such people are not deprived of the need for adequate protection as consumers of banks' services.

Trusts are created for a number of reasons. Although you can't take it with you, a trust allows you a measure of control over the wealth you leave behind. The trustee is bound to follow the instructions laid down by the creator of the trust. Trusts may be established not only as a way of handling what the deceased leaves behind; living trusts may be created by people too busy to handle all the details of their own affairs. Employers may ask banks to handle trust funds that are used to provide pensions to employees.

Trusts created by individuals are often designed to lessen federal taxation on estates. It is possible to delay the imposition of such taxes for several generations through the judicious use of trusts.

A person setting up a trust is free to name anybody as trustee. Banks regard individuals as their greatest competitors for the trust business, because people are likely to name their friends or lawyers to handle their trusts. Banks hustle hard to attract that business. Some 3,804 commercial banks have trust departments. In fact, the names of many large banks reflect the importance of the trust business both in the past and now: Bankers Trust, First Pennsylvania Banking and Trust, Cleveland Trust, Irving Trust. There are only thirty-nine trust companies that are not associated with banks.

The trust business carried on by banks is not just big, it is enormous. At the end of 1971, the assets of commercial bank trust departments represented 22 percent of the assets of all institutional investors in the United States. These trust-fund assets were greater than the assets of all insurance companies and all mutual funds. They now amount to some $400 billion.

According to the staff of the House Banking and Currency Committee, "Banks control the management of over 70 percent of all pension fund management, and it has been estimated that by 1980 total assets of pension funds will reach $285 billion."

Institutional investor trading on the New York Stock Exchange has grown to 68 percent of the dollar volume of shares traded, and trading by commercial bank trust departments accounts for half of it all.

The trust business is dominated by a handful of New York banks. Five banks control about one-fourth of all trust assets: Morgan Guaranty Trust Company, Bankers Trust Company, Chase Manhattan Bank, First National City Bank, and the United States Trust Company. Only 1.8 percent of all banks with trust departments have 72.3 percent of all trust assets.

Trust departments have a variety of customers, depending on the type of account. The most typical of all trust accounts is the personal trust. By a living trust, a living person transfers assets to the bank to administer in line with a specific agreement. The person can usually terminate the trust. A testamentary trust is created by the will of the deceased. The bank may be trustee on its own or with an individual. It makes decisions, in line with the instructions of the deceased, if any, on how the funds will be invested.

A will may also name a trust department as executor or administrator of an estate. The bank will then take on a variety of tasks in connection with settling the estate and paying taxes.

An employer can hire a trust department to handle an employee benefit trust, most often a pension trust. In theory, the creation of such a trust is an act of generosity by the employer. As a result, the employer has full discretion over how the funds are managed. Occasionally, the company shares control with its employees in recognition of their having earned at least a part of the funds in the pension trust.

Finally, a person who is a trustee may hire a bank as his or her agent. With an agency account, the trust department may be required to consult the trustee before making any investment decision. If not, there's not much practical difference between being an agent and being trustee.

Aside from those who create trusts, the beneficiaries must also be regarded as customers of the bank. They fall into two general categories: family members and close friends in personal, estate, and some agency accounts, or employees in the case of employee benefit and other agency accounts.

What the banks do with the funds placed at their disposal can determine the standard of living and the kind of retirement of a great number of people. In 1972, there were 1,218,236 separate trust accounts. The average size of a trust account was $331.30.

Obviously, trust departments, taken together, have clout. What they do can have a major impact on the national economy, and that, in turn, comes home to virtually everybody.

The giant

With enormous assets under their control, trust departments can obviously purchase large blocks of stock in major American corporations. This potential power is accentuated by the policy of most trust departments not to overdiversify. Stock purchases can usually be made only from a limited list, and the trust departments tend to follow the conventional wisdom. They, and not the beneficiaries, vote the shares they hold, thus giving them a powerful tool to influence corporate policy.

A Twentieth Century Fund report on commercial bank trust departments, based on a survey of about seventy such departments, found, in fact, that such control is rarely exercised. Instead, the trust departments tend to support management's own decisions or to dispose of the stock they hold. Nonetheless, occasions such as planned corporate mergers and acquisitions arise where the trust departments can have a great influence on management's decisions.

The extent of the possible leverage that can be exercised by the trust departments is even greater than might appear by their sheer size. The commercial side of the bank may make loans to a corporation. It obviously has an interest in seeing that firm succeed and be able to repay that loan. How it performs in the stock market is one indicator of how well a firm is doing. When the bank's trust department buys stock in that corporation, the price of the stock rises. Or if a corporation leaves major deposits with the commercial side of the bank, it may get its reward in terms of purchases of its stock made by the trust department.

The Twentieth Century Fund report found that "in many cases" trust departments obtained corporate customers as part of a reciprocal business relationship that "may lend itself to a subtle form of coercion. Business customers may simply be afraid of" displeasing a powerful creditor. So they come partially under a bank's control by giving up their discretion about who will manage their funds when they place those funds in a trust department, not by choice but under pressure.

Bank trust departments are the single most important kind of institutional investor. In fact, it may even be inaccurate to consider them investors rather than traders, because they are in and out of the market so frequently. Their trading represents about 34 percent of the dollar volume of all shares traded on the New York Stock Exchange and is probably also of great significance in other exchanges and even the over-the-counter market.

Trust departments depend to a great extent on other people's research, and they tend to go with the crowd. As a result, the investments are not highly speculative, but they do represent a major influence on those very companies that are considered the bellwethers of the economy.

When prices of these stocks begin to climb, the trust departments hurry into the market to buy, not wanting to miss a good thing. As a result, they drive the prices up even further. Exactly the reverse takes place in a falling market. Clearly, this pattern of buying and selling disrupts the market and penalizes the smaller investor, who inevitably will be further behind the trend than the banks.

In short, for the average investor, who is likely to buy some of the same stocks as the trust departments, a part of his or her wealth is, in effect, under the direct and considerable influence of those departments.

Personal trusts

Of all the aspects of banking activity, the banks are less willing to talk about their trust departments than about any other aspect of their operations.

Often, those who establish trusts to be handled by banks don't know what they are getting themselves into. Initially, their lawyers draw up the trust agreements, and they often suggest that the settlor, as the person creating the trust is called, turn over management to a bank. Some lawyers steer business toward banks because they are virtually guaranteed that the banks will turn around and hire them as counsel for the estate or trust. If an individual is named trustee, he may choose his own lawyer to carry out that job.

For a number of reasons, this is one time when following a lawyer's advice may amount to a costly mistake. While a relative or friend may not accept an executor's fee, the bank will insist on the amount the law allows and probably more. What's more, some lawyers will simply accept the standard trust form prepared by the bank and pass it on to their clients. The trouble with the standard form is that it gives the bank complete discretion over the funds placed in trust. That means that the bank can even invest in its own stock and, of course, exercise the voting rights. Such a policy raises the question of whether the settlor's wishes are being followed and whether such a trust really is in the best interest of the beneficiaries.

The major problem is the untrammeled nature of the rights that trust departments hold. The deceased are hardly in a position to complain, and the beneficiaries can complain all they want for all the good it will do them.

Trust departments usually receive a portfolio of investments. They almost never leave them unchanged. As indicated earlier, they may convert some of the assets into holdings of the bank's own stock or that of its holding company. Usually, they will liquidate all or part of the portfolio in order to invest the funds in the banks' own common trust funds. These are the same as mutual funds, but are operated by the bank and with the bank's own trusts as customers. Like mutual funds, the common trust funds permit diversification, and a bank may have several of them, each tailored to a specific need; growth, income, or tax-exempt. The bank will give particular importance to the investment performance of these funds. To that extent, a trust with money invested in a common trust fund is actually getting more attention than if it were handled separately, simply because of the limited number of management personnel available to look after trusts.

Acting on behalf of a client, a Boston lawyer once visited a bank and asked to see the holdings of a trust account. He expected to see the actual shares of the corporations in which the trust had invested. Instead, he was handed a computer printout. Gone are the days when banks maintained separate portfolios, supposedly tailored to the specific instructions of the settlor and the specific needs of the beneficiaries.

The desire of the trust department to realize the economies resulting from lumping trusts together is nowhere more evident than when the trust includes shares of a small family-owned company. Holding on to such shares will mean more work, for the bank may have to become involved in the affairs of the firm. Whenever they can, banks liquidate these holdings, often to place the money in common trust funds. The family business may suffer from the rapid disposal of a large block of its outstanding shares, and other members of the family, including some of the trust's beneficiaries, will lose income.

Perhaps all of the activity in a trust account may consist of no more than liquidating holdings and placing the money in a common trust fund. A study by the Securities and Exchange Commission revealed that in 1969, 44 percent of the personal trust accounts they examined had no activity whatsoever. Many of these appear to be small trusts where it may not be worth the bank's efforts because of relatively small fees. The result for the ignored funds is that increasing sums turn out to be held in noninterest-bearing accounts. This cash buildup, if it gets too far out of hand before somebody blows the whistle, can be an indication of inept management. But trust departments are seldom relieved of their trust accounts on the grounds of mismanagement.

Some beneficiaries would probably be happier with inactivity than with investment in a common trust fund. When the original portfolio holdings are liquidated prior to putting the money in a common trust, a capital gains tax is due. It's due again when the trust is distributed, because there's no way to hand out stock to the designated recipients. The trust account's share of the common trust fund must be converted to cash and tax paid before the holdings can be distributed.

Acting as sole trustees, banks can play down beneficiaries' interests in favor of playing up to their commercial customers. When trust departments find closely held companies—those owned by just a few people—in their trust accounts, they will often dispose of them. Unfortunately, the banks may well not get the best price, which would best suit the beneficiaries. Instead, they may sell to a purchaser who is a "friend of the bank." In addition, they may invest trust fund assets in "private placements"—shares sold directly by the issuing company rather than through the stock exchange. In this way, the banks can use investments by the trust department instead of loans by the commercial department to extend credit to the customer. The return on such investments is often lower than could be obtained from stocks that are traded on the market. Customers may actually force trust departments to invest in their shares as a condition of leaving funds on deposit in the commercial department. In none of these cases would the bank place the beneficiaries' interest above those of the commercial customer.

One Chicago bank reports that its trust department has its

large stockholdings in some fifty companies, 75 percent of which borrow money commercially from the bank and 37 percent of which have outstanding credit of more than $5 million each. This information does not prove that the bank places the customer ahead of the beneficiary, but the opportunity exists.

Yet another way that banks can harm beneficiaries in order to help commercial customers stems from the banks' desire to support management. They will vote proxies in favor of management positions even if beneficiaries lose. In one case, a trust department opposed a proposed corporate rule that would have reduced its voting power and hence harmed the beneficiaries. But it was forced to acquiesce in the new rule by the commercial department. The trust department could not have sold its shares in the corporation because its holdings were so large that merely starting such a sale would have sharply reduced the value of shares not yet sold.

It might appear that many of the problems resulting from the complete freedom of action given banks under trusts that they manage alone could be eliminated by the creation of co-trusts. In such cases, the trust department would be obliged to share the decision making on investment. This course is almost certain to be more costly, because the trust will have to pay both trustees. Usually the bank will not cut its fee, even if it has a share of authority. Said one unfortunate person who found himself in an uneven partnership with a bank: "The bank likes to act on its own even if you are a co-trustee. They don't accept suggestions on investments other than their own. Many times I've suggested good income stocks, but they wouldn't go along, so I finally had to accept their choices."

Perhaps the most appealing reason for installing a bank as trustee is the virtual certainty that it will go on operating even after close family and friends are no longer around. As a trust reaches across the years, the bank is expected to be the one constant and reliable future.

But the bank is people, especially as far as the beneficiaries are concerned. Those trust department brochures say: "In effect, our entire investment staff will be placed at your family's disposal." In fact, with all the different faces they will see, it may actually seem as though they are served by the entire staff—one after another.

At one bank there are sixty portfolio managers for 10,000 personal trust accounts. That works out to 160 accounts for each manager. The chances for advancement are not considered attractive because there are only limited opportunities within the department. The Twentieth Century Fund report found: "In the larger trust banks, personal trust portfolio managers have had relatively low status."

Personal trusts are not personal. The recipient of income from one may feel more like a victim than a beneficiary.

Pensions: you bet your life

More than thirty million people participate in pension funds. Everybody contributes to them indirectly through tax laws that favor their creation. Commercial bank trust departments handle the great majority of these pension funds. Pension trust funds are big business and, as with personal trusts, the ultimate beneficiaries often seem to be given little consideration by the bank.

Employers generally determine what they want or plan to accomplish in terms of benefit level and have an actuary determine the funds needed to accomplish this goal. They then turn to the trust department to manage the pension fund. An agreement is signed between the employer and the bank. In relatively few cases do the workers themselves have a voice in the agreement. Then, worker representatives sit on the board of the pension fund. But most employers regard their contributions to a pension fund as entirely their own money. They do not see it as money that would otherwise have been paid to the workers in the form of wages. As a result, the workers have no right to examine the trustee's work, except when it may be too late.

A pension fund is similar to a living trust in that the settlor in the form of the employer remains on the scene. Does that mean that the bank, even though it is the trustee, is relieved of certain responsibilities? For example, if the money placed in the fund is inadequate to provide the promised benefit level, is it up to the bank to say so, or can it remain silent and hope that the employer will inform the workers in time? If the bank is relieved of this responsibility, it has been relieved of a basic obligation of trusteeship—accountability to the beneficiary.

The pension reform law that was enacted in 1974 was designed to eliminate abuses that resulted from the employer's having too great a control over the funds placed in a pension or profit-sharing plan. The management could divert the funds

out of the plan, leaving inadequate money in the till and caus-
ing people who retired to lose the pensions they had earned
over a period of years. Although not so directly as the employers themselves, the trust departments had participated in actions that had the same result.

The bank is in the best position to know if the amount the
employer says he is putting in the pension fund is actually being deposited. If the bank remains silent, it could become as
implicated as the employer in the failure to pay out adequate
benefits later.

Sometimes firms would open pension trust accounts at certain banks in the belief or on the understanding that the bank
would invest a portion of those funds in those firms. This is
called self-dealing. While perhaps no more than 5 percent of
the fund might be invested in the employer's company or its
affiliate, if that company went broke, its own employees were
unduly penalized. Studies indicate that self-dealing in profit-
sharing plans may be as high as 80 percent of the stock in the
pension fund.

Obviously, just how well trust departments do when they
invest the pension funds determines how adequately pensions
will be financed and the amount of resources employers will
have to draw from other purposes in order to feed the fund.
Often those funds will come out of planned pay raises, so the
workers will have to accept less satisfactory contracts because
the trust departments have not done as well as they should
have.

Performance studies indicate that the employee benefit
funds were not able to outperform the market during a period
when stock prices were rising steadily. In other words, the
trust department managers did no better than an investor
would have done, investing in the stocks included in Standard
& Poor's 500 index. Almost half the bank-managed employee
benefit funds did not do so well as the market as a whole.

According to a Twentieth Century Fund report on the management of pension fund assets, the trust departments claim
that simply keeping up with Standard & Poor's 500 is a prodi-
gious accomplishment. They say that they purchase so much
stock that they can only buy shares in the largest companies.
Even then, they must proceed carefully in trading the large
blocks of stock they own for fear of disrupting the stock market. They envy the small investor who has greater flexibility to

purchase issues in smaller companies that undergo periods of rapid growth. The trust departments fail to mention that they have access to the kind of research about potential stock investments or sales that is unavailable to the smaller investor. He or she may find out about a change in the fortunes of a company only after the trust departments have already acted to buy or sell as a result of their better access to information.

Misplaced trust

Trust departments have been under pressure from the House Ways and Means Committee, the SEC, and increasingly from the press to eliminate a number of practices that appear to undermine their ability to operate according to "the punctilio of an honor the most sensitive." In fact, most of the reformers would even accept a close approximation, because the list of problem areas is so long.

Trust departments must conduct their stock transactions through stockbrokers. Banks can send their business through those brokers who keep their accounts in the commercial department, increasing their business with a given brokerage firm as the balance in its account increases. The trust department can increase account activity as a way of increasing broker commissions. The broker then puts his increased profits in the bank. In that way, the bank can bleed a pension fund, which pays the brokerage fees, for its own profit. In addition, it may carry out transactions through brokerage firms when it could conduct trades where their services were not required. Finally, banks can choose brokers, not on the basis of their ability, but because they have accounts in the bank. All of this can cost beneficiaries money. And it is illegal, simply because a trustee is not supposed to profit from a trust. In September 1973, Jeffrey M. Bucher, a member of the Board of Governors of the Federal Reserve System, could report: "The mere threat of Justice Department action, along with some journalistic criticism of the practice, has led to the voluntary elimination of 'tie-in' practices of this type by most institutions." Obviously, banks got pretty public-spirited under the "mere threat" of federal prosecution.

Trust departments can, as we have seen, allow cash balances to build up without such funds earning any income. Such cash results from the receipt of dividend payments or employer contributions to pension plans. The banks can lend this cash, usually to themselves, at no interest. The Twentieth Century Fund report on commercial bank trust departments found that "for the large banks, between about 50 percent and over 90 percent of all in-bank trust deposits seem to be classified as noninterest bearing. . . ." The Federal Reserve Bank of New York found that in 1971 ten New York banks made a profit of $114 million as a result of using these cash balances to make loans. This profit ensured that the trust departments would do more than break even on their operations. Almost all of this money should, under the law governing trusts, have gone to the beneficiaries of trust accounts.

Purchases of stocks in firms having a commercial relationship with the bank can also drive down income. Of course, a trust department can also fail to sell when it does not want to depress the stock of a commercial client, whatever the effect on beneficiaries. Finally, as mentioned earlier, the bank can obtain for itself authorization to invest in its own stock.

Other abuses can arise if banks discriminate among their trust customers. The banks can buy and sell among accounts. If a favored account has undesirable stocks in its portfolio, the situation can be improved by dumping the "dog" into another trust account. Here is one story recounted in the Twentieth Century Fund report on commercial bank trust departments:

> One customer, highly dependent on credit from a powerful trust institution, was virtually forced to place its pension fund with the bank. Approximately 10 percent of the assets of this fund were shortly thereafter placed in the stock of a financially stricken customer with whom the bank was deeply involved and whose stock was of less than investment grade. Almost immediately after acquisition, this issue fell to a small fraction of its original price. The investment banker (who told this story) believes that a very strong and alert pension fund customer of the bank learned of the coming debacle and insisted that the shares of the sagging company be removed from its portfolio. Because the market was thin, the shares were placed in weaker portfolios. The investment banker claims that the customer knew this but was too dependent on bank credit to withdraw, sue, or even complain.

Many of these practices that cost beneficiaries money result from the obvious overlapping of trust and commercial functions, which are, theoretically at least, barred by law. But this overlap has been the cause of the most serious charges against banks.

Most of the practices have brought on lawsuits. As a result, banks have taken steps to reform for fear of continued pressure in the courts. But there's still room for change.

The road back toward trust

One study group after another has recommended major changes in the operation of trust departments. These prescriptions for purity come mostly as a result of the abuses having reached a point where pressure from beneficiaries could no longer be ignored.

The Presidential Commission on Financial Structure and Regulation, known as the Hunt Commission, has suggested that a wall be built between trust and commercial departments in banks with trust assets greater than $200 million. Just why smaller trust departments were not included is not clear. The Hunt Commission also asked for rules banning the purchase or sale of securities on the basis of inside information. "At the present time," it said, "if bank trust officers have inside information they are in a dilemma. If they use it in a transaction, they may be charged with misconduct. If they have information and do not apply it, they may be charged with not doing the best they can for their clients. A clear rule on correct behavior should be enunciated."

The staff of the House Banking and Currency Committee went much further. It called for the complete separation of trust and commercial departments in banks where the total trust assets exceed $200 million. A Federal Trust Management Commission was recommended to regulate the management of certain funds, including pension plans.

Whether the ultimate barrier be a wall or complete separation, with the new trust company part of the same holding company as the bank, the critical issue will be how much information is communicated back and forth. The regulators will have to do a better job monitoring such exchanges.

There is no doubt that the trust departments could make it on their own. While banks wail that trust departments lose money, very few are closed down. The independent trust companies, those few not linked with banks, seem to be able to operate, although some critics claim they can do so only because they charge higher fees than the trust departments. They may also provide better and more personalized service.

Points to consider

These reforms will not come overnight and there is no assurance that they will work. In the meantime, millions of persons may continue to find themselves at the mercy of trust departments. Individuals and institutions should take steps to protect their own interests:

1. Lawyers should be required under standard practices of the bar to disclose to their clients all of the possible advantages and disadvantages of a trust agreement and their own present and potential relationship with the bank. All of this should be in writing.

2. Banks should be banned from advertising that they provide personalized or individual services unless they actually do.

3. Whatever they advertise, banks should pay greater attention to ensuring some continuity of service to beneficiaries.

4. Trust departments should not be allowed to liquidate the assets of a trust fund for the purpose of investing the money in a common trust fund unless they first obtain the consent of the settlor, if possible, or the beneficiaries.

5. Banks acting as trustees for employee benefit funds should assume the responsibility for preventing self-dealing. Trust departments can simply refuse to execute the orders of employers to purchase company stock. If this were the standard for all trust departments, there would be no risk of losing clients to other banks that would execute self-dealing orders.

6. Trust departments should also take the responsibility for informing potential beneficiaries of pension plans when the plan is not fully funded. The bank is, after all, maintaining the funds for their benefit, often as a result of a collective-bargaining agreement. It owes the beneficiaries this information. Otherwise, it is aiding in a serious breach of contract.

7. Employees should assert their rights to have a share in the ultimate control of pension funds. The myth that the employer uses his own funds to start a trust fund benefiting his employees has been discredited. The pension reform law of 1974 recognizes the lack of faithful execution by employers of their obligations to employees. Clearly, the federal government will assume a new enforcement role. But employees

must be certain to protect themselves. This includes seeking specialists other than banks to handle pension funds.

8. Banks should be required to turn over any profits from holding cash to the trust funds. If this change affects their profitability, they should reexamine their rate structure. Perhaps settlors and beneficiaries would be willing to pay a higher price if they felt they were receiving better service.

9. Banks should be required to greatly improve their disclosure practices. People thinking of creating trust accounts should determine which trust departments would be willing to provide them with detailed information about their operations. In particular, the banks should be prepared to indicate the major investments of their common trust funds and major holdings of stock outside the trust funds. In addition, the banks should reveal the performance of the common trust funds. They should disclose interlocking directorates and outstanding loans to companies whose stock is held in the trust departments. All of this information will help those directly involved in a trust account.

10. Settlors should make clear their wishes about how stock will be voted. Obviously, banks should not be allowed to vote their own stock. But the broader problem relates to social and environmental issues. Many people feel that shares should be voted not only with corporate profits in mind but also with respect to matters ranging from antipollution efforts to accomplishments in bringing women and minorities into positions of responsibility. In 1973, the American Bankers Association adopted Guidelines for Dealing with Corporate Responsibility Issues. These state, in part:

> If as an investment manager the fiduciary believes that a given corporation's activity or inactivity with respect to social or environmental issues is likely substantially to impact the earnings of the corporation or its long-term investment performance, the fiduciary should make an investment decision based upon those investment factors.

In other words, unless what a corporation is doing helps its earnings, sell the stock. It will take a direct order by the settlor to change the orientation.

11. While beneficiaries cannot simply assert new rights for themselves, there seems little doubt that they should have a

greater say over the control of the funds on which they may depend. Of course, the basic concept of the trust cannot be defeated. Most are created because the settlor believes that the beneficiaries will not be sufficiently capable of managing the funds to ensure that his or her wishes will be carried out. But beneficiaries should be able to take legal action to have a trustee changed when they become the victims of incompetence or management not in their best interests. In addition, the decision of the beneficiaries about what they wish from the fund ought to be required to be followed by the bank. If a group of children want income stressed so their widowed mother will have an adequate income rather than growth issues that will ensure a larger inheritance for them, their wishes ought to be followed.

12. Finally, any person thinking of setting up a trust and turning it over to a bank to manage ought to review that decision carefully. Obviously, as long as federal tax laws encourage the creation of trusts, people should use them. But it may be questionable whether a bank can do any better than a settlor who leaves fairly explicit investment instructions with an attorney or other qualified individual.

8

The
Regulators

At 3:00 P.M. on Thursday, October 18, 1973, about 300 men and women, looking for all the world like conservative bankers, converged on the sixty-three offices of the United States National Bank of San Diego. Although the bank offices were closing just at that hour, they had no trouble getting past the guard. They worked for the bank's new owner.

As these people moved through the door, 165 men and women, who formally moved onto the premises just twenty-four hours earlier, began to pack their belongings and make ready to leave. Most of the bank staff just watched the proceedings, although they were listening to orders from their new owner's representatives and answering questions.

At that moment, ownership of the United States National Bank, with assets of $1,265,868,000, had passed to the Federal Deposit Insurance Corporation. The 300 were bank examiners and liquidators of the FDIC. The 165 were national bank examiners who work for the Comptroller of the Currency, the man who had just decided to close the bank.

The dramatic event at 3:00 P.M. was the result of careful and clandestine planning. Secrecy was essential to prevent a run on the bank that might result from a sudden loss of confidence.

As we shall see later, the Comptroller, an official of the Treasury Department, had through the reports of his bank examiners come to believe that the USNB no longer had enough cash on hand or the ability to come up with the cash needed to meet expected demand for withdrawals. While bank assets substantially exceeded the amount that depositors had left with USNB, some of those assets were in the form of loans that would probably never be repaid. In any case, they couldn't be repaid when their proceeds were needed. If those people who wanted to make withdrawals could not get their money, panic would spread, and others, who had not planned to touch their deposits, would also seek to get their money out of the USNB. The result would be a run on the bank, which would not have time even to convert its loans into cash to meet depositors' demands.

The Comptroller of the Currency knew the time had come to act. That's why on October 17 he had sent his own examiners, who had entered the bank before it closed and had worked through the night and the next day, checking the cash, the loan collateral, and the items kept in safekeeping by the USNB. They had also supervised the bank's closing that day and had monitored its activities all the following day. In that way, the Comptroller could know exactly the condition of the bank when he declared that it was "insolvent"—out of cash. Then the FDIC took over as the bank went into receivership.

But the FDIC was to keep control of the bank for a very short time. At 3:00 P.M. on October 18, just as the FDIC people were taking over USNB, the FDIC itself was putting the bank on the selling block. Within an hour, three bids were received. They were opened, and at 4:30 P.M., the FDIC accepted the high bid of $89.5 million from the Crocker National Bank. Crocker National would assume many of the USNB's obligations. At 6:15 P.M., the deal was final. The next day, all of the USNB's offices opened as branches of the Crocker National Bank. For 335,000 depositors, there was little difference. The 300 men and women of the FDIC packed up their attaché cases and left. The largest bank failure in the history of the

United States until that time (before the collapse of the Franklin National) had taken place and no depositor had lost a cent.

But what of the bad loans? Crocker had assumed all the "clean" assets and liabilities of the USNB. As receiver, the FDIC did not sell some $240 million in questionable assets. The FDIC had to turn many of these assets into cash to meet outstanding claims against the bank. But none of these claims comprised deposits, which are insured by the FDIC.

All of this happened because a national bank examiner, together with some colleagues, one day tapped discreetly on the doors of the USNB and said they had come to look at the books. When bank examiners arrive on the scene, they assume actual control of bank operations. Their job is to verify that the bank is operating soundly and safely and within the law. Above all, they represent the depositors and other bank creditors.

But bank examination to prevent bank failure is only a small part of the activities of the regulators.

Who they are

Bank regulation has grown slowly over the years until there is now a confusing array of supervisory organizations. In the nineteenth century, after a brief flirtation with the First and Second Banks of the United States, through which the federal government itself got into the banking business, all commercial banks were privately owned and chartered by the states. Actually they were subject to only the loosest supervision by state authorities.

These commercial banks issued currency because there was no truly national currency. When, during the Civil War, it became necessary to raise funds nationally to wage a national war, a law was passed creating such a currency and also providing for the federal chartering of "national" banks that would also be privately owned. The Comptroller of the Currency was given the power to issue the charters and to supervise these banks.

Throughout the nineteenth century, the notion of "money" meant just that—the national currency. For decades, the debate raged about how much money there ought to be. If gold alone backed the dollar, the growth of the money supply would be limited. If silver were also used as backing, more dollars could be printed. With the increasing industrialization and urbanization of the United States, the need developed to be able to expand and reduce the amount of money by government policy and not by the printing press alone.

In 1913, the Federal Reserve System was created to "furnish an elastic currency." It would act through the national banks, all of which would be members, and through those state banks that wished to become members. Because its interests would be different from those of the Comptroller of the Currency, it was given its own supervisory powers over its members.

After the Great Depression and the collapse of many banks, yet another federal agency was created, the FDIC. State banks, not Federal Reserve members, were authorized to purchase deposit insurance, which made them subject to federal regulation for the first time. Because the FDIC has to provide insurance, it was authorized to examine insured banks to make sure that they would not go under and draw on the insurance.

Since 1933, then, there have been three federal supervisory bodies, plus the state authorities. In order to keep out of each other's way, the federal agencies have divided the primary responsibilities for supervision of commercial banks. Most state banks are subject to supervision by state and federal agencies. They may work independently of each other or they may carry out their examinations concurrently or, as in the case of New York, they can carry out a joint examination.

The trio of federal regulatory agencies can be confusing for the banks themselves, let alone the customer who has a question or a complaint about a bank. Each of the three federal agencies has its headquarters in Washington. In addition, the Comptroller of the Currency operates through fourteen national bank regions, each headed by a regional national bank examiner. The FDIC has twelve districts, each with a supervising examiner at the top. There are twelve Federal Reserve banks, each with its own district. None of the districts is identical. Thus, for example, if a national bank in Evansville, Indiana—subject to all three federal regulators—were to contact each, it would have to turn to the regional chief national bank examiner in Cleveland, Ohio, the Federal Reserve Bank of Saint Louis, and the FDIC district supervising examiner in Madison, Wisconsin. Of course, the Evansville bank would be likely to know exactly which office to contact on a specific matter. The bank's customers would probably not even be aware of the variety of regulatory bodies, much less know where to reach them.

What examiners do

Bank supervisors at both the state and national level have a wide range of responsibilities related to the operation of banks:

- chartering and organization of banks
- periodic examination and requiring banks to correct unsatisfactory or unsound conditions
- review of periodic reports on earnings and expenses
- advising banks, on request
- approval of changes in banking activities and capital structure
- authorization of branches and of trust operations
- approval of bank mergers
- regulation of bank holding companies
- regulation of bank service corporations
- issuance and enforcement of regulations pursuant to law
- liquidation of banks

Not all agencies conduct all activities. Not all agencies that have the same responsibilities carry them out in the same way. Not all agencies require the same degree of proof of the same operating standard.

The principal tool of the regulators is bank examination. In fact, most of the officials of national and state regulating agencies are examiners. The chief task of the examiner is appraisal, and not, as many believe, audit. The examiner's job is to determine above all if the bank is competently and honestly managed, so that it will not fail, nor, as a matter of policy, cheat its customers. An examination for this purpose may also entail some auditing. For example, some state examiners will check the bookkeeping on checking and savings accounts and require remedial action if too high a level of error is found. But no regulator checks the math in all checking accounts or the calculation of interest in all savings accounts.

When the examiner knocks at the bank door, he or she wants to check on the bank's assets and liabilities (sometimes even by talking to the bank's creditors), determine if all laws are being obeyed, appraise the qualifications of directors and the competence of officers and some employees, and get a general feel of how the bank is being operated. Banks that differ from the norm get recommendations for remedial action.

Perhaps checking of assets is the most important part of the job. If somebody has absconded with funds, some of the assets will be missing. If the bank has been poorly managed, some assets, probably in the form of bad loans, will be of doubtful value.

The Comptroller of the Currency and his examiners are the principal supervisory agency for about one-third of the banks, those with national charters. Indeed, the Comptroller issues the charter and can remove it. By issuing a charter, the Comptroller automatically admits banks to the Federal Reserve System and FDIC insurance. In addition, he authorizes national banks to carry on trust operations and open branches. He must also approve mergers involving national banks. In the case of a national bank (identified by the word "national" in its name or the letters "NA" [National Association] after the name), the first place a customer with a complaint ought to go is the office of the Regional Administrator of National Banks.

While the Comptroller examines national banks and has the greatest supervisory authority over their activities, the Federal Reserve also has considerable direct powers. For both national banks and state member banks, it determines how much money they must hold in reserves. For all banks of any kind, it approves or disapproves the formation of or acquisition by a bank holding company and regulates all loans secured by stock. And except where an entire state has a waiver, it supervises compliance with the Truth-in-Lending law. For state member banks, it exercises the same powers that the Comptroller has over national banks, including the power to charter them. For a customer to know whether he should address a complaint to the Federal Reserve, he would have to ask the bank if it is a member or turn to the state regulatory agency. About 9 per cent of banks are classified as state member banks.

The FDIC authorizes branches and mergers, in addition to examining state-insured nonmember banks—more than half of all banks. While it has no chartering power, its regulations extend to all banks with FDIC insurance, including all those directly supervised by the Federal Reserve and the Comptroller. For example, rules governing advertising are issued by the FDIC.

Finally, each of the states has a banking agency that carries on its own examinations of all state banks and authorizes all branches and mergers involving them, and the assumption of trust powers by them. For the few noninsured, nonmember state banks, the state banking agencies are the sole examining authority. State banking agencies vary in size and expertise. In New York, the banking department would be large enough to meet the needs of most independent nations. In Nevada, the banking department must worry about only four state-chartered banks.

Even this is not a complete list of regulators. Savings and loan associations may be either state or federally chartered. State-chartered savings and loans, more than 60 percent of the total, are chartered and supervised by state banking departments or by special savings and loan departments. Federal savings and loans are chartered and supervised by the Federal Home Loan Bank Board, roughly analogous to the Federal Reserve Board. The Federal Savings and Loan Insurance Corporation performs the same functions as the FDIC. For customers who want to find the proper regulatory agency, most of these thrift institutions have the words "savings and loan" in their name. In some states, other names are used— Massachusetts uses the name "cooperative banks," Louisiana uses "homestead societies," and a few other states call them "building and loan associations." FHLB members all have the word "federal" in their name.

Mutual savings banks are all state banks. About two-thirds of them are insured by the FDIC, with all but one of the others insured by the Massachusetts state insurance system. Just to confuse matters further, about 10 per cent of the savings banks are members of the FHLB. For the consumer, the appropriate regulatory agencies to turn to would be the FDIC and the state banking agency.

Credit unions are chartered either by the National Credit Union Administration or by state banking authorities. Federally chartered credit unions (the word "federal" appears in the name) have deposit insurance provided through the NCUA on the same basis as the FDIC. Some states authorize their credit unions to obtain NCUA insurance, and others provide their own mandatory insurance programs. For consumers, the regulatory agencies are either the NCUA or the state banking department.

Of course, even before you've been through the maze of agencies to determine the proper one to which you, as a consumer, should appeal, you may wonder what are proper matters of concern for the regulators. The answer is, anything. Because regulators are interested in determining how well banks are run and because they have the authority to order banks to correct their actions in all phases of their operations, any matter where you feel the bank has dealt unfairly or dishonestly with you is properly brought before a regulator.

The first step is to take a complaint to the bank itself. Frequently errors are made through inadvertence and will be immediately corrected. In other cases, the bank may be testing consumer reaction to its efforts to alter or reduce its services, and the bank will generally back away quickly if the consumer complains. In other cases, the bank may actually be cheating on its contractual agreement with a customer (as in calculating interest in a way not indicated when the account was opened) and may also change course if called on its action. The worst situation, of course, is when the depositor is, for any reason, deprived of his or her funds. In addition to all these cases where your immediate interests are concerned, the regulators would be glad to learn of any information you might have that would help in evaluating the overall management of the bank.

If the bank fails to respond satisfactorily to your complaint or inquiry, you should immediately contact the proper regulatory agency. It's important to explain calmly and systematically the situation and what has happened in your contacts with the bank. Try to remember dates, amounts, and the correct location of the branch. Include the account number or the number on the loan agreement. The regulator should be able to proceed quickly to straighten the matter out. Where both a state and a federal agency have regulatory authority, try the state banking department first.

Because of the nature of their work, banks constitute one of the few totally regulated industries in the country. Government has provided somebody to help you.

Why banks fail

In the years between 1930 and 1933, 9,096 banks failed or were suspended from operations. About four-fifths of the deposit loss was sustained by the depositors themselves. This was one of the most devastating effects of the Great Depression and involved the greatest number of bank closings in the shortest period in American history.

The Great Depression was characterized by a steady reduction in the amount of money. Money had been rapidly "created" through the 1920s by the extensive use of credit. The collapse of credit meant that the amount of money or what would be accepted as money was reduced. Credit depends upon confidence. When confidence withers, so does credit. The shortage of money spelled doom for many banks that had failed to spread their loan risk sufficiently or had simply made bad loans. When borrowers defaulted, banks did not have enough money to cover deposits. The banks that failed were the weakest, but even they could not have been expected to foresee the economic collapse that others had not expected.

After the depression reached its low point, federal regulatory agencies were created and strengthened with the goal of preventing a similar situation from ever happening again. Among the measures were the creation of deposit insurance and tighter controls on just how much money banks could loan to finance stock purchases. With a steadily expanding economy and with these safeguards, the bank-failure rate fell precipitously. In the worst years of the depression, 11.3 per cent of the banks had been closed. In the 1958-71 period, only 0.3 percent suffered a similar fate.

About two-thirds of recent bank failures were due to outright fraud and absconding with funds by bank officers. There is little chance for examiners to prevent such cases unless they stay on the bank's premises at all times. Most of the rest of the closings resulted from banks soliciting deposits through brokers who actually go out and beat the bushes for accounts. The banks must pay them a fee in addition to the normal interest payable to the depositor. To meet these payments, banks have to make high-risk loans that pay higher interest. Often these loans are made outside the bank's usual business area and the bank simply doesn't know what it's doing. Only four closings, representing 7 per cent of all failures, were due to inept management.

Beginning in 1971, the situation began to change noticeably. Larger and larger banks began to fail. And in the case of two of the three largest bank failures in American history, inept management was the cause.

The case of the United States National Bank was a classic case of illegal and improper use of bank funds by ownership. These funds were not only from individuals but also from big savers who bought certificates of deposit. If a few of these certificates were not renewed, the bank could quickly run short of cash.

In May 1974, the beginning of the collapse of New York's Franklin National Bank became public. In fact, the problem was not new or sudden.

Franklin National revealed in May 1974 that it would skip a dividend and that its profits had turned into losses because of setbacks in foreign-exchange transactions. Just as had the USNB, Franklin National had expanded rapidly. Originally a suburban Long Island bank, it had expanded first into New York City and then into international operations. In fact, it was ready for neither. As must all new banks, Franklin National accepted the riskier loans in order to corner a share of the New York market.

By May 1973, Franklin National was beginning to be regarded with some doubt by the Federal Reserve. It refused to allow the merger of the holding company that owned Franklin National and a finance company. The Federal Reserve thought Franklin would be spreading itself too thin.

Finally, as deposits continued to pour out of Franklin National, the Comptroller was forced to admit that the bank was not solvent. He also admitted that he had been "remiss" in handling Franklin National because his office had not kept up with changes in the banking industry in the past decade. In October 1974, just one year after the USNB closing, the Comptroller and the FDIC closed Franklin National down and sold it. This time the European-American Bank picked up the pieces. The FDIC was left with a great many of the less desirable tidbits of the collapse of the twentieth largest bank in the United States. These were mostly loans that would be difficult, if not impossible, to collect.

It took only three months for the next giant to fall. Security National Bank, which also started out on Long Island, fell because it, too, had a large portfolio of bad loans resulting from too rapid expansion into New York City. When Security National began borrowing extensively from the Federal Reserve, the Comptroller wasted no time and began pushing the bank to find a merger partner.

Finally, Security went to Chemical Bank and asked what it would offer. Chemical, which had already put a team together at the time of bidding on Franklin National, was ready to make a rapid judgment on Security. Within ten days it said it was ready to gobble up the forty-fourth largest bank in the United States.

People were obviously worried that banks would fail as they had during the depression. Could they lose the savings they thought were the safest?

The short answer is no. Deposit insurance really does work. Under the FDIC, each depositor is now insured for up to $40,000 to cover each account bearing his or her name. A *New Yorker* cartoon, published at the time of great worry, showed a bank with a sign in its window, reading: "Only money in the bank is like money in the bank."

Almost no bank, except a very small one, is likely to be a total shambles. When there is something of value to salvage and where state laws permit, the failing bank will almost certainly be acquired by a stronger bank. Depositors will hardly know the difference. If that doesn't happen, the FDIC will dip into its funds to come up with enough money to protect insured deposits. Admittedly, the FDIC has less than $6 billion, and with such big failures, people might worry about there being enough to make good on the insurance.

It would take a mighty big bust to run out the string on the FDIC. But should that happen, the Federal Reserve could do now what it could not do during the Great Depression—print more money. As people came into the bank to close their accounts, checking and savings money could be turned into cash money. This might actually result in less money rather than more. And once people got the psychological satisfaction of "touching" their money, they would probably stop closing their accounts. In short, both the Federal Reserve and the FDIC have learned that in case of serious problems, their action does not save banks so much as it saves the whole economy.

So while the average person can be assured about the consequences of bank failure, he or she has every right to wonder why bigger banks are failing more frequently and why the closings are due increasingly to bad management.

It's possible that bank management is no worse now than it has ever been since the depression. But never, since then, has the economy been in such trouble. The money supply was consciously reduced as a way of fighting inflation, and then a major recession took over. A slowdown in the economy inevitably weeds out the financially weak, and some of them undoubtedly owe banks money. When they can't pay, the banks find themselves short of needed cash. Banks that are sufficiently diversified and have avoided too many high-risk loans can ride out hard times. The banks where bad management judgments have been made are under greater pressure.

Many banks, but especially those which run into trouble, have taken part in a recent trend in financing loans that amount to a significant change in banking practices. In the past, loans were not allowed to outstrip deposits. But with loan demands increasing in recent years and the banks' desire to maximize profits, they have gone out into the market themselves to borrow money to relend. As opposed to deposit money, this is "hot money." The bank knows that it will have to make good on its loan—money on which it may be paying more interest than on deposits. If the bank's own loans run into trouble, it still must pay back the money it has borrowed. A bank may be tempted to go too far into loans backed by "hot money," and the Comptroller doesn't like to see the amount involved go beyond 6 percent of assets. But this can be a dangerous business.

Indeed, despite all the regulation of banks, they can take a great many risks affecting their depositors' money. The regulators cannot stop banks from currency speculation. They cannot prevent unwise loans, although they may end up pumping funds into the banks to make sure that the banks themselves are not closed down because of the weakness of their customers. Since 1970, when the Federal Reserve poured money into the banking system to ensure that Penn Central would not be allowed to bring down the entire economy because it couldn't pay back its loans, the Federal Reserve has been in the business of covering doubtful loans, not to save the companies concerned or even the bank, but the economy as a whole.

Thus, there are some major loopholes in what regulators regulate: banks are doing things they haven't done before. Above all, they themselves are behaving more like businesses and less like public utilities.

The other obvious problem is with how the regulators do their job. The members of the Federal Reserve Board, the chairman of the FDIC, and the Comptroller of the Currency are all politically appointed, but only the Comptroller turns out to be a political figure most of the time. Perhaps that's because the Federal Reserve Board is just that—a board—and professionals—economists, bankers, and businessmen—have been appointed to it. The chairman of the FDIC is also a member of a board on which the Comptroller sits, and again the tradition has been to name a professional. The Comptroller exercises his functions without benefit of any checks. In cases of bad judgment, there's nobody who can overrule him, even the Treasury Secretary to whom he nominally reports.

While it might make sense to take a look at the complex federal regulatory system that now exists with a view to some streamlining of functions, there's a great deal to be said for allowing specialized agencies to carry out specialized functions. If a single, unified agency were incompetent, there would be no other lines of defense.

For the time being, it would seem wise to break with precedent and create a Board of Administrators of the National Banks to replace the Comptroller of the Currency (except maybe for the limited function of controlling the currency, which is mostly a historic relic). The board should be financed, at least in part, by Congress. Now the Comptroller is totally independent of Congress because his operation is financed by a levy on banks. He is not, therefore, totally independent of them. Staggered terms would help insulate the board from political pressures.

An economic lesson: the Federal Reserve

While all of the regulatory agencies affect people at least indirectly, one of them has a powerful and far more direct impact on their lives. This is the Federal Reserve, known in financial circles as the Fed, which has the task of controlling the supply of money in the American economy. Sometimes banks are blamed, as in the case of high interest rates, when a development is really the result of a conscious policy of the Federal Reserve.

We all recognize that there's more to money than simply coin and currency. Banks can actually create money by putting on their books a credit to the account of somebody who, for example, has just been granted a loan. That person is not actually given cash but may make withdrawals from a loan account by writing checks that are accepted as though they were cash. Just how much money a bank can create in this way is determined by the amount of reserves it holds.

Reserves take one of three forms. First, reserve dollars may be created by gold or "paper gold." "Paper gold," or special drawing rights, is now accepted to settle debts among countries just as gold itself is. Each country has a certain amount of paper gold in relation to the amount of gold and dollars it holds. Paper gold has become more accepted around the world as the dollar, whittled down in value by inflation, has become less desirable. When gold or paper gold flows into the United States, the selling country gets dollars, which are credited to its account at the Federal Reserve Bank of New York. When those dollars are spent in the United States they move into other banks where they can be counted as part of the reserves that the Federal Reserve requires them to hold.

A second source of reserves is, of course, money in circulation. Actually, because of population growth, more cash has been needed in circulation, leaving less that the banks could hold as reserves. Neither these reserves nor dollars resulting from gold transactions can be controlled by national policy. Naturally, more money could be printed, but that would represent, in any case, only a small part of the total reserves necessary to back the enormous money supply of almost $1 trillion. Because these two sources of reserve money can fluctuate on their own, the Federal Reserve was given other more sophisticated instruments that enable it to influence directly the amount of reserves.

Most required cash reserves are held by banks in their reserve accounts with the Federal Reserve banks. If the Federal Reserve makes a loan to a member bank, it will increase the reserve account by the amount of the loan. That increases a bank's reserves. The interest charged by the Federal Reserve is called the discount rate.

In addition to making or refusing loans to banks, the Federal Reserve can also influence the overall amount of reserves by its investment policy, known as open-market operations. If a Federal Reserve bank purchases a government security, it pays by check to the seller, who deposits that check in his bank. When the check comes back to the Federal Reserve, that amount is credited to the bank's reserve account, thus reducing its reserves. The decision to buy or sell government securities is made on the basis of the Federal Reserve's decision whether it wishes to increase bank reserves or not.

Where does the Federal Reserve get the money to lend and invest? Like any other lender or investor, the Federal Reserve hopes to make a profit on its loans in the form of interest, and on its investments in the form of a higher selling price than purchase price. Its excess profits go to the U.S. Treasury.

The Federal Reserve has two additional tools for influencing reserves. It can set the interest rate it charges on loans—the discount rate. By raising the rate, it can discourage banks from borrowing to grant loans and thus prevent their reserves from growing. In the past twenty years, the discount rate has fluctuated considerably, with an overall low of 1.5 percent and a high of 8 percent. Each time the discount rate sinks back, it never goes back quite as far as where it started from.

The reserve requirements—the amount of reserves banks must have as a percentage of their checking and savings accounts—can also be varied by the Federal Reserve. When the dollar-reserve requirement is lowered, that means that one reserve dollar will back more dollars created by the bank. If the reserve requirement is increased, each reserve dollar backs fewer dollars available for loans. The Federal Reserve does not, in practice, vary this rate too widely, with large banks having been required during the last twenty years to hold between 16.5 percent and 18 percent of the checkbook deposits in reserve.

It's obvious that by determining the amount of reserves banks have—most frequently through its open-market operations—the Federal Reserve actually determines to a considerable extent just how much money there is. It can safely be presumed that banks will create as much money as the Federal Reserve allows.

During periods of "easy money," the Federal Reserve may be lending more to banks, investing more in government securities, and lowering the reserve requirements and the discount rate (indeed, it could not lend more without lowering the interest rate on those loans). Because banks pay lower prices for their reserves, they can charge their customers lower prices for the money they lend. The Federal Reserve may adopt such an easy-money policy when it wants to restart a sluggish economy where unemployment is high and business activity is in a slump.

The only problem with an easy-money policy is that it's hard to know when money has become too easy. Then there is more money around than there are goods to be bought. When money chases goods, inflation results; that is, the price of goods becomes artificially high because of their relative shortage.

At this point the Federal Reserve will embark on a "tight-money" policy. It will sell government securities, the reserve requirement may be increased, the discount rate will be raised, and thus the amount of loans to banks will be cut. As a result, the amount of reserves will decline and each reserve dollar will back fewer dollars at the banks. Because banks have to pay high interest for their reserves, they will charge high interest for their loans to discourage would-be borrowers.

Frequently, in recent years, people have blamed the banks for high interest rates. Here was one kind of inflation that could be remedied if only the banks would be willing to make smaller profits and lower their interest rates. What those people do not realize is that the high interest rates are the result of a Federal Reserve policy. Of course, that policy has the effect of contributing to inflation itself.

Banks have been ingenious in devising ways to get around Federal Reserve rules and policies in order to keep on lending to the many borrowers who will pay any price for a loan. For many, their foreign operations have been a source of funds that escape federal controls.

Finally, the entire economy begins to slow down because of the inability of people to pay the high prices that are charged. When they stop buying cars, cars stop getting more expensive, but at the same time, auto workers may lose their jobs. Thus, a tight-money policy can lead back to the need for an easy-money policy—to get the economy moving again.

Of course, the Federal Reserve's monetary policy is not the only way the government influences the economy. The levels of government spending and of taxation also have a powerful impact. However, during the Nixon years, the administration largely abandoned these measures of "fiscal" policy and left the Federal Reserve to try to keep the economy on an even keel through its monetary policy.

Obviously, the big problem for the Federal Reserve is knowing when to shift gears. If it keeps an easy-money policy too long, it can bring on inflation. If it keeps a tight-money policy too long, it can bring on recession. It has to be looking ahead and trying not only to solve the crisis of the moment but also to be seeking the proper method of returning to an even keel. It should also be attempting to close loopholes that allow banks to evade their obligations to fall in line with Federal Reserve policy. But the Federal Reserve has not been aggressive in doing this.

The Federal Reserve has taken a lot of criticism recently for its failure to change gears at the right time. Most economists would argue that the Federal Reserve should not be left by itself to try to influence the economy, that there should be a "mix" of fiscal and monetary policy. In recent years, government policy has been like a car with one front wheel that can be turned; the other just keeps going straight ahead. That causes a lot of drag and makes it difficult to control the car—or the economy.

The authority for the Federal Reserve to control monetary policy comes from the Congress, which has been reluctant to try to take a collective guess on monetary policy. But as discontent with the Federal Reserve's handling of monetary policy rises, the Congress obviously becomes more tempted to intervene or at least give the Federal Reserve some direct orders.

From the individual's viewpoint, the bank is actually an instrument of a major national policy to influence the economy. So the whopping loan rate on a new car may be more than a symptom of bad times; it may be part of the cure.

There's a Great Day Coming

American banking has evolved just about as much as the American automobile. The car was first powered by the internal combustion engine, and it still is. The basic design of the car has actually changed little, and it hasn't become much safer over the years.

By the same token, the business of banking hasn't developed much since 1933. The only big change is that, like cars, bank facilities are now accessible to a greater number of people. And in the same way that a degree of auto safety has been forced on manufacturers, the banks have been required to provide their customers with more information and to reduce outright discrimination.

The real revolution in banking lies ahead. It will come gradually, in line with the ability of the mammoth financial sector to absorb change. Banks will increasingly take advantage of technology to streamline their procedures and eliminate the billions of pieces of paper that threaten to dominate and ultimately choke the financial system. Government will alter the conditions of competition, removing artificial requirements that are relics of a historical evolution, and thus increasing the choices available to the consumer. In addition, passage of the Truth-in-Lending and Fair Credit Billing Acts and the creation of consumer offices in banking regulatory agencies indicate that government is becoming increasingly aware of inequities in the treatment of customers. But the consumer, too, must be better educated, both to take advantage of the services that exist and to protect himself when disclosure is inadequate or practices are illegal.

You and the computer

From the consumer's viewpoint, the biggest changes in banking result from the advent of the computer. Just as the check has replaced cash as the principal medium of exchange, the computer entry will replace the check for many transactions. With the card providing access to the computer system, banking will pass from the age of paper to the age of plastic.

The bank card is the opening wedge. Its more traditional function is to provide credit. A purchase can be made without the instant outlay of cash. Indeed, a purchase need not be covered by funds then in the bank account. Even more significant over the long run is the access the card gives to cash. It means the end of bankers' hours. The card is used in conjunction with banking machines that can take the place of the teller for many operations. At present, the automatic teller is used mostly to provide cash at any time of day or night. Yet it has disadvantages. It performs no other functions, it is not conveniently located, it provides only a limited amount of cash each day, and it involves an additional charge.

All of these inconveniences may disappear. Clearly, automatic tellers will be able to carry out a variety of services—perhaps as many as 90 per cent of all transactions now carried out by tellers. Transfers among accounts, loan repayment, and even bill paying are possible through the use of the properly equipped automatic teller. If these machines become more accessible and more heavily used, banking, one of the most labor-intensive industries, will at last begin to realize the economies of automation. Some of those savings should be passed on to the consumer.

The most important next step will be something called DPD—Direct Pay Deposit. Instead of paying each employee individually, employers deposit pay directly into the employee's account. The employee receives the paycheck stub, with the complete information on deductions, either directly from the bank or from the employer in the traditional way. The employee is no longer put to any inconvenience in obtaining his paycheck and is not required to take it to the bank in order to obtain cash. There are no lost or stolen checks, and the money is credited even if the employee is away from work. From the bank's viewpoint, the employee is a more attractive credit customer because of the continuous and permanent relationship created by DPD. And for Social Security and welfare recipients, the system eliminates waiting for the regular check in the mail.

This system is already in use in some places. While it provides added convenience to the depositor, its greatest significance is that it opens the door to a variety of other services. While DPD has traditionally been limited to deposits that are simple transfers from the employer's bank account to the employee's account in the same bank, now it is possible for the money to be credited to an account in another bank. New Automated Clearing Houses, which allow for transfers among participating banks through a common computer arrangement, are budding all over the country. Once this arrangement exists for the purpose of crediting paychecks, all of the customers of all the participating banks can be linked to each other through the computer.

The next step is the preauthorized transfer. This, too, is not really a new idea because checking account customers have long been able to direct the bank to make automatic deposits in a savings account. The concept can be expanded to authorize the bank, once it has received your pay deposit, to pay automatically certain fixed and regular bills such as your mortgage, insurance premiums, or consumer loan payments. The bother of writing checks and the risk of late penalty charges would be eliminated. It would even save on postage. Such a system would also be possible for payments of regular bills even if the amount varied from month to month. Of course, if customers encountered billing inaccuracies from the power company, for example, they would not want to have their electric bills paid in this way. Yet the kinds of bills that could be paid is almost limitless, ranging from the oil company's budget plan to property taxes.

Two other innovations will make it possible for consumers to use electronic funds transfer instead of the traditional check. The multicheck is already in use in some places. A depositor instructs the bank to make payments to a number of merchants by means of a single document. With the Automated Clearing House system, a great many merchants could be covered. Both cost and effort would be reduced for the customer.

The bill-check works in about the same way, but only involves a single merchant. He sends the customer a bill, part of which is actually a check. The customer fills out the check to indicate how much he wishes to pay. When he is ready to pay the bill, he returns the bill-check to the merchant, who can then enter it into the banking system. The flexibility provided the customer is especially appropriate for one-time and variable charges, where the consumer wishes to review the bill and withhold payment until he has enough money in his checking account to cover it and his other expected needs. The bill-check saves the customer the trouble of writing a check.

Once electronic funds transfer is available, a variety of uses becomes evident. In Lincoln, Nebraska, customers of Hinky Dinky supermarkets can withdraw money from their savings accounts with the First Federal Savings and Loan Association when they are ready to pay at the checkout counter. This enables them to earn interest on "checking account money" right up to the moment they need to use it. The store simply has a computer terminal that can almost instantly verify the customer's account information and balance and transfer the funds. The Hinky Dinky personnel give the customer a bank record of the transaction. Similar systems were set up by 14 commercial banks in nine states and 117 savings and loans in seventeen states within months of the Hinky Dinky plan's inauguration.

At the Farmers and Mechanics Savings Bank in Minneapolis, perhaps the most sophisticated use of plastic credit is being tested. Called Pay by Phone, it turns the customer's home or office telephone into a computer terminal. Using a push-button telephone, the customer transmits instructions directly to the bank's computer about payments he wishes to have made to participating merchants. A number of codes are used to ensure security. The customer receives a daily statement show-ing transactions, and each merchant receives a consolidated payment from the bank. This system enables the depositor to collect interest on funds until they are needed. The thrift gains deposits that would otherwise have remained in noninterest-bearing commercial accounts. People's Savings Bank in Bridgeport, Connecticut, operates a similar system, but one where the customer gives instructions orally to a phone teller. What is more significant about this process is the radical reduc-tion in the amount of paperwork. The bank is given an order by the customer, withdraws funds from one account and de-posits them to another, and prints confirming statements, all automatically.

Perhaps the ultimate step is the point-of-sale service. Al-ready tested by the City National Bank of Columbus, Ohio, this system will permit a customer to present a card at the store at the time of purchase. The card is not the traditional credit card. It is a "debit" or "cash" card, because it enables the pur-chaser to debit his own account and transfer payment to the store automatically. Use of the card would also make more traditional transactions easy. If you chose to pay by check, the card would be inserted into a terminal connected to your bank's computer that would verify that you had sufficient money in your account to cover the bill without the cumber-some procedure of presenting several pieces of identification to the salesperson. In the case of merchandise to be shipped, you might prefer to make a credit purchase and the card would then serve the function of a normal retail credit card.

The consumer should find that point-of-sale bank service could do everything from eliminating bounced checks (checks would be eliminated and the funds would be transferred im-mediately) to earning a cash discount, now reported to be at 2 percent, for actually ordering the transfer. What's more, wait-ing time in line should be cut, because there would be no checking of identification, no completion of forms. The process could take a matter of seconds. And bankers' hours would be of no relevance; the bank would always be open.

In addition to convenience, electronic funds transfer would push us a lot closer to the cashless society. If nothing else, that should reduce muggings, because no cash would be used at any point. Even bank robbers would be likely to find far less cash in the vault.

The greatest disadvantage is that the customer is forced to deal with a machine, not people. Many people place a high premium on dealing with a small, local bank because they come to know the personnel and expect personal service. If there are any problems concerning an account, the customer can expect them to be resolved by people he knows. While people are quick to recognize the benefits of the dial telephone, those who remember when the operator asked: "Number, please?" recall that they were not at all unhappy with a system that provided them a degree of human contact.

In addition, the general public attitude toward computers is far from favorable. Stories of checks being sent out in the wrong amount or of people being harassed for nonpayment of an astronomical bill they did not incur leave a feeling of mistrust and real concern about being left at the mercy of the computer. In addition, the Equity Funding scandal demonstrated that the public may, in future years, have more to worry about because of sophisticated electronics defrauders than because of muggers. In that case, company officials were able to use the computer to record thousands of insurance policies, which, in fact, had never been sold. This false information artificially inflated the company's assets, enabling it to make unjustified loans. The real losers in such a case could be honest customers—in the case of a bank, its depositors. While the regulators would have to be able to cope with such a fraud, it is clear that today they do not have the capacity to do so and that there may be no known method of defeating certain kinds of fraud.

Consumers also believe that where a new and simpler system is installed, there should be economic benefits. Banks profit from electronic innovations and some of that gain should be returned in the form of lower charges.

Electronic funds transfer can, by its very nature, end up costing the customer money. Because funds can be transferred instantly, the "float" will be eliminated. For the individual, "float" means that you can write a check on Saturday without having the funds to cover it in your account. Then, the following Monday, you can deposit enough to cover the check when it is presented for collection. Of course, both banks and merchants will also lose the advantages of the "float." Customers for whom electronics are supposed to improve service will not be happy about losing the "float."

Customer resistance is now the greatest obstacle to an electronic funds transfer system. A national commission has been created by Congress to deal with this new phenomenon, but its membership has more representatives of the banking industry than of consumers. Only when banks can prove that the new system is virtually error-free and protects individual privacy, and that lower charges compensate for the lack of personal contact and the loss of the "float," will consumers be ready to accept the coming revolution in banking.

A new structure for banking

With the exception of the oil industry, perhaps no other industry has been the subject of so much scrutiny, official and academic, as banking. Although the findings of all of these studies do not agree in every detail, they all indicate the need to revise the banking structure as it has evolved over the years. Artificial distinctions between institutions and services stifle competition and thus limit the choices available to consumers.

Three major studies have been conducted by the federal government. The Presidential Commission on Financial Structure and Regulation, more frequently known as the Hunt Commission because it was headed by Reed O. Hunt, former chairman of Crown Zellerbach, was published in December 1971. The approach of this study is admittedly that of the banking institutions themselves, not of consumers. In fact, one member, Lane Kirkland of the AFL-CIO, refused even to sign the report because of its slant. Yet the Hunt Commission report was surprising in that bankers were willing to admit the need for major structural changes.

In August 1973, Congress provided its response. In a staff report prepared for the House Committee on Banking and Currency, headed by Wright Patman, long a critic of banks, a far more consumer-oriented series of proposals was made.

Finally, late that month, the White House and the Treasury published their own suggestions, which took the form of draft legislation. Perhaps this was the most surpising of the three documents, because the White House was prepared to back significant changes in the banking structure.

These proposals on the federal level spurred considerable state activity, and financial reform became the topic of the hour. In New York, the banking department created its own version of the Hunt Commission, while the New York Federal

Reserve Bank came up with a study and recommendations specifically related to mutual savings banks.

Reform has focused on limits on interest payments and restrictions on the functions of thrift institutions. Probably it was the thrifts themselves that prompted this concern, because of the creation of NOW accounts—in effect, checking accounts on which interest is paid. Because of the novelty of what turned out to be a perfectly legal act, Congress quickly limited NOW accounts to Massachusetts and New Hampshire, the two states where they were first established. But in order to freeze the accounts, Congress was forced to argue that they were an experiment and the results would have to be analyzed before they would be opened elsewhere. At best, that amounted to a holding action while the various study commissions could come up with suggestions on how to deal with the new conditions of competition.

The interest-paying checking account, by whatever name it may be called, appears inevitable. Even the Treasury legislation provides for it in the form of the NOW account, on which the bank may technically require that the depositor wait thirty days before having his money. This is a mere technicality, and there is no practical difference between the NOW account and the traditional demand-deposit account, on which interest would still be banned.

Clearly, the payment of interest on checking accounts would move the relationship between the bank and consumer closer to the notion of fee-for-service. The customer would be compensated for leaving his funds in a checking account. But the almost certain corollary of this development would be the ultimate lifting of interest-rate ceilings on both commercial banks and thrifts.

The differential in rates between banks and thrifts was designed to ensure that savings institutions would have enough funds to finance mortgages. Commercial banks have long smarted under this distinction and argue that they assume a portion of the mortgage loan even now. They favor open competition on equal terms for the saver's dollar. If the interest rates paid went up, so would the cost of mortgages. If resistance to high mortgage rates by home buyers began to be felt, the interest rate on savings would have to be adjusted. In short, the market rather than government regulators would establish interest rates. Of course, through its continued impact on monetary policy, the Federal Reserve could also influence, though not control, interest rates.

Because each step of reform leads to another, thrift institutions will probably be allowed to take on more of the functions of commercial banks. Of course, they may also have to give up many of the advantages they enjoy as compared with commercial banks and maintain reserves on the same basis. Equity would require that if thrifts lost their advantage in paying higher interest than banks, they should gain the advantages of being able to provide the same kinds of services.

Savings and loans and mutual savings banks would acquire the authority to provide checking accounts. In addition, they would probably be able to offer personal loans in relatively small amounts, an activity that has generally been prohibited to them. The thrifts might also be permitted to provide a number of other services such as selling mutual funds, financial counseling, management of trusts and estates, and supervision of real-estate investment trusts. Indeed, it would be possible for these thrifts to convert to stock ownership and even to become commercial banks, as they came to provide the same services.

This step-by-step development, from paying interest on checking accounts to eliminating the distinction between banks and thrifts, may seem inevitable and logical. How well it serves the consumer interest remains to be seen. In particular, the distinction among institutions may have served to increase rather than limit choice. Because mutual savings banks see the world differently from commercial banks, they may provide the kinds of services that some customers feel they cannot obtain at the bank where they maintain a checking account. The competitive urge to develop services not provided elsewhere could diminish in a situation where all institutions were alike.

Whatever the ultimate evolution of commercial banks and the thrifts, the recent studies have focused new attention on the unique role played by credit unions. As a result, proposals have been aimed at strengthening them without necessarily turning them into commercial banks. Credit unions are closely circumscribed because of their exemption from federal taxes. As lending organizations among "friends," they are designed to reduce illegal loan-shark operations. In addition, they have no stockholders who must be paid a share of the profits, and thus there are no profits. Whatever is earned in interest is returned to savers and borrowers. Provided these conditions are maintained, even though services are increased, credit unions should be able to avoid increased taxation.

Above all, credit unions will continue to be open only to members of affinity groups such as members of the same church or employees of the same firm. While some states allow mere geographical residence in the same state to qualify a group to form a credit union, recent proposals call for closer ties in the future. On the other hand, starting a credit union is not very difficult, and the Credit Union National Association provides advice. The amount of funds required for the operation of a credit union is not large. Thus, those who might be eligible for membership in a newly created credit union should be encouraged to investigate the undertaking.

Credit unions will probably be authorized to offer checking accounts, just as other financial institutions do. In addition, they will also be able to service larger loans than are now permitted. Just how high this ceiling might be raised depends on the length of time for which the credit unions would be prepared to make loans. In general, they have made loans for relatively short periods, but when loan amounts increase, so do loan durations. Conceivably, credit unions could eventually write mortgage loans. And as interest-rate ceilings are lifted for banks and thrifts, they will probably also be lifted for credit unions.

Branching out: delivering bank services

Over the years, the barriers against statewide branching have been falling. The tide toward large banks with many branches or subsidiaries seems irreversible. The day of the unit bank is fading, and with it the familiarity that came of everybody in town knowing the bank president and the entire staff. If there is any advantage to this trend, it is that banking services are being offered in more convenient locations. But it would seem unwise for bank regulators to simply abandon any limits on branching. Expansion into unprofitable branches could endanger all customers because inevitably the bank would be weakened financially.

Some bank regulators and officials believe that state lines are artificial barriers to bank competition. Under existing law, it is now impossible for a bank to extend its operations across state lines except for representative offices that can be used to solicit business for the home bank. Now New York, the nation's financial capital, is considering approaching other states to allow interstate banking on terms of reciprocity. The use of interstate branches or subsidiaries would be attractive to New York banks, which are eager to gain access to the large and growing market in states such as California. Obviously, the major New York banks are confident they could withstand competition in their home market from out-of-state banks. But even some smaller states would favor interstate banking as a way of attracting a portion of the large pools of capital held by major banks elsewhere into their own economic plans.

At the same time, branch banking will take on a new meaning with the use of automatic tellers. Regulators will probably not consider them ordinary branches. Already the Comptroller has said that banks in one state can place automatic tellers in another. This is the first step in recent years toward interstate banking. And a bank will have to make less of a capital expenditure to reach an even greater number of people than if it had been required to create an entirely new branch.

In what may turn out to be the most revolutionary decision in the banking revolution—if it stands—Comptroller James Smith ruled that electronic terminals are not bank branches. His decision means that a New York bank can have terminals in Iowa or a California bank could reach into Florida. The transaction is considered to be made at the computer, not at the point where the terminal's buttons are pressed. Small banks worry that the giants in New York and other big cities will be able to push them aside because the big-city banks would be freed from limits on "branching" across state lines. The small banks may get some support in Congress. Meanwhile, development and planning of extensive terminal systems goes on. Each could handle several common operations. If customers perceived that banking by computer is the best deal, Congress would be hard put to stand by the smaller banks.

Mortgages and trusts

Both mortgage and trust services are likely to come in for more critical review.

The crisis in mortgage money availability resulting from high interest rates and the portion of loan portfolios composed of older, lower-interest mortgages has fueled a debate over variable-rate mortgages. The interest rate would change over time to reflect changing interest rates in the marketplace. Banks and thrifts argue that variable-rate mortgages are fair to the borrower and ensure a steady supply of funds for the mortgage market at all times.

Consumers see variable-rate mortgages quite differently. The mortgage loan is almost certainly the largest borrowing by an individual in a lifetime. Repayment of that loan becomes a permanent part of family budgeting over the long haul. To have the amount that is to be repaid constantly shifting could have a major disruptive effect on the budget. In addition, the Patman report attacks the proposal on the grounds that it shifts all of the risk from the lender to the borrower and that it will probably discourage homeownership. Patman reports that if payments were kept level, the term of the mortgage would have to be varied and that as little as a 1-percent rate increase could transform a thirty-year mortgage into one running forever. The Hunt Commission, which favors variable rates as an option for VA and FHA mortgages, admits that the borrower has few alternatives in obtaining a mortgage and would be unlikely to bargain with the bank. Thus, even the Hunt Commission suggests that the terms of such mortgages be carefully explained in advance and that borrowers be given the option of terminating the variable-rate system at any time they become unhappy with it.

In 1975, the Federal Home Loan Bank Board proposed authorizing variable-rate mortgages that could not increase more than 2.5 percent over the life of the mortgage loan or 0.5 percent in any six months. Under pressure from consumer and minority groups and from organized labor, Congress moved to block this proposal from being implemented.

Home Savings and Loan in Los Angeles, the largest savings and loan, is already making variable-rate loans. And balloon mortgages, such as offered by New York's East River Savings Bank, amount to much the same thing. Banks and thrifts say they may have to go this route, whatever consumers want, just to be able to make mortgage loans. Of course, such statements indicating that the only kind of mortgage loans they will be able to offer will be unpopular with consumers, may be nothing more than a form of pressure intended to convince the government to subsidize mortgage loans by paying part of the interest.

Both state usury laws and ceilings on government-backed mortgages dry up mortgage money. When interest rates rise to or above these levels, banks and thrifts simply refuse to make loans below these ceilings when they can make other loans at higher rates. Numerous proposals have been made to allow these rates to move in relation to the general level of interest rates instead of having them set by law. While these proposals seem reasonable, some may wonder if the existence of such limits does not serve to brake somewhat a flight toward even higher interest rates.

The abuses of trust departments have brought the Hunt Commission to the point of making recommendations that would substantially transform their operations. The commission favors a wall between trust and commercial departments when total trust assets exceed $200 million. In addition to closer regulation, the commission would require an annual report detailing stockholdings, dollar values, and interlocking directorates. The Patman report goes even further and proposes "the complete separation of trust departments from commercial banks, except possibly for the very smallest trust departments." Clearly, concern about trust department inefficiency and disregard for the interests of the beneficiaries is increasing and has reached the banking industry itself, as shown by the Hunt Commission report.

Reforming the regulators

Regulation itself comes in for reform under the various proposals. Patman suggests that finance companies engaged in interstate business be subject to federal chartering. He and others foresee similar treatment for mutual savings banks and savings and loans owned by stockholders.

At the same time, some proposals call for a single federal regulator and others for a rationalization of the current system in which three federal agencies—the Comptroller of the Currency, the Federal Reserve, and the Federal Deposit Insurance Corporation—share regulatory responsibility over commercial banks, and other agencies deal with savings and loans and credit unions.

Consumers will be less concerned about the form of regulatory supervision than its results. Clearly, the present system in which the Comptroller, a politically oriented official, has the ultimate authority over the largest commercial banks has proved to be inadequate if not downright dangerous to the public interest. But consumers would do well to be suspicious of the panacea of a single federal regulator. If that regulator did as poorly as the Comptroller, without being subject to pressure from other agencies, the consumer might well be even more poorly served. While the studies have not dealt with state regulation, a good case can be made for strengthening such regulation on the obvious grounds that it is closer to the people whose interests must be protected.

Finally, the debate over the Federal Reserve's independence in determining monetary policy can be expected to continue. Patman has long argued that the Federal Reserve should be required to set monetary policy in the light of guidelines laid down by the President. In addition, Congress could strengthen its own authority over the Federal Reserve by the power of the purse if it were made dependent on appropriations rather than contributions from member banks. Although Patman is no longer the central figure on the House Banking Committee, his views have gained increasing acceptance as the tight-money policies used by the Federal Reserve to combat inflation have been blamed for the ensuing recession. While the Federal Reserve's policies are certainly worthy of criticism, there is no indication of superior wisdom either in the White House or on Capitol Hill. In effect, the Federal Reserve has been attacked for failing to do what others did not do.

The consumer and the bank

In a recent study for the American Bankers Association, a survey organization found increased consumer skepticism about banks. "While the image of banks as solid and reliable still exists," it said, "it is in the process of change. In-depth interview results indicate that many respondents have gradually come to view banks as large, impersonal, bureaucratic, even exploitative institutions."

Of course, banks have been changing in recent years. Surprisingly, only in the past decade have they come to regard themselves as businesses. The growth of assets has become their dominant goal. As a result, in many cases, customers have felt that services were actually reduced or that charges were increased. In general, smaller banks have not gone along with this trend as rapidly as major institutions.

At the same time, bank customers have become more consumer oriented. Where previously they felt it improper to question bank policies and even doubted that there were differences among banks, they now are more concerned with looking out for themselves. Bank policies are watched with more suspicion and doubt, and the collapse of Franklin National raised real fears about the ability of bank managers.

The survey done by the ABA reveals a broad spectrum of discontent. Customers believe that management is rigid and that dealing with a bank is like dealing with the government bureaucracy. They complain about inadequate staffing and about the rapid turnover of the poorly paid bank personnel most of us come in contact with regularly. Even bankers' hours, certainly nothing new, draw a lot of negative comment. Customers feel that the bank's hours suit the management and the employees far more than the consumer. People who have been used to dealing with local bank officers are unhappy with branch banking, because the local manager may have to check with the main office on decisions that previously could easily have been made at the local office.

Perhaps most important, customers complain that they cannot obtain information about bank services and help in dealing with everything from balancing checking accounts to reading statements and passbooks. The cold, businesslike attitude of the bank coupled with the frequent refusal to disclose information that would help the customer make an informed decision has led to the kind of reaction of one person interviewed: "We don't trust our institutions today. . . . The institutions are getting bigger and man is getting smaller."

Help is on the way. With cumbersome slowness, public institutions are gradually beginning to recognize consumer demand for better service from financial institutions. Even those who would question the need for a growing government bureaucracy can see that a regulatory system that is largely self-enforcing—where the consumer himself can take action if the bank or thrift fails to follow the law—is both economical and desirable.

The first step, and probably the most important, is disclosure. That does not mean more fine print. Instead, it means more explanation and more attention to informing the customer of the meaning of those explanations. For the moment, banks seem to have adopted the attitude that it's better to take the money and run than to take a chance on a friendlier attitude toward their customers. There is no proof that banks would do worse using a more open approach. If they continue to spurn it, the government will inevitably be pushed to lay down stringent disclosure requirements.

But the consumer's best safeguard remains himself. Only Oregon makes consumer education a part of the public-school curriculum. Without such schooling, it's up to the consumer to get whatever information he can about the places where his money goes.

To a great extent, this book provides the kind of disclosure that should already be available from banks. Just how much money these suggestions are worth depends on the financial activities of each individual—his or her checking account, credit card, personal loan, mortgage, trust account. But there is almost no adult who does not have some relationship with a bank, and virtually all can save money by knowing more about how banks operate. Even if you forget every one of the specific points in this book, you should not hesitate to ask questions at the bank. If you don't understand a service, or it seems unfair, ask and keep on asking questions until you get a solid answer. But before you even set foot in the bank, decide for yourself exactly what service you need. You may be surprised to find that it exists.

There is no reason to be intimidated by banks. You are the customer, and you have the right to know. If you don't learn the right questions and then ask them, what you don't know can hurt you.

TOO GOOD FOR
THE RICH ALONE

*The Complete Guide to Tax-Exempt Bonds
for the Middle-Income Investor*

CHAPTER 1

The World of Tax-Exempt Bonds

I can't count the number of times investors have sheepishly said to me, "I wish I could buy tax-exempt bonds."

My answer invariably is, "Why can't you?"

Their answer, just as invariably, is exactly what I expect it to be: "I'm not rich enough."

If you have a middle income, tax-exempts are something you should know about because they very probably will fit into your investment picture.

To be specific, if you have an adjusted gross income that puts you in the 32-percent tax bracket (which means $20,000 for a married couple or $16,000 for a single person), tax-exempt bonds can be your cup of tea. There is a further bonus if your state has an income tax and you buy bonds issued in that state, because you benefit from tax-exemption increases. For instance, if your state tax is added to your federal tax, your bracket could be 40 percent. If you purchased an 8-percent bond of an out-of-state issuer, the equivalent yield you would have to buy in a taxable maturity would be 11.6 percent. If you purchased a bond issued in your state, the equivalent yield would have to be as much as 13.3 percent. These numbers make a great case for home-state buying.

If you're in the 32-percent bracket, you retain only 4.08 percent of a 6-percent yield. If you're lucky enough to get 10 percent, you keep only 6.8 percent. And keep in mind that there is practically no risk in tax-exempts. If you bought something that was yielding 5 percent with the expectation of making a capital gain of 15 percent a year, only to find six months later that the market had taken a dive and 40 percent of your principal had disappeared, you may possibly want to hear more.

Banks, insurance companies, and some of the rich have long recognized tax-exempts to be a very sweet investment. It would not be far from wrong to say that they prefer to keep tax-exempts a secret. Everybody talks about competition being such a great thing, but nobody wants it in his own business.

The obstacles of tax-exempts

Let's look at this wealth of information that has made you feel that tax-exempts are out of your league. We will take up the arguments one by one, and I think I can show you that they add up to one big bunch of nothing.

You probably have looked at many of the ads in the *Wall Street Journal* on tax-exempt bond issues and were convinced that no one wanted you to buy. The ads gave little or no information. There was no explanation of why the bonds were being sold, but the yields were listed. You may have called your broker, only to hear, "The bonds are not for you." For whom were they? They were for the banks and the insurance companies. If you asked for a prospectus, he said that he would try and he hoped that the bonds would not be sold before he mailed the prospectus to you.

You may also remember that whenever there was a large issue with a great deal of publicity, the bonds were often sold out within one day. By the time you called, the salesman or woman was saying that the bonds were now priced 101 even though they came out at 100. You were trying to buy the wrong bonds. Had anyone told you about the secondary market and the many varied bargains for sale there?

Your toughest job has undoubtedly always been getting past your salesperson. You say that you want to buy tax-exempt bonds and he or she wants to know why. You are of the opinion that the customer is always right. However, this genius who has led you down one dark road after another now decides you need some protection from the obscure recesses of the tax-exempt market.

The salesperson might well say, "After all, the pension funds do not buy them any more." What he or she does not tell you is that these funds are tax-exempt themselves and should not be buying tax-exempt bonds. If you were lucky enough to hold a tax-exempt certification from the government, I would also advise you to pass them by.

The real reason that this salesperson does not want you to buy the tax-exempt bonds is because he or she is sure never to see that money again. It is not polite to talk about "churning," but this is the device that wide-awake salespeople use to earn commissions over and over again on the same dollars of the client. Most salespeople look on tax-exempt purchases as very final. What better endorsement could you get?

Then you probably have heard the oldest knock there is against tax-exempt bonds—"You know that there's not much of a secondary market." I will show how big a lie that is.

You may also have received the knowing look and the whisper about "those defaults." There is no doubt that there have been defaults, but so very few when compared to the billions of bonds outstanding.

More myths

There are also some peole who have been scared away from tax-exempts because "they" (whoever "they" may be) are going to repeal the exemption very soon and you will lose your investment. There is not a chance that tax exemption will be repealed in the near future. It is a constitutional question. The question is not going to be decided by the IRS. However, let us concede that the tax exemption may be removed at some future time. The removal would apply only to future bonds and not to those outstanding. This, in effect, would give you what the bond business calls a museum piece, and its value would increase as time went on because of the lack of supply.

You can also be scared off by the philosophical approach. Every time someone writes about the tax system and the possibility of tax reform, tax-exempt bonds get a pasting. The idea of tax-exempt bonds seems to bring out the crusader in these people. They have been egged on by many secretaries of the Treasury (since the time of FDR, because he hated tax-exempt bonds). A former chairman of the Federal Reserve Board once said that he could not go along with a system that allowed people to loll on beaches and clip their tax-exempt coupons.

Politicians hurry to add amendments to various legislations. It is a good thing that there are some people in Congress who know that the principle of tax exemption is not for the rich to get richer but to insure that local areas are able to sell bonds to provide the improvements without having to petition Washington for them.

These charges have tended to keep some would-be buyers off-balance. Thus one of the best-developed myths about tax-exempt bonds is that they are special and are reserved for the banks and the rich, synonymous terms to many people.

Several years ago, an investment banker had a chance to learn if the wealthy really did have a corner on the tax-exempt market. It was at a dinner in Palm Beach, Florida, with an accumulated wealth of about $300 million among the twenty or so people there. Some had more millions than others, but they were all very wealthy. His poll showed that not one tax-exempt bond was owned by that group.

Does this mean that tax-exempt bonds are not considered a good investment by wealthy people? No, it just means that there are gimmicks in the tax laws such as oil depletion and various housing write-offs.

Actually, the Palm Beach story shows that the person who is in the 32-percent bracket cannot compete with the wealthy in their write-off situations.

In addition to the lack of enthusiasm of the leading investment bankers, there was also a feeling in the industry that advertising was immoral. It was all right to advertise an issue without the ratings and without mentioning any of the security features of the bond. Thus, this "tombstone" advertising, basically showing off to each other in the business rather than appealing to the investing public, became the prevailing kind.

The reasoning was that the privilege of tax exemption should not be handed out. It was good to let the banks and the insurance companies get the benefits of tax exemption, but ordinary investors need not apply. Most of the bankers and the insurance-company people could not have cared less. They were all for opening up the market.

However, some of the knights in shining armor who posed as the leaders of the tax-exempt industry thought it was better to keep tax-exempts under wraps. It must be said that they did a marvelous job for many years. It was a big secret. In fact, it was so much so that most of their colleagues within their own firms did not really know what a tax-exempt bond was, or what its possibilities were.

Therefore the investors who came into tax-exempts in the early fifties would have to be called pioneers. They got very little help from the salesman who was stock-oriented and who did not see any prospect of churning the accounts of clients who bought tax-exempts.

Then some people came along and started to advertise the fact that they wanted to sell tax-exempt bonds. The industry's comments were restrained, but disapproving.

Despite all the obstacles placed in their way, many individual investors have found out about tax-exempt bonds. Part of the credit is due to many firms in the industry who have worked on the art of communicating with investors. The committee at the Securities Investment Association (formerly the Investment Bankers Association) has done a fair job with varying results. At times this committee was more interested in maintaining the status quo of the business or setting up rules for regulation.

Just so you do not think that there are only a few individual investors involved in tax-free bonds, the table on the facing page shows a breakdown on the holders of tax-exempt bonds. Notice that I also have broken down bank holdings because many of the bonds that are purchased by banks are on behalf of their trust accounts.

While the figure of 26.5 percent of all outstanding tax-exempt bonds being held by individual investors does not look small, it should be higher. The responsibility for its lack of growth belongs to the industry and even to the issuers. The officials of the local areas have sometimes shared the feeling that they were participating in a private society. Now many of them realize that with the increased volume they must do something to help in the distribution of bonds.

The job of figuring out whether a yield that is tax-free is sufficient when compared to a taxable situation always bothers

Who Owns Tax-Exempt Bonds

There are over $190 billion in tax-exempt bonds outstanding. The following table reflects the various groupings of investors who hold these bonds:

		% of Total
Commercial banks	$ 95,661,000,000	50.3
Insurance companies	33,807,000,000	17.8
Individuals*	50,524,000,000	26.6
State and local government, various funds	3,957,000,000	2.2
Savings banks	921,000,000	.5
Corporations	4,038,000,000	2.2
Brokers	1,130,000,000	.6
TOTAL	$190,038,000,000	

*This grouping includes bonds purchased by trust departments of banks for clients or held in estates.

investors. Over the years many types of tables have been developed. Most of these tables relate to single taxpayers. But most tax-exempt buyers are married and therefore need a table that refers to a joint return. In fact, all of these tables can go out of date very quickly with changes in the tax laws.

The formula for instant figuring of equivalent yield is contained in chapter 8. All you need to know is simple long division and it can be done.

There is nothing mysterious about tax-free bonds. They can be an excellent investment; they can be an important part of your overall portfolio. You may never buy more than $5,000 worth of bonds, but you ought to know what you are buying. You are not buying a U.S. Savings Bond. But you do help promote the type of local, noncentralist government that has made this country great.

There are many decisions to be made, but they are not difficult when you have decided what your goal is. You may find that your situation demands diversification even for the limited amount of dollars that you have to invest, and this might mean that you should be looking at the tax-exempt funds. However, the main point is that there is ample room for all kinds of investors under the very large tax-free-market umbrella. Therefore you do not have to wish that you could buy tax-exempt bonds—you *can*.

Get to know them better

It is easier to deal with bonds when you understand them. It seems as if there are hundreds of types of bonds in the tax-exempt market, but basically there are six different types:

General-obligation bonds. These are backed by a pledge of the issuer's full faith and credit for prompt payment of principal and interest. Most city, county, and school-district bonds have the further distinction of being secured by a pledge of unlimited *ad valorem* ("property") taxes to be levied against all taxable property. In most cases, if taxes are not paid the delinquent property is sold at tax sale, giving the bondholder a superior claim above mortgages, mechanics' liens, and similar encumbrances. Since general-obligation bonds are geared to tax resources, they are normally analyzed in terms of the size of the resources being taxed.

Limited and special-tax bonds. These are payable from a pledge of the proceeds derived by the issuer from a specific tax, such as an *ad valorem* tax levied at a fixed rate, a gasoline tax, or a special assessment. Occasionally a bond will be secured by the first $250,000 each year of a tax which annually yields $1 million, thereby giving unusual ability to withstand a weakened economy. Limited and special-tax bonds are frequently bargain-priced.

Revenue bonds. These are payable from the earnings of a revenue-producing enterprise such as a water, sewer, electric, or gas system; a toll bridge; airport; college dormitory; or other income-producing facility. They are usually analyzed in terms of their earnings, historical or potential, compared with bond requirements. They have built up a good record over a long period of time, and are sometimes considered to be better than the general obligations of the same issuer. The yield is generally higher for this type of bond.

Authority issues. These are bonds issued by authorities and agencies which can be created by a state or local government. The purpose of an authority is to fill a need that cannot be filled via general-obligation financing. Thus when a bridge, tunnel, or toll road is needed, an authority is usually formed. Authorities have been used to build water and sewer systems, electric power plants, gas systems, hospitals, baseball parks. In most cases the idea is to have a self-liquidating project, thus relieving the taxpayers of liability. Some authority issues need subsidies from the state or local unit. This type of authority is usually set up to avoid inflating the debt of the issuer. It should be noted that authorities are the most criticized of all issuers.

The reason for this is the autonomy that some of these authorities have. In some cases there is little control by the local body that created the authority in the first place of what is built or how a project is run. Authorities have their value. The problem occurs when the authority will not recognize its true place.

Lease-secured bonds. These are backed by a pledge of a fixed dollar amount by a party other than the issuer to make payments to the issuer over the life of the bonds to cover the principal and interest requirements on the tax-exempt bonds. Normally the payment is made pursuant to a lease-and-trust agreement.

These bonds are the type that we use when we set an industrial-bond issue. It is also a way that some public bodies have of using the "lease-back" theory to build city halls and libraries and to pay back by the lease-payment method.

Double-barreled is a term applied to tax-exempt bonds which are backed by a pledge of two or more sources of payment. For example, many special-assessment or special-tax bonds are additionally backed by the full faith, credit, and taxing power of the issuer. Similarly, one occasionally finds a bond secured by the joint pledges of several parties, any one of which would give adequate protection.

You do not find too many double-barreled situations around today, but if you come across one, take a good look at it—it might be a very rewarding situation.

Over the years I have seen municipal-bond issues for convention centers, marinas, baseball stadiums, roller skating rinks, swimming pools, golf courses, campsites, motels, factories, bus terminals, wheat silos, ski lifts, CATV networks, airplane hangars, airport terminals, sugar mills. . . . Whenever a community needs something it will ask, "Can we float a bond issue?" Sometimes they can, and sometimes they cannot, usually depending on the state's laws.

Some of the issues described above might make you think that they did not qualify. How about that roller skating rink?

Actually, it was built for all of the people in a town and is nonprofit; thus it has a public purpose. Golf links are the same, so long as they are public and open to all. The CATV situation was for a college in Indiana, in a town shut off from decent TV reception because of the terrain. Public purpose means that the project must do something for the community, such as adding jobs, increasing the area's net worth, furnishing enjoyment to the local citizens, or, of course, providing services as an airport or a bus terminal does.

Most stadiums are built to accommodate the local entry in a professional football or baseball league. It is usually a matter of subsidization, but even the boosting of a team is thought to be public purpose in some areas. In fact, Congress thought so too, and specifically named stadiums as being exempt from any restrictions they put upon industrial-revenue (lease-back) bonds.

Some of the lesser-rated priorities could be called better risks. I point this out because an investor should be an investor and not be carrying a banner. Let your causes be separate from your investments. The best thing about tax-exempt bonds is that there will hardly ever be a project that will not outrage the most devoted believer in causes.

I also think it is good objective thinking to accept the bond attorney's opinion as to whether a bond is tax-exempt or not. As long as you have that opinion, you are safe. There is no reason for you to make a concentrated effort to find out if the tax exemption is really there or not.

The art of buying

Investors usually need a course in the art of buying tax-exempts. It is no different than finding out about art or music. You need some instruction. Now you may be a great art collector and a wonderful judge of property. In fact, you may be (or may have been) the craftiest of stock buyers, but what do you know about buying tax-exempt bonds?

The basic problem is that there are so many of them. Not only are there many issues, but each issue can have up to forty or more different maturities. This is why so many people shy away from tax-exempts. The problem starts with the salesperson who handles your securities. He or she sometimes does not understand the subject, and this is a sure sign that you will never get to understand it either unless you are persistent.

You start with the idea of earning tax-exempt dollars consistent with quality. This seems to be inconsistent to some people who insist on knowing what you really want—yield or quality. The disbelievers are usually salespeople. Unfortunately, not many bond salespeople know very much about bonds. This is especially true in the houses that do not specialize in bonds, but it is also true of many bond houses.

I have always resented lazy bond salespeople because they are dangerous. The crooked bond seller can be weeded out, but the lazy one hides under the guise of being prudent. These are people who think that the selling of an AAA bond to an investor when excellent bonds are available in lower ratings constitutes doing a good job.

There are many good bonds available in the A and even Baa (BBB) ratings. These are credits which have never had a problem as far as a default is concerned. However, the lazy salesperson retreats to the AAA bond and the investor can lose as many as fifty basic points in yield. To put it more strongly, the investor may get a 6.5-percent instead of a 7-percent yield. On a $10,000 investment you would lose $50 tax-exempt income each year.

The only time that a lazy salesperson helps you is when the prices of bonds are low. That is when you should be buying high-grades.

This is not inconsistency. This is being adaptable, and this is one talent that a tax-exempt investor needs. You need not possess any degree in economics to have this talent, but there are a few strings attached. You must know what is going on in the financial world. A brief glance at the *Wall Street Journal's* bond column would help. Each Monday an index—a simple averaging of yields—gives you the relative position of the market. If that index is over 6 percent, then you know that the market is at a low point and you should be looking at high-grade bonds. If it is below 5 percent, then you know that it is at a high point and you should be looking for the best value that also has yield.

Many people have a problem because some uninformed salesperson convinced them that only general-obligation bonds are any good. There is a lot to be said for the notion of the full faith and credit of a community, but you first have to ascertain that the community is credit-worthy. You might find that a revenue bond is just as good or better, and you will be earning more yield (i.e., tax-exempt dollars).

Many investors assume that their investment goals are similar to those of insurance companies and banks. There is only one point on which your aims are the same as an institution's: in the hope that the investment works out. However, there are very few other goals that can be matched. For instance, banks usually have to make short-term investments, but you do not unless it makes you comfortable. Insurance companies usually need AA bonds or better.

Their investment goals are different from your own. However, you can join them in their search for quality. There are some excellent A-rated situations and many Baa (BBB) bonds that have never had a default. Check that out. It is always a good item to check, and the information can be obtained in minutes. For instance, the cities are never given high ratings, but I believe that some of our city bonds will do just as well over the years as those of our suburban communities, which will ultimately be subject to the same problems as our cities.

What about unrated bonds? An unrated bond does not necessarily mean that the security of that bond is not good. In some cases the bonds have not been presented for a rating or the rating agency has some rule that prohibits it from rating this type of bond.

Look at unrated bonds very carefully. Read the official statement. If you do not feel competent to make a judgment, call your attorney and/or your accountant.

What to look for

You should feel comfortable. That may not sound like good security advice, but it is good advice for believing that you have done the right thing. Feeling comfortable might mean that you pass up some higher yield and fall back on a lower one where you understand the situation.

For many years I have been advocating the four Ws when buying tax-exempt bonds. I also added two Hs so that the formula becomes 4W + 2H. Here is how you should use them in your appraisal:

Who. This could be the most difficult of the Ws because it makes you ask yourself which bond you should buy. If you have ever seen a Blue List (a publication printed each market day that lists most offerings being made by dealers and dealer banks—not available, however, to individual investors), you would know that an average issue has about 144 pages and carries a total of $650 million worth of bonds. The question of who could also be turned around to ask yourself if you should be buying tax-exempt bonds. If you are in the 30-percent bracket and you can find an attractive yield, they are for you.

What. Should you buy a general-obligation bond or a revenue issue? We find that most people have made up their minds that they will stay in the general-obligation area because they know they have the credit of the issuing government behind the bond. Some are dubious about revenue situations because they see that the most prominently defaulted issues are the revenue bonds. You should not close your mind to revenues. However, if you feel more comfortable, then you should stay with the general-obligations. It should, however, be noted that some of the finest tax-exempt bonds outstanding are revenue situations. In fact, there are some cities whose revenue bonds are rated higher than the general-obligation bonds of the city.

When. If you were to make a poll of other investors, you would find that the problem of maturity bothers them most. They are confused—and you may be too—as to what constitutes a short-term or a long-term investment. The maturity of a bond should not be confused with your life expectancy. Life expectancy has nothing to do with an investment. There isn't much anyone can do if you feel that a five-year investment is long term. I do not consider anything under twenty years as a long-term investment. In fact, you will also hear opinions that a thirty-year maturity is a long one and that twenty years is an intermediate one. Remember that *very few bond investments are held to maturity by an individual.* You may buy a twenty-year bond today and sell it in five to ten years because you can make a profitable switch or even a long-term profit. In the matter of maturity, you will have to first settle your investment priorities. If you are in the tax-exempt market until the equity market gets well again, then you should be in dollar bonds, where you have a quick marketability. If your ideas of maturity tend to make five years a long-term situation, leave your money where it is. Just remember that after you have picked the rating and the bond you want, the amount of yield to be earned will depend on how long you initially cared to risk your money. Remember, however, that you must pay capital-gains tax on bonds sold prior to maturity when those bonds are sold at a price greater than the one you paid.

Where. The location of your bond is important, especially if your state has an income tax. It means that if you buy bonds in your state, you will be preserving all of your yield. Otherwise you could be paying state taxes on your out-of-state bonds. The importance of location might also make you more comfortable if you are familiar with the city or area where the bonds are issued.

The addition of the two Hs is also important to the formula. They are: *how* are the bonds backed; and *how many?* The first H is the most important, because it gives you the reason for buying. No matter how much yield you receive, it means nothing if the security of the bond is not sufficient. General-obligation bonds are easy. The bonds are backed by the good faith and credit of the community, city, or state involved. When you consider revenue bonds, you are looking at a more difficult subject. There are many ways that a revenue bond can secure its revenues, and you must know what makes revenue flow to the bonds of your project.

Understanding credit (i.e., security) means understanding an official statement (prospectus), explained in chapter 4. You may find that this subject is beyond you. Do not feel inadequate. Get the advice that you need.

That second H—how many—is something that only you know about. However, there is always the matter of "putting all your eggs in one basket." Do not be like the man who put no more than $5,000 in any one name. This would have been enough for a small investor, but this was a wealthy individual who was investing a total of almost $500,000. He should have been investing in lots of about $50,000, because there is some value in large blocks.

There is nothing that bothers a small investor more than the fact that his or her $5,000 investment does not mean as much as a $50,000 investment or larger. However, as good as tax-exempt bonds are, we have to face the fact that the volume buyer runs the market. Large bond issues are controlled by the big buyers. However, this should not bother a small investor. There may be a problem when you sell your bonds. The seller of $50,000 bonds might do a point or two better than the seller of $5,000.

This irritates the small investor. But the irritation is not worth it when considering the benefits of tax exemption overall. As time goes on, more individual investors will buy bonds and small blocks will be worth more in the secondary market.

Help yourself

The art of buying bonds demands some study. The most important thing demanded is the no more than ten minutes of your time required each day to read the bond column in the *Wall Street Journal* and any other information that you can find on bonds. I must warn you that some of the people who answer the questions in the Q & A columns are liable to be vague, if not actually misleading. However, there is no substitute for reading, and most of this reading can be enjoyable.

Many firms put out bond letters. As you learn more, you can advance to the bank letters and those published for the pros.

The way to invest your funds is via an offering sheet or list. It is a listing of a company's inventory of bonds which gives you all the information you will need about the bonds being offered for sale, except that information which must be found in an official statement (prospectus) or other documents. Always ask for the offering list. Do not take suggestions over the phone.

However, after the purchase your diligence should not end. It is not enough that some "expert" has advised you to buy the bonds. It is also his or her duty to supply you with progress reports. If you do not receive them then write to the issuer and identify yourself as a bondholder. If you do not get satisfaction, write to the trustee bank. All of this information is in the official statement. This procedure should be followed on all revenue-bond purchases.

When you buy general-obligation bonds, your best way of checking them is to ascertain whether the town or city has retained its bond ratings. This is something that you should check out with the salesperson. Actually, they should give you any information that might affect the rating so that you can decide whether to retain the bonds or not.

New investors often let a salesperson fit the dollars they have to a bond. For instance, the new investor may have $12,000. The salesperson sees a bond that sells for 80, and sells the investor $15,000. (A bond with a face value of $15,000, selling at 80 points on 100, sells for $12,000). However, the coupon may be low, and the investor may only get a 6-percent yield when the level should have been 7-percent. Buy only yield. Matching dollars can cause you to lose money.

It is easy to become knowledgeable, and, when you consider how poorly some of the economists have done over the past several years, you may prefer to become your own expert. This does not mean that you should forego the advice of others, especially of those with competence in these areas.

This also doesn't mean that I am ruling out all salespeople as advice-givers. There are many experienced people in the field who do an excellent job for their clients. What I am saying is that you should gain some independence so that you can stand on your own and make some of your own investing decisions.

2

Secondary and Dollar-Bond Markets

The most often repeated wheeze about tax-exempt bonds is that there is no market for your bonds when you want to sell. Those of us who have been carrying the torch all these years call it "the big lie."

I would say that the big lie got its credence in the days when the stock market was booming and when no self-respecting salesman would put his client in bonds when there was money to be made in stocks, to say nothing of the commissions the salesman earned.

In August of 1974 the president of Morgan, Stanley & Company implied that there was no market for tax-exempt bonds. Why, when over $324 million long-term bonds had been sold, did he make such a statement? It was a typical corporate bond man's attitude, combined with resentment that this end of the business had grown so when formerly it was restricted to the back rooms of investment banking houses.

Actually the secondary market for tax-exempt bonds is the best-organized and best-disciplined market we have. The truth is that you can always get a bid in the tax-exempt secondary market. There is one problem that has to be recognized: the problem of time. The bids are not instant, especially in the case of bonds that are not well known, but there are bids. Can every market make this claim?

What is the secondary market? It is a combination of things. It is the group of traders who sit at desks of dealers and dealer banks all over the country. It is a group of brokers who work with the above traders only and never do business with any institutional or individual investors. It is the Blue List, which is a listing of the bonds available in the market. It is the Muni-facts machines around the country (operated by the *Daily Bond Buyer* organization, the industry trade paper), that also helps the secondary market by listing offerings

Indeed, it is a vast network of people with many different outlooks, thus making it a wide area of interests. It is no different from any other market. It is an auction market where the seller has to find a bid. In this market, the seller has the choice of going directly (via his broker, of course) to a regional dealer or specialist in a particular bond using a broker who will funnel back the highest bid of many. The seller also has the option of asking a dealer to place his or her bonds in the Blue List, where some prospective buyer might see them. In the latter case, the seller is usually putting a price on the bonds rather than looking for a bid. The point is that the tax-exempt market has many sides.

Here is proof of how well the secondary market works. It was the "crunch" of 1966, in the month of August. (A crunch is when the financial system loses its liquidity.) Various other markets, such as the corporate and U.S. treasuries were having a tough time getting bids. I wanted to know what, if anything, was happening in the tax-exempt market. I called Jack Kenny, the founder of J. J. Kenny & Company. He looked at his pads and told me that his firm (and this did not include any other municipal broker) had traded $5 million in bonds. Actually that was a drop in the bucket, and Jack was not happy, but blocks of corporate and treasury bonds were not moving on the worst day the market had seen in many years. I will not pretend that the prices were great, but bonds were moving, and that is sometimes more important than the price.

The market works because of men like Jack Kenny who perform the brokerage duties for the municipal-bond business and are known only to people in the business. They do no business with you or with any other investor, individual or institutional. They are restricted by an unwritten code (to which all adhere) to do business with dealers and dealer banks only. Their charge is usually $1.25 per $1,000 bond. They can get more on certain odd-lot and other situations. What they do for this nominal charge is really something.

The Blue List

The Blue List is an operation that is now owned by Standard & Poor's. However, many years ago it was started by an enterprising young bond man named Roald Morton, with the help of another man who is still active on the dealer side of the market, Bill MacKay.

They set up a municipals version of the Pink Sheets (The National Daily Quotation Service) where dealers could advertise bonds for sale. The Blue List, however, has become more than that. After Morton's retirement, the president of Standard & Poor's, Brenton Harries, developed some new systems that have made the Blue List more than just a sales sheet. The most important of these systems has been the one called the Blue List Retrieval system. This allows a bond house to ascertain what is available in any Blue List by various categories. The subscriber (the Blue List is only available to dealers and dealer banks) can find out, for instance, the AA bonds in $50,000 (or $10,000 or $5,000 for that matter) lots due in a certain maturity. This information is flashed to the subscriber in a matter of seconds.

The Blue List is more than a place where your bonds may be placed by your dealer or dealer bank (if you want to sell). It is also a source of record. We all watch the Blue List volume. When the market is heavy, the Blue List is thick. This is when the market gets rough, and the dealers do not know at what price they should list their bonds.

Therefore the Blue List becomes an important factor in the day-to-day market. The totals that are shown in the Blue List are the factors that determine the state of the market.

One of the sad things about these great assets in the tax-exempt market is that you, the investor, cannot deal directly with either municipal bond brokers or the Blue List. However, the fact that you know about them and what they do for you in the marketing of your bonds can be a solace.

In addition to the Blue List and the broker, we cannot forget the regional bond dealer who makes bids for the bonds in his area. Most of these dealers are connected to the large markets by teletype systems and are also on the various brokerage teletype systems.

Brokers are fascinating people. They are the product of an evolution that began over fifty years ago, and they have grown in stature as well as in business. The first brokers were almost itinerant peddlers. They went from office to office seeking to broker bonds. Then they found that they needed telephone trunk lines to protect their clients, the municipal bond dealers. They were on their way.

In those formative years they developed the relationship which has become more sophisticated, but yet remains basically the same. It is a relationship of trust. The dealer bares his soul to this man called the broker, and the broker works to find him a buyer for his bonds. No client has ever received as confidential a hearing or a better execution. The basic thing to remember is that while the transaction is on behalf of a dealer, it might be your bonds that are for sale. This is why the bond broker is important. He is someone with whom you have no contact, but on whom you must depend if you are selling bonds. In fact, if I had bonds to sell, I would demand that the bonds be given to a broker.

Once you have established that there is a secondary market that is operative even when the government and corporate markets fall away under the pressures of a crunch or some other crisis, then you have established that it is safe to buy bonds.

The secondary market has one other important advantage for the individual investor. The investor who buys bonds in the secondary market is usually better off dollarwise than the investor who buys in the primary market.

It is no secret that most of the bidding on the primary issues in the tax-exempt market is fiercely competitive because of the competitive-bidding regulations that prevail in most issues. One aspect of these bids does not lend itself to the best interests of small bidders: the bidding revolves around the banks, who are interested in the earlier maturities, and the insurance companies, who are interested in the longer maturities. There is rarely any thought given to what the individual investor is thinking about. To be frank, it does not matter at this point (except if it is an issue that has a low rating and is pointed toward the individual market) what you and other individual investors think. To win the issue, the bidders must have a feel for what the institutional buyers think.

This is why I have always advocated that individual investors concentrate on the secondary market rather than the primary one. It gives you a chance to look at the whole market and an opportunity to be selective. Do not forget that the secondary market is not under any price restrictions. This means you have the entire list of outstanding bonds to choose from.

We are then back to the question, "How do you operate in this market?" The investor has several ways to go. You can get a list of offerings from your salesperson. You can direct your bank or broker to find a bond within certain specifications (rating, maturity, location, purpose, and, of course, amount). Using this system, and following the ideas prescribed elsewhere in this book, you should be able to find the bonds that will fit your portfolio and your income needs.

Dollar-bond markets

A dollar bond is born when an issue has a "balloon" maturity of about twenty to forty years (or maybe more). Serial bonds with limited amounts cannot become dollar bonds. After a new issue (usually a revenue issue) is sold and delivered, the term bonds (or the balloon maturity) become dollar bonds; the trading is then conducted in dollars. There are firms and brokers who specialize in this market.

Trading in dollars makes it easy to list the issues in newspapers such as the *Wall Street Journal, The New York Times* and other dailies around the nation.

The one thing that sets the dollar markets high in the estimate of many investors is the fact that many of these issues are listed in newspapers. There is a great feeling in being able to find the quote each day on the bonds you own.

The investors in this market are a breed unto themselves. What really made the dollar-bond market was the need of many investors to find shelter when they were temporarily out of the stock market. They therefore found the shelter and earned tax-exempt dollars while being sheltered.

Dollar-bond traders are also a separate breed. They have the instincts of a stock trader in that they trade supply and demand without any real interest in the background of the issue. Of course they are cognizant of reports of slackening revenues, but basically they trade the supply and demand.

Twenty-five years ago there was only one dollar bond: the New York City 3 percent bonds due in 1980 (known as the 3s of '80). The traders of that day would gauge the market based on what the 3s of '80 were doing at that particular time. Today, this issue is just another New York City bond drifting toward maturity.

The world of dollar bonds changed in the early fifties, when turnpikes (or toll roads) became a leading preoccupation of the tax-exempt market. The issues had to be term maturities to justify pay-outs, and thus a new market was born. It was soon discovered by the people who habituated the stock market. They found that they preferred investing in this part of the tax-exempt market rather than getting a low return in banks or letting the money lie idle in checking accounts when the stock market was in the doldrums. They also preferred trading to be in dollars rather than in yield to maturity. These people were not interested in the yield twenty-five or thirty years hence. They were interested in current return, and the use of dollars rather than yield was convenient.

Over the years, the dollar-bond market has given the tax-exempts direction. It has indicated what shelter investors were doing at a particular time. It has also been a barometer of what has been happening to the various toll projects revenuewise. This was shown in early 1974, when we were beset with the energy crisis. It was also apparent when the legislatures of New York and New Jersey passed enactments that would allow the Port Authority of those two states to spend money on mass transit. Whipped up by Wall Street opposition, the investors became unhappy and many of them dumped their bonds.

Actually, when the toll-road bonds were initially traded, there were some rough days. The roads opened, but did not immediately do as well as the feasibility engineers said they would, and some of the more conservative investors got out. However, in the course of the changeover, the equity investors noticed that this was probably the fastest municipal market available for the quick selling that they were used to in the equity markets.

Then newspapers began to carry quotes on these bonds,

which meant that these were the only bonds in the tax-exempt market where you could follow the daily progress of your investments. Other issues are not reported this way for obvious reasons—the vast number of issues plus the maturities within them.

Although dollar bonds originated as toll-road bonds, the list includes public utility bonds and even some bonds that have the backing (or moral backing) of a city or state. The majority, however, are still roads or bridges depending on toll revenues.

Many defaulted issues are actively traded. They are traded "flat," which means that you do not have to pay any interest when you buy, and you cash in the coupons (with interest on the late interest) when they have enough funds to pay out the coupon.

Some of the most famous defaults are in this market. Some examples (in chronological order) are the West Virginia Turnpike, the Chicago Calumet Skyway, and the Chesapeake Bay Bridge and Tunnel. What makes their inclusion in this market valid is that they are working out their problems.

The future of dollar bonds

It is interesting to speculate on the future of dollar bonds, assuming the equity markets were to continue in the doldrums. It seems that many new investors have come into the market drawn by the allure of the quick sale when needed. It is also possible that the shelter people are still there waiting for the equity markets to reverse their trend.

Many (myself included) have been shocked at the lack of interest in yield by some of these investors. Therefore we wonder whether these bonds will have to qualify more in the yield area, or if their ready marketability will make up for the differential that has always existed and still does. If this is indeed a new ball game, and the switching aspect from equity to bonds and back will not be a factor any more, then the concept will have to be rethought.

It would certainly make sense for this market if dollar bonds were placed in proper perspective. The bearish thing about it is that it would probably be bad news for the equity markets, and that is not good. As far as the tax-exempt market is concerned, however, it would bring the bonds in the dollar markets into line with the remainder of the market. It could mean adjustments in prices from present values. A look at this market shows that money-market factors have not been as weighty as the energy crisis or bad news from a project.

Switching over to the positive side, a rebirth of equity-market confidence could mean a rebirth of the dollar market as the former machinery becomes operative again. Coupled with those who enjoy ready marketability and like to read daily quotes, this could mean that the dollar market will return to being its independent self.

Aside from buying these bonds when they were originally offered, I have never considered the dollar markets as bona fide investments. Rather, I have thought of them as temporary investments to be used as a bail-out. It would take a realistic policy in pricing to change my mind. This, of course, would depend on whether enough new investors (less the equity-market shelter people) have entered the market. It could also be that some of the shelter people have become permanent investors in this market.

While anything connected with the money market has to involve questions, we may be finding that the dollar-bond market is going to have to deal with the same problems they have ducked over the past years because of the peculiar status of the market. The questions as I see them are, will there be an adjustment in yields and would this mean a price problem for the present holders of these bonds?

3

Caveat Emptor

There is one misleading idea that many people have about tax-exempt bonds: you cannot be cheated because the bonds are being sold on behalf of local governments. The truth is that this is no protection, especially when the bonds are of the revenue variety. This is not a knock against revenue bonds. It is a warning to investors to know what they are buying.You must take the same precautionary measures that you would apply in buying any other security. You have to know with whom you are dealing. If you do not want to do this, forget about buying bonds. You will be taken as easily as people who have been sold the Brooklyn Bridge.

There has been some fraud over the many years of municipal-bond history. There have been relatively few frauds when compared to other areas of the security business; however, this is no balm because tax-exempt bonds are not thought to be subject to fraud.

There is no regulation to speak of in the tax-exempt bond business. The basic theory is that bonds are issued by local areas without regulation from the federal level. This should not stop an investor from checking out what he or she buys and from whom they are buying.

As the saying goes, "Figures do not lie, but liars figure." This is true in the tax-exempt business as well. There are too many so-called bond houses (but really boiler shops) around the country that are waiting to fleece would-be tax-exempt bond purchasers. I do not say that you have to deal with New York Stock Exchange firms, but I do say that you had better have a good idea of with whom you are dealing. There is no doubt that when there is a serious fraud, it usually involves small investors.

I was very much surprised years ago when I found that a prominent law firm in Chicago whose influence spreads all over the nation had approved an issue that was nonexistent. To compound this, the bonds were sold to an insurance company. Thus there were two very sophisticated entities being deceived. The fact that a law firm that has been approving tax-exempt bonds for many years could be so deceived may seem incredible to you until you have looked at the system.

I can create an issue of bonds in a nonexistent town, but in an existing state and county. I can take the details of that issue to a bond attorney who has been involved in that particular area. I can tell him that the bonds are already sold to the XYZ Insurance Company (which, indeed, they were). Bond counsel will then look at the laws of the state and the county to see if I followed every rule. This is the easiest part of the swindle. There are no mistakes on my part—I concoct a perfect issue except for one thing: it does not exist.

A strange thing that I have uncovered in my research is that frauds involving nonexistent towns have never been sold to individual investors.They have usually been sold to institutional investors such as banks and insurance companies. The record shows that many prominent institutions have been caught, and this is not reassuring. The frauds on individuals are usually perpetrated with real issues. However, most of these real issues have very glaring potholes to begin with.

An easy mark for fraud is the industrial-revenue bond. One example is a group of issues that emanated from an industrial district called the Northwest Industrial District of Oklahoma.

It was built on the remains of an old Air Force base in north-western Oklahoma. The people in the area thought that all of their problems would be solved if they attracted industry to the area.

There are all kinds of industries and many kinds of people in these companies. Some of them make a career of going from place to place and failing. It may seem surprising that such companies cannot be detected, but then you forget the zeal of the average community, especially when faced with a great unemployment problem or a situation that spells decay.

A company seeking finance through industrial-revenue bonds must have some history and a net worth. It should have at least as much net worth as the amount of bonds it has issued. Thus if a company is issuing $1 million in bonds it should have a minimum of $1 million in net worth.

The companies involved in this industrial district in Oklahoma were new, and they had no net worth. The authority members were outstanding people in the community. (A local bank president was the head.) It did not seem wrong to them that the bonds were sold at 70 cents on the dollar. They thought that this represented the risk factor involved since the companies were "start-ups."

What they did not know was that the underwriter sold the bonds through other dealers and the bonds were sold at 100 to individual investors all over the country. In other words 30 points, or $300 per $1,000 bond, was split up by all the middlemen before the investor received the bonds.

The bond underwriters in question were not known to the usual bond community. However, they were known to a bank in the South that financed the operations and took a major share of the profit. This southern bank was not linked to anything in the deal except for providing the cash to transact the deal. If you were to look for any direct evidence that this bank was involved, you would not find it. The bondholders found that they were holding worthless paper. The only people who could be "blamed"(the bond counsel traditionally only passes on the legality of an issue) by the bondholders were the attorneys who gave a legal opinion. They were the only ones who could be found.

Investors cannot expect to be protected by law when bond situations are vague.

The crooked bond dealer is aware that most investors will

take a higher rate of interest and not ask any questions. Thus they know that they can come to an investor with a very weak security and sell it on the basis of yield. Yield is good consideration, but if you do not have security, then you have nothing. All the yield in the world will do you no good if that bond does not pay out, and the only way it can pay out is if the bond has security. What you should be looking for:

1. Know the bond dealer. Check him out through your bank or through a regulatory body such as the NASD (National Association of Securities Dealers). There should be an office near you.

2. If it is an industrial-revenue issue, find out what the security is and check out the net worth of the company or find out if the company has put up any additional security.

3. Find out the exact costs of the issue, and find out what the bond dealer has paid for the bonds. Anything over 10 percent (which is also too high) should be rejected. In some issues, however, the 10 percent covers all legal expenses.

4. Check the trustee bank and find out what safeguards it has set up and whether it has checked out the company and its principals.

You cannot have any inhibitions when you are buying bonds. Do not be afraid to ask the necessary questions. Do not be fearful of hurting a salesperson's feelings. There is no doubt that many firms and salespeople resent what they consider prying questions. If they do, you should find another company willing to tell you what you want to know—whether it is about the bonds being offered or about themselves.

The feeling of being overwhelmed is the biggest problem that most investors have. Add to this the human weakness of hating to admit that we do not know something about a particular subject. You can also add the naïve belief many people have that no bad tax-exempt bonds can be issued, and the idea that all issuers protect themselves from bad issues, so that you, the investor, are protected as well. This nonsense is also perpetrated by many salespeople. There is a selling slogan that is used in the business, which describes tax-exempt bonds as second only to U.S. government securities as far as safety is concerned. This is generally true. But there may be times when bonds, such as industrial-revenue issues, might not qualify for that imposing description.

It is true that most tax-exempt issues that have problems

eventually work out. In today's market, however, there is a breed of people hustling bonds that may be just as worthless as some stock floated during the boom days of the OTC market. You have the means of seeing that this does not happen to you if you insist on the right information.

When it comes to buying anything but rated bonds you should have some extra help, such as your attorney or tax accountant, in your corner. You need someone with an open mind. Such a person is not too hard to find. Some people will take some glib excuse for the lack of printed information on an issue. For instance, one investor was told by a salesperson that "the issue is too old for the prospectus to have meaning." The investor accepted his word that "everything is doing great. . . .I even spoke with the president of the company this morning and he told me so." If you accept this kind of assurance, then you are in trouble.

There is no reason why a salesperson cannot supply you with an official statement (this is the municipal description of a prospectus), or at least with an updated report concerning the project. In the case of an industrial-revenue bond, the most up-to-date information is the balance sheet of the company. Nothing else really matters, because the balance sheet contains the whole story of how well or how poorly that company is doing. The balance sheet is the most important part of the official statement on any new industrial-revenue bond issue. The official statement may describe the city or county and the economic area, but the credit is 100 percent dependent on the company itself.

If you have one of the following problems, most of what I am trying to warn you about will not mean much:

• If you are looking for a tax dodge as well as tax exemption by using "hot money," or trying to buy bonds under an assumed name by trying to pay for the bonds in cash, you should be warned that it does not work. If you also refuse to give your Social Security number, you certainly will have problems. If the salesperson who is handling your account suggests that you need not give your Social Security number, then he or she is the one for you to watch very closely.

• If you are serviced by a lazy or stupid salesperson, then you have a problem as serious as if the salesperson is dishonest. These people can cause you to lose money by letting you buy very highly rated bonds, when a lower rating would have been adequate; also their lack of knowledge of the bonds that they are selling could cause you serious loss.

There is another interesting situation that you should know about. There are many undercapitalized firms who will use your money to finance their operations, especially in new-issue situations. They do this by requesting that you send your money a week before delivery of the bonds. This allows them to clear your check and to accumulate the money they need to pay for the bonds that they have purchased. Thus you become their partner with no profit to you, and they usually pay no interest.

I suggest you write a letter to the salesperson who wants to sell you tax-exempt bonds. If the following questions are answered, you will have a fairly good idea of with whom you are dealing:

1. Can you send a balance sheet or a D & B report on your company? (Note: some companies may object to a balance sheet, but they should be able to give you bank or other references.)

2. Can you supply a list of the officers of your company?

3. How long has your firm been in business?

4. Does your company belong to a regulated group, such as an exchange or the NASD?

5. Are investors protected with investor insurance?

6. Has your firm or any member of it ever been cited for a violation involving clients or their accounts?

7. If I pay for new-issue securities, what safeguards do you have to protect my payment in case the delivery is not made either to you or to me?

8. What are your criteria for hiring new salespeople?

9. Does your company have a continuing educational program for its sales personnel?

10. How long have you been in the bond business?

11. What was your previous experience?

12. What is your academic background?

13. Are you personally registered with the NASD?

These questions should not be regarded as an invasion of privacy. However, you will find that some salespeople will resent them and may drop you as a potential client, which will be good news for you. Actually, many firms have such material ready to mail to their prospective clients.

I do not advocate that you deal with a firm because of its

size. In fact some large firms do not do as good a job with individual investors because their emphasis is on the institutional investor. You have to make up your mind based on the following requisites:

- The reliability of the firm.
- The type of service that they can give you when they are requested to supply official statements, performance records, and other pertinent data.
- Are you and the person who is trying to sell you bonds congenial? This does not mean that you have to be old buddies. It does mean that you should have mutual respect, and that there are clear-cut channels of communication open.

The businessman's risk

No one seems to know how the term "businessman's risk" originated. It became part of the bond jargon in the early sixties as speculative issues came to the fore in greater numbers. There were other projects which basically were unproved issues. However, these bonds were not all bad. In fact most of them are well regarded in today's market. The problem was that they were new and the market traditionally shrugs off anything new and makes it pay some sort of penalty, usually in the pricing.

Thus every high-yielding bond is not as bad a deal as some of the writers who conduct those Q & A columns in your favorite newspaper would have you believe. I recently saw one where an investor said that he could get a high rate of interest on a tax-exempt. The response was "back off, you are looking for trouble."

His answer did everything but suggest that the questioner call up the Better Business Bureau. His yardstick (and that of many other people) is that a bond whose yield is much higher than most other bonds has to be suspect. This is not always true. (Although the bonds that have defaulted, it must be said, have usually been of the higher-yield variety.) The point that I am making here is that there are many good high-yielding bonds available.

Where does price or yield come into the picture? There is usually a differential of at least 2 percent between the Baa- or BBB-rated bonds and the so-called businessman's-risk bonds. Of course in a very tight money market when Baa or BBB bonds begin to sell at 8½- or even 9-percent yields, there isn't much room for a differential because usury laws prohibit very high rates. Therefore most of these projects stay under wraps until rates return to more "normal" conditions.

It is also true that many of the bonds that are well regarded today began as businessman's-risk bonds. In fact most of the bonds of the state of Florida were considered high-risk at one time, not to mention those of Alaska and Hawaii. So were some assessment bonds in Orange County, California. The same is true of some airport bonds, and there are countless under-priced (when they were originally offered) issues in the pollution area. Then there are the small bond issues of small towns that the big underwriters do not bid on. These become yield bonds too, because they are small in amount.

Remember another basic rule: The market always makes a new issue go through an initiation period. This is true even if the new type of bond has a good rating. Of course ratings do not always do the trick.

I do not urge that you buy businessman's-risk situations as a matter of course and fill your portfolio with them. However, I do recognize that many investors look at the high yields with envy, and would like to have some. Therefore I am giving you some guidelines on how to approach these bonds and still be happy at a later date.

First, the more bonds that you have in your portfolio, the more chances you can afford to take. If $10,000 in bonds will be your entire investment in the tax-exempt market, you should be in something very comfortable. However, if you have followed a circumspect course in investing in tax-exempts, and have accumulated several blocks, you would buy some higher-yielding bonds.

Hospital and nursing-home bonds

There is one type of high-yielding bond that merits special attention: hospital and nursing-home bonds (sometimes called health-care projects). The best type of health-care projects are nonprofit ones. This may sound confusing, but keep in mind that there are many private institutions funded via industrial-revenue bonds that are tax-exempt. There is nothing wrong in this procedure, except that I have not seen too many issues that look good when they are using the credit of their sponsors, because not many of these sponsors have healthy-looking balance sheets. Sometimes this is because the sponsoring company has a string of nursing homes. Thus when you total the bonds outstanding (or mortgages) against the net worth of the sponsor, it does not always measure up to the one-for-one theory. (That theory insists that the total net worth of the company equal the amount of the bonds being issued.)

The counter argument to this approach is that even though those sponsors are the guarantors, the basic dependence in such issues (nursing homes) is on the third-party pay. These are the payments made by federal, state, and local agencies on behalf of the elderly people in these homes. However, I insist that the profit-oriented (as differentiated from church and real nonprofit groups) sponsor think only about that profit. Some of these sponsors will walk off and leave a project if it is not working out or if it is not spinning off enough profit.

This is true of hospitals, too. In these days of higher wages and costs, the problem is whether or not an institution can make it. To you, this has to mean whether it can make enough money to pay its overhead plus the principal and interest due on its bonds. Look at the bottom line and worry whether your bonds are going to be paid or not.

The most important document in any revenue-bond issue, whether it be a hospital, health care, or any other type of revenue bond, is the feasibility report. The most important part of any feasibility report is the conclusion: whether the issue will earn enough revenues so the bonds can be paid. Many reports actually sidestep the question. These reports are written so that you can take either side of the question. If this is true of any report you see on a new issue, pass the issue by. Do not bother to find out why the language is vague. The only thing that you are interested in is whether the bonds will pay out.

Also, make sure that the producer of the report is a nationally recognized company. If you do not recognize the name, or cannot find any background material on the company, pass the deal by. Most companies will give a rundown on themselves in a report—except for some of the larger CPA firms whose names are almost household words.

The basic investment question in a feasibility report is coverage. You cannot be interested in an issue that can just meet its debt service after all expenses are paid. You need more than that. You need one-and-a-half times the total debt service (and the highest debt service). If the debt service is $100,000 per year, there should be $150,000 left after all expenses. This is minimal. To go any lower would be taking a chance.

Always remember: Unless certain facts are laid out very clearly, you should avoid the issue. The coverage factor is one. Another is whether the report maker has considered the rising costs of wages and prices in the years ahead. You must assume inflation will continue to some degree.

Know who the sponsors are and who the bond underwriters are. There are too many good people in the latter category for you to do business with some fly-by-night. Just as important are the sponsors. These things are easy to check out if you have the time, and you should make the time when investing. There is one thing that I cannot say too often: buy bonds of the projects that you know. This is especially true in a small issue (small being anything under $1 million in bonds). I would never buy a bond of some place that I had never heard of.

There are so many high-yielding bonds available; you do not have to reach out as though there were a shortage. You can make some excellent investments in high-yielding business-man's-risk bonds.

There are many detractors of these bonds—perhaps the salesman or woman who covers your account, or possibly your banker who does not handle them. I look on all their no-nos as being constructive, because they will make you think and read before you make a decision. This is also an area where you should have your attorney or accountant do some work.

Occasionally some elderly investor interested only in tax-free income and not so concerned about the principal acquires some of these bonds. This is not good investing, but it is a fact of life. Many elderly men who pursue this policy argue that it will be up to their heirs to worry about the soundness of the project. If they see several years of capitalized interest (the setting aside of funds for interest for a year or more when the issue is originally financed, thus making the interest for a stated period a sure thing) plus debt service (similar to capitalized interest, except that a reserve fund for debt service is extra insurance in case the project has some problems), they are ready to go.

The purchase of businessman's-risk bonds depends on how well you are doing financially. They should not be your only investment in tax-exempts, but should be an adjunct to your portfolio. You administer the same tests to this type of bond as to other tax-exempts. The key word is objectivity.

The protectors

There are people in this business whom I call your protectors. As tax-exempt bonds are free from most regulation, I am not referring to the SEC (Securities and Exchange Commission) or the NASD (National Association of Securities Dealers), although the latter organization has authority to regulate the selling practices. The people I refer to are in the private sector. They are the bond attorneys, the feasibility experts, and the bank trustees. The people in the public sector who can be counted among your protectors are the various public officials such as the city attorneys and the courts.

The feasibility expert

The first protector you encounter in a revenue-bond issue could be the engineer whose job it is to declare an issue feasible or not feasible.

The feasibility report gives an investor an unbiased look at a project. It would be silly to pretend that there has not been criticism or hints of hanky-panky on some reports.

Feasibility studies can get off to a false start and never get back onto the road. The problem haunting the feasibility report makers is that they must deal with people. If a representative of a feasibility report maker asks you or me whether we will use a bridge or go to a motor speedway, we invariably say yes, but frequently we never do.

Must we avoid feasibility report deals based on popular response? Not all. A feasibility report should be a part of your decision, but it does not relieve you of the responsibility of making the decision, nor does it relieve the underwriter of his obligation to delve into all of the facts about an issue.

The people connected with an issue are putting together information for you and me. Sometimes the results can be great, and in some cases they can be horrible.

One last word. Know the feasibility firm; check out their record; ask the underwriter on which other issues the firm has given opinions. If all of this seems like too much trouble, avoid the issues where feasibility is a major factor.

While there may be controversy about how ratings are determined, there is no doubt that the raters should be included in the group of protectors.

What goes on behind the scenes of a bond issue may also seem tedious. If you ever go to a bond closing (where the bonds are delivered to the underwriters), you might have a hard time staying awake while the attorneys pass around documents and quibble about the wording in various clauses. All of these people have a function, and it is to protect you, the bondholder. In fact, knowing that this great array of talent has been involved in the bond issue should make any bondholder feel more secure.

The bond attorney

It has been said that bond attorneys *make* laws as well as interpret them. Most bond attorneys would deny this, but when you consider the nature of their job the making of some law is almost inevitable.

The nation's bond attorneys have been in the forefront of new legislation on bonds. The leading attorneys in a state (those who give opinions on the bonds of that state) will usually write the legislation for new laws, or point out the holes they find in a proposed law. To my knowledge, I do not think that any legal opinion issued by a bond attorney has ever been reversed. This is especially true in some of the industrial-revenue financing, where it has been rumored that the IRS has on occasion disagreed with the opinion, but has held its tongue.

How can a man or a law firm be the means of getting an issue to be called legal or vice versa? It all started out over one hundred years ago, when the railroads were making their big move across the country. So many towns were built and financed illegally that investors began to look for legal help. The principal investors of those days hired outstanding attorneys to decide on the legality of the issues. The investors liked the idea and felt secure, and that, after all, is about 90 percent of the sales process.

As time went on the cities, counties, and communities began retaining bond attorneys themselves. They not only received the legal opinions, but they also had someone to lean on for advice in the consideration of new issues. This is still the case today. Bond attorneys work on a contingency basis—if there is no bond issue, they don't get paid—only when the bond is issued are they paid.

It is well to remember that even though the bond attorney is hired by the municipality and has a close working relationship with the underwriter, he and his firm are your attorneys. He views the transaction as if he were acting for one bondholder.

The bond attorney's fees are small when compared to the expense of marketing the bonds. In other words, the bond salesmen get the big money, not the bond attorneys. The job of the bond attorney is an intensive one. It is in many respects similar to that performed by the attorney who acts for you on the closing of a home sale. He must check all new laws. He must see that no court decisions have been rendered that would tend to make the bond issue not legal. In the industrial-revenue bond area, he must check to see if the issuers and the sponsors are conforming to the many and tangled regulations set up by the IRS. The various decisions by the courts are as important as the basic law, and his opinion is in trouble if he misses an important court decision.

Another of the important jobs of the bond attorney is to write the lease (where needed) and the trust indenture. The latter document basically sets the ground rules for the project and instructs all parties as to their duties. There is no doubt that some of this work (as has been noted by critics) is boiler-plated (copied or duplicated). However, each issue has its own problems which cannot be boiler-plated. The bond attorney can show his ingenuity in the lease and can show his respect for the bondholder in the indenture. In the majority of issues, this is just what he does.

Another of the bond attorney's jobs is to examine the bond itself. In actuality, it is the bond attorney who composes the form of the bond. It is also his job to ascertain that no litigation is pending against the financing in question. If there is any, he will not issue his legal opinion. He will also not release his opinion until the treasurer of the issuing body has furnished him with a receipt showing that the bonds have been paid for.

No underwriter will ever pay for the bonds until he knows that the bond attorney has issued an unqualified opinion. This is important for a bondholder. Never buy a bond where a bond attorney has issued a qualified opinion. It does not happen too often, but it can happen.

No delivery of bonds is good without a legal opinion. Thus an older bond, issued before opinions were printed on bonds or where the opinion was too long to be printed on the bonds, must have the legal opinion attached to the bonds to make it a good delivery.

A very important function in the bond-issuing process is the continuing job that must be performed by a bank trustee. This is one of the badly neglected components of the bond business. There are too many banks that have the necessary trust powers and can legally act as a trustee, but do not do a good job. This is another job that has been set up to protect the bondholders. Not all bank trustees do a poor job. But if even one bank trustee is not doing a good job, then some bondholders are at least potentially in trouble.

The selection of bond trustees is not a very reassuring process. The most important factor in selecting a trustee is the amount of influence that a bank has in a particular area. The fact that the bank buys a good deal of the area's bonds is also a consideration. In many cases the ability of the bank to act as an advocate for the bondholder has never been tested. The only time it will be tested is when there is a problem with an issue.

From my studies of how bank trustees act when the chips are down, the majority of them do not act fast enough. They become bogged down and look for the officials of the project to do something. This is not what they were hired to do.

I believe that poor bank trustees can be made into good trustees. It takes constant prodding by bondholders and by underwriters. If you do not receive information that should be sent to you, scream for it—you will be making that particular bank into a better trustee. Most of the trustee banks that do a bad job do so because they think of their assignments as routine clerical situations. Some trustee banks do not know what their job really is. This is a damning indictment because it means that they have not read the indenture that was drawn up by the bond attorney.

The local attorneys and the courts

The protectors that you have on the public side are the city and county attorneys and the courts. The local attorneys usually do not want a bad issue to be sold. They feel that it is their job to protect the publicly elected officials from bad deals. Thus they are defending potential bondholders.

Most local attorneys do an excellent job. These incorruptible people make your job as an investor easier. It is the lazy people who do more damage than the crooked ones.

In the end, the courts are the bondholder's best friend. In many states where revenue-bond issues have to go before the courts, the bondholder is given the full protection of the system because the district attorney or the county attorney has to argue against the issue. The judge then decides whether to approve it. This is the system used in the state of Florida, and it works out well there. I would advocate it for every state.

The bondholder is therefore not without friends, especially as far as the bond attorney and the courts plus most public officials (local attorneys) are concerned. They are usually in good hands with most trustees. However, there are trustees who like to handle the funds of the project and get the money for paying out the interest and other expenses, but will not rise up and take a stand when the project has problems. Always remember that you have a right as a bondholder to make your ideas known to a trustee. If you speak up, you will be heard and heeded.

CHAPTER 4

The
Fundamental
Facts

Reading tax-exempt ads and tax-exempt official statements (the equivalent of the prospectus) are not the favorite sports of most investors.

An ad is not essential to buying a tax-exempt bond. In fact, most tax-exempt bond issues are not advertised, and this is no great loss. Most of the ads printed in publications do not give you much of an idea of what the issue is about. Also, most of the ads are for the successful issues, and they do not have any bonds available when you get around to calling. The only ads that really say anything are the selling ads. Be careful: some of them sell too hard, and make more use of the yield they offer than of any information on the issue.

Over the years I have come to feel that tax-exempt new-issue ads are not really meant for investors. They are run for the purpose of impressing the competition within the industry or to make the senior officers of the underwriting firm happy.

The ads as you read them are a mixture of what the lawyers and the industry group, the Securities Industries Association, have ordained. The latter group came up with the real winner in advertising ideas—not showing the ratings—still adhered to by many.

Outside of stating the name of the issue, and the fact that the bonds are tax-exempt, the ad doesn't do much more than show the amount, the coupons, and the yields. What's wrong with that? Most people cannot easily translate yields to dollars. Also, those facts are not much to go on, and in the absence of other information would provide a poor reason to buy the bonds.

There is rarely any information about the credit or the security involved, although this is important to you.

The tax-exempt people have come up with some tantalizing ads. Of course there are a number of "straight" ads, where you know what you will be looking at in case you are tempted to fill out the coupon or make that call the ad insists you should. In fact, some old-line companies are now advertising in advance of issue, wherein they explain the issue and ask that you send in a coupon to receive a full prospectus. But the bucket-shop boys merely say, "We have 9-percent bonds!" When you call, they will want to sell them to you over the telephone. Who ever heard of anyone asking for an official statement (or prospectus, if you will)?

Any attempt by bond dealers to sell you bonds on the basis of a come-on ad and yield is unconscionable.

Reading an official statement is not as difficult as many people think it is. It is necessary that you understand the importance of an official statement. Everything that you need to know about a bond issue is contained in it. It is also the place to confirm what the salesperson told you about the issue in his or her sales pitch. If you do not find a reference to what he or she claimed, then you know that you have the wrong issue, to say nothing of the wrong bond salesperson.

Some official statements translate the yields to dollars, but most still do not. Of course, if it is a 6.5-percent coupon at par, then that is a 6.5-percent yield and needs no translation. However, a 9-percent coupon at a 6.8-percent yield might throw you a curve—in fact, it would make an old pro run for his basis book.

Here are the most important items to check out in an official statement:

1. Whether the bonds are tax-exempt in your state as well as federally.

2. The ratings.

3. When are the bonds callable, and at what rate.

4. The date of the issue and the due dates.

5. Who or what backs up the bond.

6. The disposition of funds—look to see that too much money is not being spent on underwriting fees, etc.

7. In revenue-bond issues, check to see if ample reserves are set aside.

8. Check to see if additional bonds can be issued—if they can, check under what circumstances—additional bonds can dilute your investment.

9. Any good official statement has a layman's version of the indenture and the lease (this applies to revenue-bond issues especially).

10. If it is a revenue-bond issue, look for some projections— these projections may not pan out, and no one can be held to them, but at least you can find out what the project hopes to accrue in the way of revenues—remember, it's the revenues that pay off your bonds.

11. Also look at the table that shows how the bonds will be paid off and whether there is a chance of an early pay-out.

12. A feasibility report should be printed *in full* if there is one available.

There are parts of an official statement that are not important to you, but that must be included for full disclosure. Full disclosure is required in every issue. If you see an issue that has an official statement that is not complete, then you should not bother considering it. You are entitled to know everything about an issue. You may get the excuse that the underwriter was trying to make it easier for you to read. Do not be taken in by this so-called concern.

Some of the official statements that used to be issued on tax-exempt bonds contained the minimum amount of information that could be given. There were few bad deals. Marginal issues have increased, however, and we also have more "bucket shops."

How does lack of disclosure work? A case in point was a 1972 health-care-project issue. The developer in this issue had connections with one of the firms that ordered a feasibility report and, through members of his family, also owned the bond underwriter. There was nothing wrong in this situation (although some bondholders might have been scared off if they had known about it). The wrong was committed in not making the disclosure.

In many cases the use of a developer who has connections with the contractor may be beneficial to the project. Of course the feasibility report should be by a neutral third party. Full disclosure is to your benefit. So look to see that it is there. Do not take verbal assurances. Demand that everything about the issue be in print.

What the ratings mean

You may question whether the bonds you buy will default or not. It is not a bad habit to assume a pessimistic attitude, the traditional stance of an investment banker. The investment banker usually takes the role of the devil's advocate, and so does the rating agency. So should you.

There is always the question of what link there is in ratings and defaults. Most studies have shown that there is not much evidence of any connection at all. The record shows that since the depression most defaults have been in the nonrated areas. The rating system might get a real test if we have another depression.

There is also the question of how ratings affect the pricing of bonds. This is a definite fact. Tax-exempt bonds comprise a business of comparisons. The bonds of a certain city rated A are compared to the most recent city which was also rated A. There is always the problem of quality within a rating bracket. In other words, there are AAAs which are deemed better by the market than others. However, this is where the market apparatus of supply and demand takes over once the rating is established.

It is rare to see the market upgrade a bond from where the raters have placed it; however, it is possible that the market will *downgrade* a bond. New York City is an example of this. A combination of bad publicity and a very high volume brings this about.

No doubt those who buy rated bonds have a great deal more to rely upon than those who pick the unrated situations. This does not mean that unrated issues are bad, but the investor does have a rationale for picking a certain issue when it is based upon a rating.

There are a number of issues that are now being passed over (such as hospital and nursing-home issues) because the agencies do not see proof of continued third-party pay which involves the paying of the principal and interest of the issue. Here we have to make some independent judgments, because regardless of proof that this kind of aid will have to continue, no rating agency will see it since there is no legislative fiat that future congresses and state legislatures will continue the aid. This is where a sense of history and social progress must take over. It is also why you can never completely rule out an unrated bond.

As one who has created considerable discussion over the years about whether rating agencies did the right thing in certain issues, I still believe that your lot as an investor is a better one because they are there.

The best thing that has happened to the raters is that they have become more commercialized by charging for their ratings. When this was first thought of in 1968, there were those who worried that the ratings were in danger of losing their value. There was never any chance of that. Now the issuers pay for their ratings whether they like them or not. The truth is that no issuer ever likes a rating. They always feel that they should be at least two notches higher.

There is always the question of whether an investor is not better off with a lower rating for a good bond. It would be great if all the AAA bonds were rated BBB from a yield viewpoint, but this is where the rating system makes sense. The bond under review is considered from the standpoint of security and not of value. Thus the system tries to reward those issuers who do the right thing. Of course the best of all worlds, for an investor, is to buy a bond that begins with a low rating and improves by the time you are ready to sell it.

Those moral obligations

An investor wrote to me some time ago asking why I was against moral-obligation bonds. He had purchased some bonds that his salesperson had told him carried the moral obligation of a state. He told the salesperson of my remarks, and was told that I did not know what I was writing about. In addition, the salesperson had asked whose word his client would take, mine or the governor of the state?

I have never claimed that any of the bonds that carry the so-called moral obligation are about to default. What I am concerned about is some future time when things may not be good. What will happen to the moral-obligation bonds when the direct debt of the state demands payment, especially if there are limited funds to pay out with?

This is how investment bankers approach any bond issue, even those in which they have great confidence. You should always approach an investment from the negative side. It means that you are looking at the investment with your eyes wide open.

The moral-obligation craze began in New York State. The federal government is another practitioner of this form of bookkeeping. It floats about $1 billion of notes each week for various federal agencies, and it keeps them out of the federal budget.

New Jersey is another state that went the moral-obligation route when it was financing its sports complex, regarded as necessary because the New York Giants needed a place to play. You will find other instances of the so-called moral-obligation bond in other areas of the country as well.

There are many articles being written about "back-door" financing. Many investors found out for the first time that they did not have as good a bond as they had thought. If they had read the official statement, they might have seen a disclaimer that would indicate that getting the money from the state to the corporations might not be easy if some future state legislature does not go along.

Some salespeople talk about these bonds as obligations of New York or New Jersey. They do it with that knowing wink face-to-face or that voice inflection on the phone. There is no way of knowing how many people with these bonds think they have direct obligations of New York or New Jersey.

My fear about these bonds is not for now but for tomorrow, when priorities could become tougher and tougher to set. I am not sure that a legislature twenty years from now, faced with tough decisions on budget, will continue to subsidize these authorities. This can be regarded as a bearish outlook, but when you consider the changes of the past twenty years, you must take the possibility seriously.

I see nothing wrong with buying these bonds, but I do worry about the bonds being sold to investors under false pretenses. However, some of the moral obligations issued, such as for the

Albany Mall by Albany County, depend on the state to pay rent. This has to be considered a very binding contract because the state will pay rent as long as it is viable.

There are also some bonds that have fairly binding contracts because, again, these contracts are between a locality and an authority such as the New York State Dormitory Authority. These involve state aid, and are legal and binding contracts.

However, the project that is bound by nothing but an understanding that the state will step in if all does not go well has to be considered a bond that cannot enforce its obligations. You must decide before you buy. If you already own bonds of this type, you owe it to yourself to check on them. I am not advocating that you dump them. If, however, you bought them under a misapprehension as to what their true security is, then you might ask yourself whether you should hold on to them.

Those who are looking to invest should be careful that every city and state bond they buy (unless it is a revenue situation) is a *general obligation* of the governmental unit. In other words, be very diligent.

5

The Building of a Tax-Free Portfolio

Many people do not worry about building a tax-exempt portfolio because they believe that they are buying their tax-exempt bonds on a one-shot basis. However, if circumstances permit, you will probably find yourself adding to that portfolio at least once. You want to avoid a hit-or-miss portfolio.

In September of 1974 we looked at the tax-exempt bond portfolio of Nelson Rockefeller, exhibited at his confirmation hearing for the vice-presidency.

We do not know the maturities of these bonds except in the cases of the Florida Turnpike, New Jersey Highway, New York State Power, and New York State Housing Finance. However, from the valuation which was made as of August 30, 1974, it looked as if most of the bonds were long-term.

Mr. Rockefeller, a New York State resident, had 59 percent of the portfolio in bonds that would receive a New York State tax exemption (including the Puerto Rico bonds, which are exempt in all states due to its status as a commonwealth). Did Mr. Rockefeller have enough local tax exemption? I do not believe so. In New York State, where there are many issues to choose from, I would have had more in New York State issues. You might ask, What about diversification? That might have been a factor, but I really do not see that as a very important factor when you look at the portfolio.

Here is the Nelson Rockefeller tax-exempt portfolio:

New York State Bonds
$3,000,000—N.Y. State Housing Finance Agency
 3,550,000—N.Y. State Power Authority
 1,000,000—Port of N.Y. Authority
California Bonds
 1,000,000—Metropolitan Water District
   250,000—Sacramento Municipal Utility District
Connecticut Bonds
   805,000—Hartford, Conn., Public Housing
              Authority
Florida Bonds
 3,000,000—Florida Turnpike Authority
Missouri Bonds
   445,000—Poplar Bluff Public Housing
              Authority
Montana Bonds
   320,000—Helena Public Housing Authority
New Jersey Bonds
 1,000,000—New Jersey Highway Authority
Puerto Rico Bonds
 2,000,000—Puerto Rico Water Resources
              Authority
_____
$16,370,000—TOTAL

My reaction to his portfolio is that he could have used more yield. Although 62-percent A and Baa is good, a man in his position could have used 75 to 80 percent of the lower ratings. Using Moody's as a barometer, his rating classifications were: Aaa, 15%; AA, 23%; A, 43%; Baa, 19%. However, this was a judgment of the people who bought the bonds, and there is no clinker in the lot. This is the kind of block buying that takes place when a large trust or group is involved, and, from what I have been able to find out, the buying was usually done on an across-the-board basis. I think this is fine for the Rockefellers and some others who buy in family or business groups.

Of course this is the way that bonds are often purchased by the trust departments of banks. They make a decision on a particular bond, and buy it for those who have money and for those who they think should have the bonds. While I am sure that many trust departments give each account as much attention as possible, I have always worried about this mass-production method of bond selection.

Each investor's problems are different, and this is why a small or average investor is better off in many ways with a firm that watches out for his interests. If the investors know in which direction they would like to go, it helps. You must be careful of many things, such as liquidity. This might mean not putting all of your eggs in one basket.

Let us tackle one of the big questions: how long? There is nothing about tax-exempt bonds that bothers people more than length of maturity. There is no consensus about what is considered long. Long-term can be one year, or it can be forty years. Actually the latter is right, but I would never be able to convince some people of that.

Selecting maturities

Maturity comes back into focus when you talk about a portfolio, since if you do not consider maturity, then you cannot begin the work of putting a portfolio together.

Suppose you select a program that begins short and goes out as far as twenty-five years. This is the way it would work. For instance, the investor has $50,000 and he or she decides to buy A-rated bonds in five bond amounts and five-year increments. This means $10,000 in bonds per year. It is not a large amount, but it is not exactly an odd lot, even though some of the pros might think so. Here is what we would do, assuming we are investing in 1975: We would have $10,000 each of bonds (rated A) of locations in your own state (if there is a state income tax), due in 1980, 1985, 1990, 1995, and 2000. This gives you an average life of fifteen years. It also gives you a runoff every five years.

This is the most successful of portfolios because it gives you the best of all worlds. You are not too long on the average life of the bonds, and you can diversify as to coupon. It also usually works out well as far as average yield is concerned.

If the twenty-five-year situation (until 2000) bothers you, you can shorten up by having $15,000 in bonds in the fifteenth and twentieth years with $10,000 in the fifth and tenth years. This also accomplishes the job and makes you comfortable.

If you are fortunate enough to have $100,000 for investment, you can use $20,000 a year under the first plan or $25,000 per year under the second. The $25,000 amounts would certainly be attractive if you were looking forward to the secondary market.

To figure out average life, you multiply the amount of your bonds by the number of years to maturity. Add all those figures and divide by the amount of bonds, and you have the average life of your portfolio.

If you have $100,000, you might want to strip your bonds $10,000 every two years, which would also get you to 1995. This would give you some great runoff possibilities. This arrangement would give you an average life of eleven years on the bonds. Of course this would be reduced each time a bond matured, unless, of course, you have replaced a maturing bond with longer bonds.

There is always the person who has what is best described as a bunch of cats and dogs in his or her portfolio. If the strength of the bonds is okay, they usually have a hodgepodge of maturities. An orderly portfolio is the best. Any portfolio that is all over the place is usually not productive.

This means that you might have to switch some of your bonds. The first thing to do is to get an evaluation of the bonds you now own to see if you want to sell them and replace them with others. You might want to tax-swap them, although you most likely would be trying to change maturities more drastically than the tax regulations allow under tax swapping (see chapter 6).

We started at the top with the Nelson Rockefeller portfolio, and now we are talking about relatively small ones. However, they are all big to the individual investor, since he has worked hard to build up the portfolio. No one can afford the win-a-few-and-lose-a-few attitude. You did not see it in Mr. Rockefeller's portfolio, and you should avoid it in yours.

This does not mean that if you are so disposed (and have an adequate amount of capital), you should not go for a high-yield situation once in a while. However, don't just throw $10,000 (or whatever amount is involved) into the air and let it fall on some issue without checking it out. You should show the same due diligence with this situation as you would with any other issue. Do not let the salespeople know that you are taking a flyer or they may help you fly higher than you really want to go.

Remember that the above paragraph is predicated on your having the money to lose. It is not for widows and orphans, nor is it for those whose portfolio represents their life savings.

The one thing that I think of as being important in setting up a portfolio is to remind you again that you should be comfortable with it. If there is anything that bothers you about any bond or even about the subject of tax-exempt bonds, *do nothing* until you have it squared away. Just be comfortable in what you are doing.

Retirement provisions

How about that time when you are ready for retirement? Perhaps you will still have profit-making situations that will keep you in a high bracket. However, most of us have a rapid change in salary whenever we do decide to retire.

It is a good idea to put that portfolio in shape, so that it can be dismantled easily. As you approach retirement age and have a fairly good idea of what the economics of your retirement will be, you should arrange your portfolio so that it is maturing when you are retiring. This is relatively easy, but it does mean that you have to keep a close eye on those maturity dates.

You do not have to do all of this yourself. If you can get competent help from your salesperson, that is fine and you should consider yourself lucky. Do the principal thinking and let others work out the details of what has to be done. In this way, the building of a portfolio can be fun because it is a challenge. It is something that you should do and not leave to a trust department or to a salesperson.

Over the years, I have met many investors (in the over-sixty age group especially) who buy bonds for immediate income and profess not to care if the bonds fail years in the future, so long as they get their nontaxable income. If a person is interested in leaving a viable estate he can still have his income and a good portfolio, too.

If the investor has sufficient assets to buy long bonds, he can get that high current income and know that his or her heirs will have good bonds which might be held until maturity or could be traded for others or even sold.

Some people put clauses in their wills that prohibit the selling of their bonds. This is bad business. I have seen estates stuck with bonds bought in 1950 at 1.5 percent which do not mature until 1980.

Short-term investments

The short-term investments that look so good when money is tight can be classified under that great overall heading, the good-and-bad-news syndrome.

The good news is getting all of that tax-free income for such a short time. The bad news can come when you wait too long—the tight money market subsides—and your notes are not yet due for payment. This can all be avoided. For one thing, you can sell your notes, no matter how short they are. If they are a month away from maturing, any good bond dealer will take them and hold them until they can be redeemed.

However, the prevention for this may be found in chapter 9. It does not take that much background to find some of the answers. Just as any of us can see a thunderstorm approaching, or knows that a rainbow heralds the end of a storm, you can also detect changes in the bond market.

The industrial-bond revolution

The industrial-bond era in the tax-exempt bond business has brought about major changes in the attitudes of the bond business and in the investing habits of individuals. The important point is how these changes have affected the individual investor.

Industrial-revenue bonds should be considered suitable for investment. This means a good hard look at the company for which the project is being built.

It can be said that industrial bonds are similar to corporate bonds. The difference is the tax-exempt exterior of the industrial-revenue bond. The usual basis for deciding to buy these bonds depends on whether you like the company or not. This makes it similar to the common stock of a company.

The basic thing to remember when investing in an industrial-revenue bond is that the company for which the project is being built and which will be responsible for lease payments (which go to paying the principal and interest when due) is your biggest concern. Too many investors worry about the town in which it will be located, but it is the company's health you should be checking. What has the company been doing for the past several years and what is its net worth? This is the most vital statistic, and it can be found in the balance sheet in the prospectus. If there is no balance sheet on the company, forget the bond.

I have developed a formula (which I consider a minimum) that the net worth should be equal at least to the amount of bonds being issued. Some people argue that the formula rules out proper consideration for sales volume. Nevertheless, old-timers question what could happen if the economy runs into a recession or worse. In that event, net worth will stand up far better than sales subject to the times.

IDR issues

The popular name for industrial-revenue bonds when they are being sold is IDR—Industrial Developing Revenue. It is a type of bond that can be most deceiving because of the mistaken notions many investors have of the guarantees on the bonds. Many investors see that a county or town is sponsoring the issue and think they have a local guarantee, when what is really happening is that the locality is serving as a conduit through which the bonds can be offered. Unfortunately too many communities, in their eagerness to snare industry, forget to do a proper "due diligence" on the company. It hardly profits a community to bring in a poor company that folds and leaves an empty building and many people out of work. Add to this investors who probably did not show too much due diligence either.

It is shocking to find that many IDR issues around the country are ready to default or have already defaulted. If you check out the companies involved, you will find that most of them have no net worth at all. Just as remarkable are the people (such as bankers and merchants) who serve on industrial boards and allow these issues to be sold.

A further look at these issues shows that some of them have been sold to "underwriters" at seventy cents on the dollar, but resold to foolish investors at one hundred. Then when the issue has problems, the irate bondholder looks for the culprits. All who can be found are the board, the bond attorney, and the trustee bank. There are cases where these people are being sued, although the responsibility for the security of the issues did not belong to them. The real culprits are the underwriters and the salespeople who sold the issue to the public. They could have had someone check out the company if they were too busy to do it themselves. The truth is that they were probably dazzled by the high rate of interest.

While pollution bonds are usually issued under IDR regulations, they are also usually issued on behalf of utility companies for the companies with excellent balance sheets. They don't yield as much as the run-of-the-mill industrial-revenue bond. However, they usually represent a concession to the market and can be obtained for better yields. An objective look at pollution-control bonds (again depending on the guarantor) is highly recommended for good investing.

Industrial-revenue bonds are structured in the same way as other revenue issues. There are usually some short-term maturities which are called serials, and the bulk of the bonds are due in twenty, twenty-five, or thirty years. The setting of maturities usually depends on the leasee, because the payments are tailored to the company's needs. The payment that they make to the trustee bank must cover all expenses of the issue—the principal, interest, and other costs such as trustee fees. Remember that the issuing body has no part in any payment; it acts merely as a conduit in having the bonds issued.

This is something that can never be emphasized too much. Bondholders have no recourse, either to the city or the county that issues the bonds. However, I advise that you buy bonds of a city or county in preference to those of an authority. This is because the city and county will make sure that some due diligence has been performed as to whether the company has the ability to pay. Even though they are not themselves liable, most cities and counties would rather not suffer the embarrassment of default if they can prevent it.

Industrial-revenue bonds are great investments if approached correctly. However, there are people who could destroy the concept because of the issues they sponsor. Naturally it behooves all local officials to be careful. Investors have to realize that an IDR bond is the easiest type to check out, if they will just look at the balance sheet to see if the bond can meet the one-for-one test. Make sure that the balance sheet is audited by a competent accounting firm. Even the question of whether the bonds are rated becomes secondary to the security. Following the one-for-one formula takes the mystery out of it. If balance sheets confuse you, however, or if your record of buying common stocks has been bad, then think about general-obligation bonds or tax-free funds. The main thing is to be comfortable.

Tax-free funds

So you are the kind of investor who doesn't want to fool around with clipping coupons, even tax-free ones. You also say that you do not want the problem of picking out your bonds. I am going to introduce you to tax-free funds, because they afford you diversification and convenience.

Tax-free funds came into existence because of the persistence of the original sponsors. Any changes that have been made occurred only after some very difficult bargaining sessions. This is why all of the funds are identical in their structure and in what they have to offer. This is fine for investors because they know that the various funds are all the same.

I believe that the tax-free fund is just what this volume-increasing market has needed. It is a godsend to those investors who just do not want to be bothered with choosing bonds. It is also a great thing for the investor who is mutual-fund-minded but would also like to invest in tax-exempts.

But the greatest benefit of tax-free funds will be the demand they create for bonds that will alleviate the volume that is pounding this market day after day. However, this is no reason for investors to buy. Their only reason should be based on the yield. I believe that this type of security passes these tests, but there have been some criticisms.

Now and then someone will write an article that casts doubt on the security of tax-free funds. The emphasis is always on the portfolio which has been gathered to create the fund. In most cases these portfolios have not contained the very best bonds that could be purchased. However, they were bonds that could be defended and bonds which had enough yield to make them interesting to investors.

Load charges

Most of the critical articles about funds concentrate on the load, and there is no doubt that this is an area that must be brought into range. The managers of the funds would do most anything in their buying to fill the fund with bonds that would have a satisfactory yield level after the fund was able to take its four or four-and-a-half points load. Some critics have also questioned the rating that Standard & Poor's have given some bond issues, which allowed those bonds to be purchased by the funds. In other words, these are basically sweetheart ratings.

I would say that this charge is baseless.

There is no doubt a load charge of 4 or 4½ percent still charged by some funds does affect the current return that an investor can earn on these funds. One-half percent in the load takes away a negligible amount of your yield. However, there is also a plus point. The load is a one-time situation. These funds do not have annual management fees. There are critics who will say that the low price you get on selling units is actually equal to another load charge. They argue (and rightly so) that if the units have to be resold, the penalty is usually absorbed by the seller of the units.

The Municipal Investment Trust Fund managed by Merrill Lynch has charged a 3½-percent sales charge for some time now. This has to be regarded as a breakthrough in the load area. It will be difficult to get much lower. In fact, most of the MITF competition is still at 4 and 4½ percent. It is difficult to get below 3½ percent because of the expense involved in floating one of these issues. Merrill Lynch has the advantage of being able to underwrite large issues. This brings about a smaller cost per unit and thus a lower sales charge.

The purchase price of a unit in tax-free funds is determined by the evaluator (Standard & Poor's in most cases) once each week. The price arrived at becomes the price of the units for the following week.

There is an element of profit and loss in the gathering of a portfolio that does not affect unit holders. When a sponsor is gathering bonds for a fund, these bonds could go up or down depending on the market. This does not affect the worth. If there is a loss then it is absorbed by the sponsors; it also follows that they receive the profit if the bonds move up in value.

This sometimes disturbs critics of tax-free funds. They seem to want a one-way street. They want the investors to share in the profits but to be free of any losses.

Diversification and convenience

The two most important attributes of tax-free funds are convenience and diversification.

There is no doubt that diversification can be the greatest attribute that any fund can have. As the markets get lower, there is more diversification as to rating. In July 1974 one prominent fund was advertising that 90 percent of its bonds were rated A or better. In fact, 44 percent of their portfolio was AA and AAA. This means that when the market is lower, the funds upgrade at almost the same price previously paid for lower-rated bonds. I would have to defend convenience when that convenience does not hurt what you are doing. The convenience, aside from the gathering of a portfolio in one security, comes in having your bonds evaluated at least once per month, and the fact that your interest is mailed to you sometimes as often as once per month.

Just to prove that something extra can be worked into the tax-free fund market one underwriter recently underwrote an insured fund. This means that the principal and interest on the bonds in the fund are insured, thus guaranteeing payments to the holders. Standard & Poor's has awarded this fund an AA rating even though some of the bonds are rated as low as BBB.

The insured funds that I have seen indicate that the yield to the investor is not too far off the yields of the funds that have no insurance. Is there a catch? No. However, if you want to be technical you would have to say that there is no assurance that the insurance company is going to be able to continue meeting its obligation through the life of the various bonds.

There also has been a certain amount of experimentation in funds where all bonds are located in one state, usually to get a tax exemption. However, the reaction of investors has not been overwhelming and therefore you do not see many funds of this type being marketed.

The tax-free fund is a readily saleable security. The apparatus provides that the sponsor makes bids; but if he does not, then the trustee will buy the units. The result of such an action could be the sale of bonds in the portfolio. Until June of 1974 this has always been avoided but a group in Los Angeles which was sponsoring a fund of 10,000 ($10 million units) decided that it could not sell any more than about 6,000 (they had begun the selling operation in February), because the market had moved down too far to justify the sales at the prices the sponsor needed.

Thus for the first time (to my knowledge) a fund had to sell bonds from its portfolio to redeem the unsold units. This, of course, hurt all the unit holders. It also brought home a lesson in this area. The underwriting of tax-free funds requires that the sponsors have the capital to sustain necessary losses if they occur.

Another thing to remember about all existing tax-free funds is that they are closed-end funds. This means that they cannot be extended. This also means that if any bonds are called in advance of their maturity, then the fund has to make a distribution to the holders and the fund is reduced by that much. There is no reinvesting of the funds.

Despite my assertion that tax-free funds are good vehicles for investment, each fund must be looked at from the standpoint of what that fund contains. You must still exercise reasonable judgment about the portfolio. You must agree with the judgment of the people who have purchased the bonds for the fund. If you do not like just one of the bonds, pass it by and wait for the next one.

As I wrote earlier, the lower the market, the better portfolio a sponsor can get. In the higher markets the sponsors are forced to lower-rated situations to maintain yield. Therefore it has to be apparent that yield is the most important factor, although it must be yield based on security.

Do not forget that there are always tax-free fund units on sale. There is constant movement in the secondary market which allows you to pick some good bargains. As in the basic tax-free market there is a good chance that your best bargains might be in the secondary market. The factor that works on your behalf is that the evaluator, not the bond dealer, sets the price that you pay for the units in the secondary market. It makes for a very fair way of operating a market.

I have reproduced a glossary for tax-free funds (Appendix 2) which should give you some help in dealing with the principal factors of tax-free funds. Potential investors will find it handy when dealing with their first purchase.

Current return

You usually see bonds computed on a yield basis to maturity. However, since all funds are sold on a dollar basis per $1,000, yield is stated as current return. To figure a current return, you simply divide the net annual income per unit (which is found by dividing the net annual income by the number of units outstanding) by the public offering price that you pay. Of course any change in the net annual income will affect this current return. This is the way a hypothetical fund would look:

Annual Interest Income .... $ 68.00
   Per Unit
Less Estimated Annual Expense .... $ 1.50
Net Annual Income Per Unit .... $ 66.50
Net Annual Interest Rate Per Unit 6.65%
Public Offering Price .... $100.25 Per Unit
                               [$1002.50]
Current Return 6.63%

CHAPTER 6

Some
Definite
No-Nos

There are several warnings which need repeating. The most important ones involve having loans outstanding when you own tax-exempts, tax swaps, and the evaluations that you are given for your bonds by some bond houses.

Let's take the evaluations first. Too many times false evaluations are given, especially by the firm of origin. This is why it is a good idea to go to someone not connected with the particular bond issue that you bought. Of course a firm not in the underwriting where your bonds originated may make it sound like the worst bond ever issued. You sometimes wonder which is worse—the protective evaluation or the tear-down technique. You may wonder whether an evaluation would mean anything.

There is no doubt that bond traders are notorious for hiding bonds or their true prices. Some years ago a bank officer lost his job with a Chicago bank because he was involved in something called "the daisy chain." This was a plot to hide the fact that certain bonds had lost quite a bit in value. The scheme was to keep passing the bonds among a group of dealers and dealer banks. Finally the scheme was discovered and several houses almost went out of business.

Many people ask for evaluations when they really want a bid. Evaluations, working indications, and bids are three different things. If you are asking for an evaluation, then you are trying to get a bid for the purpose of knowing what your portfolio is worth. A working indication is nearer to selling the bonds, and the bid is something that the dealer making the bid must stand behind.

You should be able to know what your bond is worth at any time. Of course the absence of any posted market makes some investors nervous. It is not enough to say that they should not be in the market if they are going to be that nervous.

The expense of going out and getting bids for bonds can be a problem. If one of the computerized brokers is asked to get a bid for a client but it is really only information for the client, he will not be too eager to do it again. If the request is made almost daily, the dealer handling the account will make the estimate himself. All evaluations, whether done for firms or for clients, should be performed by people who have no axes to grind. There are several firms who do this work and they have no connection with any bond issues.

There is an excellent system for evaluating bonds. It is a book called *White's Tax Exempt Bond Market Ratings*, published by Standard & Poor's. It lists most issues and it numbers each issue; there is a yield level that is available each week and which you can key into the numbers assigned the bond issue. The people at Standard & Poor's tell me that this book can be obtained for $180.00.

Those who buy bonds and need a day-to-day evaluation should not buy bonds in the first place. Bonds are a long-term investment. Bonds should be purchased for the income—in this case, the tax-exempt income. I am not saying that an investor should not have the right to know what his or her bonds are worth. An evaluation, if given honestly, is enough.

Tax swaps

Tax swaps are among those very misunderstood situations where the misunderstanding extends to the so-called experts in some of the bucket shops, who do much swapping and make a big deal about it. The truth is that most swaps, if placed under the scrutiny of the IRS, would not stand up. However, the IRS sets no guidelines.

There is a group of bond dealers who have set themselves up as experts in the area. They make swaps which my grandchild could tell you were wrong, and yet people fall for them. Many of these swaps are made between customers.

A good swap, as I know and understand the procedure, is one where bonds swapped are similar in type, rating, and purpose. For instance, a swap of a city and a state bond of two different ratings should not be done. The maturities should be very similar and the yields used in the exchange should be very close.

When you are advised to swap New York City (rated A) versus Syracuse (rated Aa), or if the coupons are 4 percent and 5 percent, or if the maturities are about ten years apart, that is an open invitation to the IRS to move in.

When you are swapping you should consult your accountant and your lawyer, or at least one of them. Let them tell you whether they would do it. If they say no, repeat that *no* loud and clear to the salesman who tried to arrange the swap.

Tax swapping in tax-exempts, as in other areas of the business, is a legitimate situation when done right. Make sure that you are getting the right information from the right people. Also, check on what profit they are trying to make on you. They are not taking a risk on your transactions. Therefore there is no need for them to make a big profit.

Borrowing to buy: beware

People are shocked when the IRS calls them and questions them about mortgaging their house to buy tax-exempt bonds or the fact that they have borrowed money to buy tax-exempt bonds. The problem comes because the taxpayer is trying to get tax deductions too. You might ask how the IRS found out about the tax-frees when the interest does not have to be reported. In these days, when the Social Security number is used for all purposes in order to better identify all of us and what we do, it is easy for the IRS to find out this information.

Not too long ago a man outside of New York wanted to retain me to help him prove that the IRS was wrong in denying him one of the deductions that he was claiming. He was claiming a deduction on a loan for a mortgage yet was also taking his tax-exempt interest. He was certain that I could find precedents among my records showing that the IRS could not tax his tax-exempt bonds. He was most disappointed when I told him that I could not take the case because he was lost before we began.

The record will show that the IRS has won case after case when they can prove that a loan was taken out to buy tax-exempts. Therefore do not get excited when someone tells you how you can get the government two ways by mortgaging your house and buying tax-exempt bonds. I do not say that you will not get away with it, but I do say that the rate of ripping off the IRS is decreasing all the time. If it is up to the computers there will be no loopholes. Trying to get both sides of the interest deal (getting tax-exempt interest and getting a credit for paying it) is the perfect tax loophole that is being closed and in truth should be. Such deals give tax-exempt bonds a bad press and give some politicians a chance to expound on how evil tax-exempt bonds are. The truth is that there is nothing wrong with the principle except when the unprincipled try to slip through loopholes.

Those defaults

Default is an awful word, whether you are talking about bonds or any other loan. Some critics of tax-exempt bonds have taken several prominent defaults that have occurred and have blown them out of proportion. There have been defaults, but the defaults are very minor when compared to the amount of tax-exempt bonds outstanding.

There is no doubt that you will hardly ever find a default in a rated issue although one such issue in the state of Maine (rated AAA by Standard & Poor's) did default several years ago. However, very few rated issues have failed since the Great Depression. All issues that did default have paid off (or are in the process of paying off). Not only have they paid their back interest but most of them have paid interest on interest.

You should protect yourself by checking or having the salesman check the default section of the indenture of any issue that you may have under consideration. Do not buy an issue where the issuer has the right to deny you interest on interest if and when there is a default.

The principle also works well for investors who buy after the bonds are in default. Many people have made excellent buys in projects that they correctly assessed were at the bottom. They buy the bonds with coupons, which have not been paid, still attached to the bonds. The return can be very generous. Most investors consider this negative investing. It is really not negative at all; in fact, it is fairly positive. What you are doing is making a decision that a certain project is going uphill.

The most famous of all tax-exempt defaults in the last twenty years was the West Virginia Turnpike. Over the years many plans were put forth for setting the West Virginia issue on its feet. I do not believe that there was any fraud in the bond presentations but there sure were some big holes. There is doubt whether the issue should have been sold.

It has been said that the West Virginia issue was sold because some politicians, engineers, contractors, and bond men wanted to make a profit. It was a project that was many years before its time. The feasibility report was glowing and the bondholder bought. It wasn't long before it became evident that not enough drivers wanted to drive over the road. Over the years there have been many ideas for West Virginia to bail out the project, but the state (like other issuers of like projects) found that its credit rating was not hurt by having a sick child hanging around. Then there were the purists who insisted investors take their medicine when they made a mistake. However, the purists never advocated punishment for the greedy contractors, engineers, and some managing underwriters.

The Chesapeake Bay Bridge and Tunnel Authority was a tremendous issue of $200 million. The issue had a lot going for it: It had Merrill Lynch, Pierce, Fenner & Smith; the First Boston Corporation; and Allen & Co. heading the underwriters. There were all kinds of reserves built into the issue—they funded money for four and a half years of interest payments plus other reserve funds. This enticed a number of underwriters into the deal. They never intended for themselves or their clients to be around for too long.

It was not too long before many firms in the Street realized that after the cushion (the reserve fund for interest payments) became deflated there was not much that could be said for the issue. Most of these firms were advising their clients when to sell. Actually, if tax-exempts had been under the SEC some of the information might have been considered insider stuff.

The managers indignantly issued denials. Some investors did

not know what was going on because the biggest seller, Merrill Lynch, maintained a position in the bonds and tried to hold the market together. Therefore their clients never heard a discouraging word on the bonds. Their ability to assess what was going on was bad. In addition, there were people who held out hope that, because this project was an agency of the state of Virginia, the commonwealth would not let the bondholders down.

Feasibility was the problem. The traffic engineer had made no mistakes up until 1960 (the year of the Chesapeake issue) in his previous looks at future revenues of many road projects. However, many doubted his reasoning that people would wander over to the Norfolk area and motor down the seashore road to Florida when you could (by then) bypass Baltimore and Washington and zoom (very much more scenically) to Florida. In fact, very few people who made the trip to Florida each year bought the bonds. It was an omen generally disregarded by the underwriters.

Beware of the marginal revenue issue that depends on the report of feasibility and the clout of underwriters. In the Chesapeake issue, many people went into the underwriting because they wanted to make brownie points with the managing underwriters. Most of these people did not retail a bond. They sold their bonds to other dealers who liked what they read, and who believed that it was not their function to worry about those matters.

Ask questions

The inability to question is dangerous. No investor should allow a dealer to sell him or her bonds without receiving a good explanation of what the bond is all about. There is also the question of whether that dealer really believes in the project and why.

The first realization of an impending default brings chills to the market. Panic is the order of the day. Early warnings that a default might be coming are usually heeded by a minority. However, the word gets around because the lack of revenues is very obvious and figures have a way of being consistent.

Again, most of this information has been available, but most dealers do not send out reports. If you buy a bond, make sure that you get all the reports you need. Also ask if the revenues are up to predictions. You should not have to ask, but if you do not get the information, do not hesitate to sever your connections with that firm.

Despite the record that most issues in the tax-exempt area (and especially those that show increases) usually work out, the first reaction is always bad. Bonds go down to 25 or so. For instance, in October 1974 West Virginia was at 63½ bid for the 3¾-percent issue. However, this is not bad when you consider the coupon. Bringing up the rear was the Chesapeake, and here there is mixed reaction. The 32 bid for a 5¾-percent coupon is representative of the fear that it will be a long, long time before this issue works out.

However, now that I have described the bad points, it is time to look at the positive side of some of these issues. True, there are some that will never be revived. However, I have seen some pretty mangled issues come back to life and make their way to liquidity. In fact, if some West Virginia investors had held on they would not have taken the bad losses they did, and would be getting interest on interest today. Of course this is hindsight, but you would be surprised to know how many investors never did sell their bonds.

There are also the investors who join the parade when the bond is down. The interest-on-interest situation, plus the fact that they are traded flat, which means that you pay no interest when you buy, is attractive. Therefore what the investor buys is unpaid coupons and a chance to be paid the principal when due. (It is at least fourteen years away in West Virginia's case and twenty-five years in Chesapeake's.)

Issues that can make it back from the brink of disaster are remarkable in that they are still surviving. They are viable if a bit slow. Traffic increases all the time on these projects and time seems to be on their side.

Most tax-exempt investors who happen to be trapped in a defaulted issue usually "live" another day because the issue continues to pay interest, however belatedly. In addition, the principal amount of the issue is usually paid (especially on long term situations) as the problem is cured by time. Even the interest payments that are late earn interest. It is true that some tax-exempt issues have also completely defaulted, but the amount is miniscule. However, a default is not something to be brushed aside as unimportant. Each default is important because it should not happen. Because they are governmental entities, issuers have greater responsibility about the type of issues they authorize. The real responsibility lies with the investor and that investor should know the people from whom he or she is buying.

CHAPTER 7

The Anatomy of a Bond Issue

Over the years I have written many essays and delivered many lectures about how a bond issue is born. I refer to the area as Hometown, U.S.A., because this represents all cities and towns. Some people have suggested they were getting a civics lesson. Exactly. This is what municipal bonds are all about. Our way of government is being demonstrated. Too many people think bond issues are a figment of some politician's imagination, which will possibly enrich that politician.

Most issues are incubated in our minds—yours and mine—because we want, and that *want* is translated into bond issues. We want schools, roads, libraries, and hospitals.

The first step in organizing a bond issue is getting grassroots support for that project. It is necessary to prove the need for the project and to show that it is politically palatable for the elected officials. There is no use pushing a project that cannot be sustained on both counts. What many people forget is that the political motivation is supplied by the voters. Any sign of displeasure by a segment of the voters is enough to kill what you may think is the worthiest project.

Thus an investor can feel reasonably sure that the issues being financed by Hometown, U.S.A., are not necessarily frivolous issues. This assurance is essential if you are to believe that Hometown, U.S.A., can indeed pay off this obligation.

Suppose you are the chairperson of the drive to build a new library. You organize a committee and bring your petitions to the attention of the city council. A councilman or woman introduces a bill committing the city to build a new library. This is the beginning—but only the beginning.

Now the city council must hold hearings. There will be those who do not believe that a new library is necessary because you already have one. However, the city council says yes, there will be a new library. Its studies show that the library can be erected at a cost of $4 million. It authorizes a bond issue for the project. It decides that the bonds should mature equally— $20,000 bonds per year for twenty years.

If you live in a city that has to have elections on these matters, then an election is set. However, the number of cities and towns that call for referendums on these matters is growing smaller.

Notices must be printed. The city attorney and the bond counsel are called in to work out the legal snarls. A date is set for the bond issue by the fiscal officers of the city. In many cases the fiscal officer is aided in his decision by a fiscal consultant who can be either a bond house, a bank, or a consultant who specializes in setting up bond issues.

When the date is decided upon, the notice of sale is printed in the newspapers as the city ordinances require. It is also usually required that the notice be printed in the *Daily Bond Buyer*. The *Daily Bond Buyer* is the tax-exempt bond industry newspaper; the various underwriters find the issues they bid on in this paper.

In this notice of sale the terms of the sale are outlined. The prospective bidders are told when the bonds will sell and how the bonds will mature. There is also information about any maximum interest rates (because many states have ceilings on rates) which may restrict the bidders from bidding rates which are too high. It may also contain a restriction on using very high rates in the early maturities. This latter practice is legally correct because it usually falls within the average net-interest cost prescribed by the notice of sales. However, it often puts such a burden on the issuers in the early years that some states and cities have prohibited the practice; they do not allow a bidder to have more than a certain percentage between the highest and lowest coupon.

When the notice of sale appears in the *Daily Bond Buyer*, the managing underwriters go to work on structuring their bidding accounts. Actually, most accounts have already been established, although this does not stop an underwriter from forming a new account. However, most underwriters stay within the same accounts for many years. The issue we are talking about here is a moderately small issue in the context of today's market.

In addition to the manager there may be an average of nine or ten underwriters in each account. The manager and two other firms may commit for $500,000 each; five other firms or banks might be in for $400,000; while two smaller firms may have $250,000 each. As this is a general-obligation of Hometown, U.S.A., banks can bid on the issue. In fact, there probably will be many bids made.

The next thing the city and its financial advisors have to do is to visit the rating agencies. The rating agencies want to see the latest figures. After they decide what the bonds should be rated, they publish their findings. The city pays for this service and the costs are charged to the bond issue. Let's assume that both Moody's and Standard & Poor's have rated the bonds A.

Then everyone waits for the day of the sale. The sale is by sealed bids. The notice of sale contains a bidding form or at least the form to be followed. Hometown, U.S.A., might be a thousand miles from some of the bidders and therefore the account managers arrange to have local banks or bond dealers cover the sale. There is one other important item: A certified check in the amount of 2 percent (in this issue, $80,000), must accompany the bid, or the bid is not accepted.

Before the bid can be made, an underwriter must gather his fellow underwriters and decide on what to bid the issue. The process is one of comparison. They begin with what other comparable A-rated bonds are selling for. They decide the coupons and the yields for each maturity and they decide on the amount of profit per bond. In an issue like this the profit might be a little less or a little more than $10 per $1,000 bond, which is not much. Profits vary. In strong markets they are low and in weak markets they are higher. What a profit margin basically reflects is the down-side risk. Simply put, if the bonds cannot be sold at the yields decided, then the profit margin becomes the cushion. It usually isn't enough if you are wrong.

If the notice of sale calls for the bids to be in at twelve noon they had better be there or they are not accepted, even if the late bid is a better one than all the rest. The bids are opened and the tabulations are examined—many times a bid may be figured wrong. After all the bids are checked the city announces the winning bid. This may take an hour or more.

Let us say that ABC Bank has bought the bonds. The job of selling starts immediately. The managing underwriter sets an order period of an hour or two and all members must enter their orders in that period and cannot confirm bonds to clients until they are confirmed by the managers.

Group-account orders have priorities. These are orders where all members of the underwriting account share in the profit and they usually cover several maturities. For instance, a bank (perhaps the manager in this case) will take all the bonds through ten years, which is half the issue. If you had asked for $5,000 of those bonds you would not get them. This annoys many investors but it is not a legitimate complaint.

Your salesperson's firm may not be in the issue but they can still get bonds because a dealer's concession is allowable to them and represents their profit for selling the bonds to you. On new issues and most other tax-exempt situations the price to you is a net price with no commission added. Never pay a commission on a tax-exempt unless your broker is acting as an agent. Then the charge should be about $2.50 per bond.

There are other things that the managing underwriter must do. They will have to arrange for an ad. The city must arrange for the printing of the bonds and the bond counsel must begin his job of deciding whether the bonds are legal. You have about thirty days before the bonds are delivered.

The mechanics of a bond delivery

Let us suppose that you have purchased $5,000 of the bonds due in 1989. You have received your confirmation that the bonds have been sold to you on a when-as-and-if-received-by-us basis. This means that the dealer or bank who sold you the bonds will deliver the bonds to you if he gets them.

Why wouldn't he get them? There are many reasons why a delivery might not go through, although most of them do. The attorneys might find some problems with the issue. A group of taxpayers might go into court to have the issue restrained. The only problem that you should not have is the failure of the underwriters to pick up the bonds and deliver your bonds to you.

The majority of underwriters are able to pick up an issue when it is ready. The words "pick up" in this instance refer to the ability of the underwriters to pay for the issue before they have received the money from the investors. You should not necessarily help your dealer pay for the bonds. The bond business is a risk business and dealers should be able to pick up their bonds without help from their customers.

Before picking up and redelivering the bonds there is a lot of paper work and printing to be done (for instance, the printing of the bonds). A tax-exempt bond is a very complicated item. It has to have coupons attached for the life of the bond. This means different sets of coupons for each maturity. There is a great deal of documentation on a bond, plus the printed legal opinion (in most cases) of the bond counsel. The bond counsel is the one responsible for getting the bonds printed; he must provide the wording that goes with the bond. He must also check out bond number one to see if it is correctly printed.

During this period the bond counsel is checking the issue completely to see if there is anything illegal about its sale. He usually does this prior to a sale, but he has to check out court decisions in order to be prepared to render his opinion that the issue is legal.

During this period, if the bonds are all sold, the underwriters wait as do the investors. You, the investor, have not paid any money as yet and the underwriters have paid only 2 percent of their bid. Often the underwriters are still struggling to sell the bonds up to the time the bonds are delivered. In fact, they may be forced to sell bonds at lower prices than they sold to you. What does this mean to you? Nothing. It points up the hazards of buying new issues.

There has been much debate over the years as to why the time lag between sale and delivery is so long. One of the problems is that some citizens, perhaps your next-door neighbors, are thinking about challenging a bond issue. These cases are usually governed by certain state laws. If a litigant can file suit against a bond issue and just have his or her own costs to worry about, then there would be more suits. However, if, as in many states, the losing litigant has to pay all costs, then it is a different deal. They hesitate before they file nuisance suits.

As the time of delivery draws near, the city or home town and the managing underwriters set a date for the delivery. This gives the underwriters a chance to bill the clients for the bonds.

In this case let us assume that the bonds were dated July 1 and the delivery to the underwriters will take place on July 15. This means that the redelivery of bonds might take place on July 16 or 17. In the days of tight money, when it is costly to carry bonds, the dealers or the banks try to get the bonds delivered as fast as possible.

When this redelivery date is set, the bonds are confirmed to the institutional and individual customers. If July 17 has been set as the date, you will receive a bill from the bank or dealer you purchased them from with the price of the bonds figured to that date plus sixteen days of interest (as the bonds were dated July 1). Of course you receive tax-exempt interest from July 1 because when you turn in the first coupon it will be a six-month coupon. Occasionally there is a short coupon because of dating problems. For instance, if the bonds were dated October 1 and the issuers wanted all their bonds due January and July, then they would attach a three-month coupon to the bond. If that issue were delivered in mid-October you would still be entitled to a three-month coupon on January 1.

Thus if July 17 is the delivery date, you must have the funds to your bank or dealer on or before that date. As you can see there is a two-day lag before the bonds are delivered. However, the managing underwriter obtains a loan for the entire account for the purpose of carrying the bonds until delivery. They have each of the underwriters deliver his funds to the bank on the day of delivery, thus satisfying the loan.

You can see why it is so important for the managing underwriter to have solvent companies in the issue. The failure of an underwriter to pick up his bonds would force all the others to do it in proportion to their commitments in the overall underwriting. Thus if company B failed to pick up 200 bonds, that amount of bonds would have to be split among the other underwriters in proportion to their overall part of the underwriting account.

Your dealer (who may or may not be a member of the underwriting group) sends you a confirmation. You should have someone pick up your bonds as quickly as possible. I recommend that the bonds be in your safe-deposit box and not in any vault unless your seller is a bank. You should make arrangements to have the bonds delivered to your bank. Of course if you handle your own bonds you can go to the underwriters' office and pick up the bonds yourself. Make sure that whoever picks up the bonds inspects them to see that they are the right maturities and that all the coupons are there.

Make sure that the legal opinion is either printed on the bond or that you have a copy of it. Also see to it, if the issue is a revenue-bond issue (the Hometown issue was not), that you receive a final copy of the official statement; in a revenue-bond issue the delivery is not complete without this statement.

You should also have a copy of the official statement even for a general-obligation issue. File it with the bonds so that you know the circumstances of the issue, in case you want to sell the bonds. I also recommend that you make a card with the pertinent data on it for your information. Write the name of the issue as it appears on the bond, and the coupon and the maturity day plus the date of the issue. Also place on this card the name of the trustee bank and the paying-agent bank so that you can decide which is more convenient when you want to cash in your coupons. This will give you a record to look at when you are attempting to get a bid or an evaluation on the bonds, without having to go to the vault.

You will probably have a bearer bond. If you lose it or it is stolen, a thief could cash in the coupons. Place your bonds in a safety box and enjoy the tax-exempt interest. Do not tear off coupons in advance. If, for some reason, you have to sell the bonds, the delivery could be flawed because of the detached coupon. If your bonds are at your bank they may tear the coupons for you and claim the interest in your behalf.

8

Situations
Bondholders
Face

In this chapter I am going to be writing about some of the situations that bondholders will face from time to time.

Bond insurance. This is a growing field in which several insurance companies are now insuring various facets of a bond issue. In the general-obligation area the insurance company will insure that the principal and interest are paid by the issuing bodies over the life of the issue. When this insurance is issued, Standard & Poor's will give either a AA or AAA rating (depending on the insurance company issuing the policy) on the bonds insured even though the bond issue without insurance might only deserve a BBB rating.

In the lease type of revenue bonds (generally industrial-revenues) there are other companies who will guarantee the lease payments, which of course lead to the payment of the principal and interest on the bonds.

Does this insurance help marketability? I am not sure that

the insurance has made that much of an impression up to now but this could be because many investors do not understand it. I know that I have been disappointed in the small number of insured issues. How dependable are the companies? I do not think that Standard & Poor's would base its rating of AA or AAA on a company's guarantee if they did not think that company was in good shape. However, the ultimate decision of whether you think a certain company has the ability to meet its commitments is a personal one. You can get help from your accountant or attorney on this question. Take a look at their balance sheets and their record. Treat them the same as you would a bond issue.

Calls. Most revenue issues have call features. The call is a device whereby the issuer gets a chance to call in your bonds by paying you a premium (which is stipulated when you buy the bonds) and can thereby retire the bonds or refinance the project. The latter case usually prevails when the project has been doing well revenuewise and there is a chance of refinancing at lower rates.

When all the bonds of an issue or a maturity are not called they are usually call bonds in inverse order. This is why some people try to get the highest-numbered bonds in a maturity.

How do investors fare in the matter of calls? I think they do well because as long as the call price is high enough you are protected. However, it is important that you take a good look at the call schedule and how it works.

Discount bonds. If you use discretion when buying them, I know of no better way to invest, especially in a high-interest-rate market, because the bargains are there.

Remember, if you do not receive the right amount of yield you could be in trouble. If you hold the bonds until maturity (which is usually the aim) then you must pay a capital-gains tax. Let us assume that you were to buy a 3½-percent bond due in five years at 7.3 percent. If you were to figure in a 25-percent capital-gains tax, then the effective yield would be 6.6 percent, which would be in line with other current coupon issues in that maturity range. If after figuring what your effective yield would be after capital gains you find that the yield is considerably lower than the yields being offered in the market, pass it by and look for another offering.

Be very careful of a discount bond that is called a fractional. It is another get-rich-quick scheme. Fractionals are the bonds

with very low coupons—one-quarter and one-half of 1 percent—which sell for very low prices. I do not consider them
suitable for individual investors. Ask your accountant how you
will fare taxwise if you buy them.

Interest dates. Sometimes an investor gets bowled over by a
salesperson who says the bonds are J & J or A & O. What he or
she means is that the interest is due January and July or April
and October in the latter case. It lets you know when your
bonds are due for interest payments, which is what this investing is all about.

There are only the following interest-date combinations, and
they can either be one or fifteen, which means the first day of
the month or the fifteenth day.

> J & J—January and July
> F & A—February and August
> M & S—March and September
> A & O—April and October
> M & N—May and November
> J & D—June and December

Tenders. A tender offer is made by a city or an authority that
has money in the bank and wants to buy outstanding bonds to
lower its interest-cost requirements. Tenders abound in bad
markets. This means that the issuer will usually be able to buy
back bonds at considerably less than the price at which they
were issued.

When a tender is advertised, the issuers usually agree to buy
a certain amount of bonds at the lowest prices tendered. The
process is similar to that used by companies that went public
and now want to buy back their stock. But those companies
usually put a price on the stock; this is different from the bond
tender. The best thing about either situation is that it is option-
al on the part of the holders.

Many tenders are printed in the *Wall Street Journal* in the
form of ads in or near the bond section. This is another service
that you can expect of the person who handles your bond-
buying. He or she should bring this to your attention, and
should also help you with the pricing and file the form for you.

Sinking-fund operations. Most revenue issues have sinking
funds. Some of them are mandatory but some of them are not.
They may have accumulated funds since they do not wish to

call bonds at premiums when the bonds are selling at deep discount if the bonds came out at a time when interest rates were low. These sinking funds are managed by the trustee bank.

It is difficult for an individual to operate in this market without the cooperation of the person who sells you bonds. The information is usually known only to the traders, who are not famous for worrying about investors. They usually have enough problems worrying about their positions and making a profit. The problem for the individual investor is not to be picked off. If you hold a bond that could be a candidate for a call and you get a bid for the bond, ask a lot of questions. Do not let some trader make a big profit on you.

Advance-refunded issues. These are not as important as they used to be because the Treasury has revised its regulations on the arbitrage of tax-exempt issues. Here is how it worked: An issuer would see that because its credit had improved, its bonds could be refunded at lower rates. However, there may have been bonds outstanding that were not callable. In other words, these particular bonds would have to remain outstanding until their maturity date. In an advance refunding, these bonds in effect are escrowed because cash or U.S. Treasury Bonds are put up with the trustee to cover their interest and redemption price. Thus the bonds become AAA. Most individual investors sell the bonds to banks at a good profit. These issues are very few and far between unless the credit of the issue moves much higher; the Treasury sets a limit on the coupons that can be set in the refunding. The Treasury caught on to the fact that there were sometimes two issues outstanding representing one project. One was the refunded bonds in escrow but still outstanding, and the other was the new issue. If it did not prove anything else, it proved that tax-exempt-bond people are great mathematicians.

Tax-exempt bond math

Some investors are bothered about all the high-sounding math of yields, percentages, and so forth, in bonds. They are impressed by their confirmations, which show the price carried out to many places. Many common-stock buyers found that the arithmetic involved there was simple. In fact they even found that doing a price/earnings ratio was not difficult. If you mention bond math, however, they recoil in horror.

This reaction is unfounded because when you strip away all the fancy frills and the sophisticated calculators, it is just simple arithmetic. Of course, there is a lot more math in bonds than this—figuring out amortization schedules, for example—but what follows is all you will need:

• Formulas for figuring out what the tax exemption means for you in your tax bracket.

• How to figure interest.

• How to figure yields—including current, to maturity, and discount yields.

The formula method for figuring tax equivalents works two ways. You can find the tax equivalent of a tax-exempt bond or a taxable security. In either case the formula begins with ascertaining your tax bracket and then finding the differential:

$$
\begin{array}{r}
100 \text{ percent} \\
\text{Less} \quad \underline{? \text{ (your tax bracket)}} \\
? \text{ (the differential)}
\end{array}
$$

Let's assume that you are in the 32-percent tax bracket. You have been offered a tax-exempt bond with an 8-percent yield. You want to know what the taxable equivalent is without looking at the chart which you probably would not carry everywhere. The differential is 68 percent, and you divide this into the 8 percent:

$$8.00 \div 68 = 11.76\%$$

Thus you have found that the equivalent taxable yield is 11.76 percent. Now suppose you were seeking to find what you must earn in a tax-exempt bond to equal an interest rate of 10.5 percent (taxable) being offered to you. Once again you use the differential, but this time you multiply as follows:

$$10.50 \times .68 = 7.14$$

So you see that you require a 7.14-percent tax-exempt yield to equal the offering of the taxable security.

Knowing how to figure interest is a skill you can use in many endeavors, not only bonds.

First of all, remember that tax-exempt bonds are figured on a 360-day year, while U.S. Treasury Bonds and other transactions such as mortgages are figured on a 365-day basis. If you would like to check the interest on your confirmation, or if you would like to find out how much tax-exempt interest you made in a certain period, just follow this example. If you buy $5,000 of 7 percent bonds you would earn $350.00 per year. The bonds are due January 1, and you are having them delivered to you March 14.

This means that you must pay two months, thirteen days interest (you always figure up to the day before delivery). One day equals approximately $.9723. Multiply that by seventy-three days and your answer should be $70.98. You should be able to come within a penny or two of the figures on the confirmation. Actually, if you were to look at an interest table you would find the official figure is $70.97.

There is another area where figuring yields can be very illuminating. Remember that the interest you earn and the discount or the premium you pay determine what yield you earn. All examples being used assume a $1,000 bond, even though most bonds are in denominations of $5,000.

One thing that confuses tax-exempt investors is that bond dealers do all their transactions in either dollars or yield to maturity. As I have pointed out before, most investors do not expect to be alive as long as some of their very long-term investments, which might mature as late as 2015. The yield most of them are interested in is the current return. You hardly ever see current return shown in an ad for bonds. However, many dealers show it in their offering sheets.

Current return has to do only with the interest that you earn. You need two factors. Let's say that you have purchased a 7-percent bond at 102. How do you determine the current return? You divide the coupon by the amount paid as follows:

$$7 \div 102 = 6.86\%$$

Thus 6.86 percent is what you are earning.

Since yield to maturity is the way bond dealers and banks express yields in ads, let us find out how this is arrived at. Let's assume that this is a bond with a 6.5-percent coupon due in ten years, and you purchased it at 105. What is the yield to maturity?

First you find the current return, which is:

$$6.5 \div 105 = 6.19\%$$

Then you divide that 5-percent premium you paid by ten

years, and you find that this reduces your yield (5.0 percent ÷ 10 years) by .5 percent per year. Subtract this and you find:

$$6.19\% \text{ (current yield)}$$
$$\underline{- .50\%}$$
$$5.69\% \text{ (yield to maturity)}$$

Now if the bond was a discount bond at 6.5 percent for twenty years and you purchased it for 90, you have two situations. You want to find the yield to maturity, but you also have to take into account that Uncle Sam demands a 25-percent capital-gains tax from you if you do hold those bonds for twenty years (which is possible). Again you find the current return:

$$6.5 \div 90 = 7.22\%$$

Taking the ten-point discount over the twenty years, you find that it is again worth .5 percent (10 percent ÷ 20 years), but this time, since it represents a discount, you add it to the current yield.

$$7.22 + .50 = 7.72\%$$

This is the yield to maturity, but this is not the yield you will earn, because you will have to pay that 25-percent capital-gains tax. Thus all you will have gained from that 10-percent discount ($100) after the capital-gains tax of 25 percent will be $75, or an effective discount of 7.5 percent instead of 10 percent. Therefore the factor becomes .375 (7.5 percent ÷ 20) rather than .5, and this is the true yield to you:

$$7.220 + .375 = 7.595\%$$

Some of the above calculations may seem bothersome, but I maintain that in addition to being a good mental exercise, it gives you a better look at bonds in the tax-exempt market. It also removes much of the mystery when you find out that these things can be figured out so easily and so quickly.

Timing

I think that I have given you enough ideas to help guide you in your choice of investment. However, timing is another matter and can, when all is said and done, be the most important one of all.

All you really need to do is read the *Wall Street Journal*

daily. There is also excellent information in *U.S.News & World Report* and in *Business Week*.

The *Wall Street Journal* on a daily basis gives you a rundown of the various sales of new issues, including tax-exempts, corporates, and governments. Do not forget that all bonds are related because they all go to make up a major section of what we consider the money market. Here are some of the things you will find in the *Wall Street Journal* that will give you clues to what may happen:

1. Each Monday they print a tax-exempt index. The *Bond Buyer Index* (published by the *Daily Bond Buyer*) is thought to be the official one in the industry, but no individual investor can afford $732 a year for a subscription to the *Bond Buyer*. The *WSJ* index runs fairly close to the *Bond Buyer* average. The fact is that most indices use the same bonds as the bases for their index. The *OTC Market Chronicle* also runs one each week that I compile. These various indices indicate the direction of the market. They run inversely—in other words, if the market improves, the yield goes down; and if the market worsens, the yield goes up.

2. The *Wall Street Journal* covers the important sales in all of the markets and gives reports on how they do. This also gives you an idea of what is going on as to yield levels and reception.

3. The *Journal* gives you capsule comments on what various bond dealers and buyers for institutions are saying.

4. The reports on the prime rate are important as well as those on the cost of federal funds. They are usually found on the bond page.

5. Each Friday there is a story on the Federal Reserve Bank weekly report. This should be studied. The total amount of loans is most important to the money market, and the money market controls the bond market. If loans are going up, then we are in for tighter money; and if they are going down, this is an indication of easier money being ahead.

If you take a few minutes each day to read these articles, you should know what lies ahead for the bond market. In this way, you can go ahead with an investment or hold back. It seemed to me that when we reached the 12-percent-rate mark in 1974, there was not much further to go. That, therefore, represented the low of the market. Conversely, as the prime rate tumbles, you know that rates are going to be lower.

The record of the past several years shows that the time spans of up markets (when yields are low) tend to be much shorter than down markets (when yields are high). Therefore the wait until yields start to move up again usually has not been very long. Of course this could change. I think it is indicative of the times we live in with the inflationary aspect and demand for capital.

I always recommend that bond investors be aware of political trends. In the past fifty years the Republican party has stood for "hard money," while the Democrats have usually been supporters of "easy money." Therefore you should keep an eye on politics. If you see a Republican trend, then you know that the old-time religion might be dominant again. If you see the Democrats moving ahead, then you might expect that money will be easier. However, nothing is certain, and these roles might even shift. They may even make the money market nonpolitical. Anything is possible.

Unemployment has a lot to do with what happens in a bond market. It is strange but the bond business depends on economic disasters to do better—you will find that yields go down when unemployment rises. It is the old theory that bonds offer a better investment shelter in bad times than anything else. This could be true, but I feel that bonds are an investment for all seasons.

Inflation is the hated word of institutional buyers. Each time the rate of inflation goes up they cringe and wonder whether they can afford bonds because of the fixed rates. While I am not an advocate of inflation, I do not get as paranoid about it as some of the people I see writing in (or being quoted in) the *Wall Street Journal.* I recommend that you do not, either. I agree with Dr. Milton Friedman on his idea of indexing bonds. This would mean a variable rate, and it has been used with many corporate bonds.

The problem is whether it can be used in tax-exempt general-obligations. I do not think it can, because most officeholders like to know the rate of interest. A rate that could float up would scare them. It can be used in tax-exempt-revenue situations, and I think that it might be a larger part of the bond scene in the years ahead.

One thing to keep in mind when you are looking at the bond market is that your outlook is not the same as the bond dealer's. To the bond dealer it is a good market when the yields are going down and the prices are going up. This is not to your advantage unless you want to sell some bonds that you bought in a lower market.

Your goal is to find the right time to buy. You also have to keep your funds active. Keeping them in a checking account will not help. When you are waiting, you should look for some short-term situations like tax-exempt anticipation notes.

Let us plot a hypothetical case. The yields in the market have been going down for several weeks. In fact the *Wall Street Journal* tax-exempt index is about as low as it has been all year. You have read that some bankers are talking about large increases in loans. Times are good, but there is a hint of renewed inflation. It just happens that you have funds available at this time, and you think that you might want to buy some tax-exempt bonds. The signs are clear: *Wait.*

You agree that you should wait, but then what should you do? You look around for some short-term notes (tax-exempt, if possible, but straight U.S. government bills for ninety days could work too) if the wait seems short. Of course, if you think that the up market has wended its course and a change is imminent, you might hold the cash and wait a bit longer. You could, however, also take the attitude that the down market has a long time to run. Then you could invest in a three-month note. The worst that can happen is that you sell out the short-term notes before they mature to get into longer-term bonds. There may be a slight loss, but in the long run it might be worth it.

In this book I have written about the short and the long term as far as investing. In this chapter I am referring to short and long term as they pertain to your investment thinking. You may read what a variety of economists have to say, and you will find that it is usually long-term. Actually it is easy to make long-term predictions. However, people who underwrite and trade bonds daily do not have the luxury of thinking for the long term. They must come up with the short-term approach because gut decisions have to be made.

You, as an investor, must work your ideas somewhere in between. I am convinced that most bond investors have more ability than they realize. I know that most of you can do as well as the salesman who is calling you and trying to sell you some bonds that his firm owns. If you are generally aware of what is going on in the market, then you are in a good position to deal with any salesperson. Establish the fact that you know what's going on—then you do not have to be following anyone.

Let what happens in your investing be your idea, and not some salesperson's. This does not mean that you should not accept suggestions; but if you are informed, then you can deal with those suggestions in an intelligent manner.

The
Future of
Tax-Exempt
Bonds

Many people fear that the tax-exemption privilege will be eliminated and they will be stuck with bonds that no longer have the exemption.

Your only risk in buying a tax-exempt is the market, not the possibility of having your tax exemption taken away.

Perhaps the idea that our local areas have the right to issue tax-exempt bonds does not impress many people.

The right to issue our own bonds is perhaps more important a part of our local government than we realize. I am not discussing whether some of the officials in local government are everything they should be, but then that is our fault and our responsibility to cure the problem via the voting booth. The fact that we have the right to issue bonds is important. The reciprocity (no federal tax on local bonds, no state tax on feder-al bonds) that has existed since Justice John Marshall's decision has to be considered a plus because of what it has accomplished. Our schools, hospitals, roads, and other projects are monuments to this system.

There is no doubt that when some people see rich individuals buying tax-exempt bonds, they think, "What an abuse." But is it?

So that you will understand what the alternative is, I am going to discuss what the Treasury would like to see. The Treasury would like all bonds to be taxable. Treasury people claim that this would save money. They do not seem to realize that pension funds and mutual life insurance companies, which pay no taxes and buy more than $20 billion in bonds per year, would probably turn away from Treasury to local bonds. The drain on the Treasury would be that much greater.

There has been a debate raging for many years as to whether the matter of tax exemption is a constitutional problem or not. The final decision could end up in the Supreme Court. A decision to bring all bonds under federal control would be a difficult one.

Congress does not want any part of the problem because of the pressure from local areas.

I would not want to state that tax exemption will never be eliminated. Remember what I said above: There is no risk that *your* bonds may become taxable. Even if future tax-exempt bonds are banned, the existing bonds would continue to bear tax exemption. In fact, if the Treasury is successful in banning future issues, the bonds that you hold would become much more valuable.

They would, in effect, become museum pieces. This would mean that you would be holding a bond that could not be replaced by other tax-exempt bonds. There is ample precedent on situations like this. The U.S. Treasury had some bonds that were tax-exempt, but after 1941 all bonds and notes issued by the Treasury and the various agencies of government became taxable. However, the issues outstanding retained their tax exemption.

Another reason why I am so convinced that the investor who buys a tax-exempt bond will not be stuck with a taxable security (which could bring on financial disaster for some people) is my conviction that we have an almost sacred regard for contracts in this country.

When you buy a tax-exempt bond (just as with any type of bond) you make a contract to lend money. The other party makes an agreement to repay you a certain amount of interest every six months and to redeem that bond from you at a stated future date. In a tax-exempt bond, the local issuing body also covenants that the interest that you will receive will be tax-free. That is your contract, and you have the right to see that it is carried out.

I cannot see any Congress, administration, or court that would deny the validity of your contract. If they did, it would be a national disaster that could affect anyone with a debt contract, which is why it will not happen.

I can see where the federal government could conceivably pay off your bonds at 100 to remove them from the market. They might even replace them with fully taxable bonds at a higher rate of interest, although I think that is not likely to happen. All I am trying to point out is that you will not be stuck. That is the basic fear that most bondholders and would-be holders have.

Therefore I can see no reason why all investors who can gain from tax exemption should not be holders of tax-exempt bonds. Remember, most of the myths about tax-exempt bonds are just that: myths.

However, I would like to remind you just one more time that you should not buy tax-exempt bonds without due thought and discussion with the people who give you financial advice. Tax-exempt bonds are a boon for this nation and they can be a boon for you, but you must do your part in performing due diligence. You must take time to consider just what type of bond you need. Make sure that you know what that bond is all about. Just as it is your (and my) responsibility to make the administration of our local areas better through electing qualified and honest officials, it is your responsibility to buy bonds with your eyes wide open. If you will, you can help eliminate the bucket-shop operators who would sell unsuspecting people defaulted bonds or other undesirable issues.

Tax-exempt bonds and funds are a splendid way to invest. They have weathered depressions and other economic disasters. If you have been on the point of buying but have had some apprehensions, I hope that I have cleared them up. As long as you recognize and avoid the pitfalls, you will enjoy your tax-exempt investments.

Tax-Exempt Bond Ratings

Key to Moody's Municipal Ratings

Aaa—Bonds which are rated **Aaa** are judged to be of the best quality. They carry the smallest degree of investment risk and are generally referred to as "gilt edge." Interest payments are protected by a large or by an exceptionally stable margin and principal is secure. While the various protective elements are likely to change, such changes as can be visualized are most unlikely to impair the fundamentally strong position of such issues.

Aa—Bonds which are rated **Aa** are judged to be of high quality by all standards. Together with the **Aaa** group they comprise what are generally known as high grade bonds. They are rated lower than the best bonds because margins of protection may not be as large as in **aa** securities or fluctuation of protective elements may be of greater amplitude or there may be other elements present which make the long-term risks appear somewhat larger than in **Aaa** securities.

A—Bonds which are rated **A** possess many favorable investment attributes and are to be considered as upper medium grade obligations. Factors giving security to principal and interest are considered adequate, but elements may be present which suggest a susceptibility to impairment sometime in the future. (See general note below.)

Baa—Bonds which are rated **Baa** are considered as medium grade obligations; i.e., they are neither highly protected nor poorly secured. Interest payments and principal security appear adequate for the present but certain protective elements may be lacking or may be characteristically unreliable over any great length of time. Such bonds lack outstanding investment characteristics and in fact have speculative characteristics as well. (See general note below.)

Ba—Bonds which are rated **Ba** are judged to have speculative elements; their future cannot be considered as well assured. Often the protection of interest and principal payments may be very moderate, and thereby not well safeguarded during both good and bad times over the future. Uncertainty of position characterizes bonds in this class.

B—Bonds which are rated **B** generally lack characteristics of the desirable investment. Assurance of interest and principal payments or of maintenance of other terms of the contract over any long period of time may be small.

Caa—Bonds which are rated **Caa** are of poor standing. Such issues may be in default or there may be present elements of danger with respect to principal or interest.

Ca—Bonds which are rated **Ca** represent obligations which are speculative in a high degree. Such issues are often in default or have other marked shortcomings.

C—Bonds which are rated **C** are the lowest rated class of bonds, and issues so rated can be regarded as having extremely poor prospects of ever attaining any real investment standing.

Con. (– – –)—Bonds for which the security depends upon the completion of some act or the fulfillment of some condition are rated conditionally. These are bonds secured by (a) earnings of projects under construction, (b) earnings of projects unseasoned in operating experience, (c) rentals which begin when facilities are completed, or

(d) payments to which some other limiting condition attaches. Parenthetical rating denotes probable credit stature upon completion of construction or elimination of basis of condition.

General Note: Those bonds in the **A** and **Baa** groups which Moody's believes possess the strongest investment attributes are designated by the symbols **A 1** and **Baa 1**. Other **A** and **Baa** bonds comprise the balance of their respective groups. These rankings (1) designate the bonds which offer the maximum in security within their quality group, (2) designate bonds which can be bought for possible upgrading in quality and (3) additionally afford the investor an opportunity to gauge more precisely the relative attractiveness of offerings in the market place.

Generally speaking, bonds in Moody's highest rating categories can be characterized as follows: **Aaa** obligations, their safety is so absolute that with the occasional exception of oversupply in a few specific instances, characteristically, their market value is affected solely by money market fluctuations; **Aa** bonds, their market value is virtually immune to all but money market influences, with the occasional exception of oversupply in a few specific instances; **A**-rated bonds may be influenced to some degree by economic performance during a sustained period of depressed business conditions but during periods of normalcy **A**-rated bonds frequently move in parallel with **Aaa** and **Aa** obligations, with the occasional exception of oversupply in a few specific instances; **Baa**-rated are more sensitive to changes in economic circumstances, and aside from occasional speculative factors applying to some bonds of this class, **Baa** issues will move in parallel with **Aaa**, **Aa**, and **A** obligations during periods of economic normalcy, except in instances of oversupply; **Ba** bonds are speculative, their market value may be affected by varying economic circumstances not necessarily geared to the business cycle; **B**-rated bonds are usually quite sensitive to day-to-day circumstances affecting the borrower's ability to service debt on schedule, especially during down trending economic cycle; **Caa** bonds reflect the market's concept of the probability and imminence of a workout; **Ca** bonds are speculative in high degree and usually indicate nominal workout value; and **C**-rated bonds appear to be hopelessly in default and usually have only a nominal speculative market value.

Unless otherwise noted, municipal ratings are for "general obligations" which are defined as validly issued and legally binding evidences of indebtedness secured by the full faith, credit and taxing powers of the issuer.

Standard & Poor's Corporation

AAA-Prime—These are obligations of the highest quality. They have the strongest capacity for timely payment of debt service.

General Obligation Bonds—In a period of economic stress, the issuers will suffer the smallest declines in income and will be least susceptible to autonomous decline. Debt burden is moderate. A strong revenue structure appears more than adequate to meet future expenditure requirements. Quality of management appears superior.

Revenue Bonds—Debt service coverage has been and is expected to remain substantial. Stability of the pledged revenues is also exceptionally strong, due to the competitive position of the municipal enterprise or to the nature of the revenues. Basic security provisions (including rate covenant, earnings test for issuance of additional bonds, debt service reserve requirements) are rigorous. There is evidence of superior management.

AA-High Grade—The investment characteristics of general obligation and revenue bonds in this group are only slightly less marked than those of the prime quality issues. Bonds rated "AA" have the second strongest capacity for payment of debt service.

A-Good Grade—Principal and interest payments on bonds in this category are regarded as safe. This rating describes the third strongest capacity for payment of debt service. It differs from the two higher ratings because:

General Obligation Bonds—There is some weakness, either in the local economic base, in debt burden, in the balance between revenues and expenditures, or in quality of management. Under certain adverse circumstances, **any one such weakness** might impair the ability of the issuer to meet debt obligations at some future date.

Revenue Bonds—Debt service coverage is good, but not exceptional. Stability of the pledged revenues could show some variations because of increased competition or economic influences on revenues. Basic security provisions, while satisfactory, are less stringent. Management performance appears adequate.

BBB-Medium Grade—This is the lowest investment grade security rating.

General Obligation Bonds—Under certain adverse conditions, several of the above factors could contribute to a lesser capacity for payment of debt service. The difference between "A" and "BBB" ratings is that the latter shows **more than one fundamental weakness, or one very substantial fundamental weakness,** whereas the former shows only one deficiency among the factors considered.

Revenue Bonds—Debt coverage is only fair. Stability of the pledged revenues could show substantial variations, with the revenue flow possibly being subject to erosion over time. Basic security provisions are no more than adequate. Management performance could be stronger.

BB-Lower Medium Grade—Bonds in this group have some investment characteristics, but they no longer predominate. For the most part this rating indicates a speculative, non-investment grade obligation.

B-Low Grade—Investment characteristics are virtually nonexistent and default could be imminent.

D-Defaults—Payment of interest and/or principal is in arrears.
In order to provide more detailed indications of credit quality, our traditional bond letter ratings may be modified by the addition of a plus or a minus sign, when appropriate, to show relative standing within the major rating categories, the only exceptions being in the "AAA"—Prime Grade category and in the lesser categories below "BB."

NCR—No contract rating. No ratings are assigned to new offerings unless a contract rating is applied for.

Provisional Ratings—The letter "p" following a rating indicates the rating is provisional, where payment of debt service requirement will be largely or entirely dependent upon the timely completion of the project.

Tax-Free Fund Glossary

It is always good to know what a salesman is talking about when you buy bonds. It is no different with tax-free funds. The following definitions should be helpful to any investor who is thinking about tax-free funds but is sometimes confused by the various terms.

Fund—The fund is an investment trust formed for the purpose of obtaining tax-free income through investment in a portfolio of bonds (usually rated BBB by Standard & Poor's and Baa or better by Moody's) issued on behalf of states, towns, cities, territories, and authorities or political subdivisions in the United States. The interest on the bonds in the portfolio is exempt from all federal income taxes (and some state taxes if they are bonds of a state or one of its subdivisions where there is an income tax law) per the legal opinions of various recognized bond counsel to the issuing governmental bodies.

Unit—This is what you buy. It represents a certain fractional undivided interest in the overall principal amount of the fund. A unit is usually issued in $1,000 pieces.

Sponsor—The sponsor corresponds to an underwriter. The sponsor has the responsibility for assembling the portfolio and monitoring the progress of the various issues in the fund. The sponsor can direct the trustee to dispose of bonds when he feels the bonds are not acting well or are in default.

Trustee—The trustee is a bank and its job is to hold the bonds and act as a general disburser of principal and interest. It also pays the various charges incurred by the fund. It redeems units when called upon to do so by unit holders or when the sponsor has a bid for the outstanding units.

Evaluator—In most funds available, Standard & Poor's acts as the evaluator. However, this is not necessarily the case in all funds. The evaluator's job is to establish the price of the units in the fund. The evaluator also evaluates the bonds in the portfolio, usually on the last business day of a week. This price becomes effective for the following week. The evaluator also makes an evaluation twice a year, usually on the last business day of June and December.

Sales charge—This is the charge that is added to the price of the units (which was set by the evaluator) and is the compensation that the sponsor and other dealers distributing a particular fund receive. It is used to pay sales commissions and is then sales profit. It usually runs from 3½ to 4 percent or $35.00 to $40.00 per $1,000 unit.

Monthly distribution—Many funds (especially the recent ones) make a monthly interest distribution.